Understanding Educationa

Much is written about both the practical issues associated with conducting educational research and the methodological controversies which are ongoing in social science research. What is often neglected, however, is the relationship between epistemology, methodology and practice. This book redresses the balance.

The writers of this book consider questions which are often taken for granted and examine them critically. The book looks at the philosophical and socio-cultural contexts of educational research and relates the latter to contemporary paradigm shifts such as feminism and postmodernity. It also examines in detail a selection of innovative and sometimes controversial approaches to educational research. These include evaluation, action research, feminist research, ethnography and biographical research.

With an increasing number of students undertaking research as all or part of their courses, these issues are now more important than ever. All those involved in the research community should read this book.

David Scott is a lecturer in Educational Research Methods at the Institute of Education, University of London. He is the current editor of the *Curriculum Journal*. **Robin Usher** is a reader in Postcompulsory Education at the University of Southampton, where he is the Head of the School of Education. He is the co-author of *Postmodernism and Education*.

Understanding Educational Research

Edited by David Scott and Robin Usher

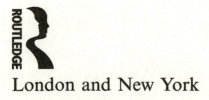

London and New York

First published 1996
by Routledge
11 New Fetter Lane, London EC4P 4EE

Simultaneously published in the USA and Canada
by Routledge
29 West 35th Street, New York, NY 10001

Routledge is an International Thomson Publishing company

© 1996 selection and editorial matter: David Scott and Robin Usher;
individual chapters: the contributors

Typeset in Times by Routledge
Printed and bound in Great Britain by
Clays Ltd, St Ives PLC

British Library Cataloguing in Publication Data
A catalogue record for this book is available from the British Library

Library of Congress Cataloguing in Publication Data
A catalogue record for this book has been requested

ISBN 0–415–13130–8 (hbk)
ISBN 0–415–13131–6 (pbk)

Contents

Contributors

Ian Bryant   is a Lecturer in the Department of Adult Continuing Education at the University of Southampton. He has previously worked as a lecturer in Social Studies at Champlain College, Montreal, and at Paisley College, Edinburgh. His research and teaching interests are in theories of adult education, professional development and reflective practice. He is co-author with Robin Usher of *Adult Education as Theory, Practice and Research: the Captive Triangle*.

Michael Erben   is Chair of the Education and Social Science Division of the School of Education at the University of Southampton. He has published widely in the areas of the sociology of education and the sociology of biography, and is currently a member of the editorial board of *Sociology*. His current research is in the sociology of biographical studies and he is Co-editor of the journal *Auto/Biography*. He is a past President of the *Association for the Teaching of the Social Sciences*.

Janet Harland   is a Lecturer in Education in the Curriculum Studies Department at the University of London Institute of Education. Previously she has taught in several London secondary schools. She has evaluated a number of educational development projects, in particular the Technical and Vocational Educational Initiative. She has published widely in books and journals on evaluation and related issues.

David Scott   is a Lecturer in Educational Research Methods at the Institute of Education, University of London. Previously, he was a research fellow in the Centre for Educational Development, Appraisal and Research at the University of Warwick, and a Lecturer in Educational Assessment at the University of Southampton. He has edited *Control and Accountability in Educational Settings* and written (with Marlene Morrison) *Libraries for Learning: Approaches to Book Resources in Primary Schools*. He is currently the Editor of *The Curriculum Journal*.

Pat Usher   is the Faculty Registrar of the Social Science Faculty at the University of Southampton. She teaches in the School of Education at Southampton and the Open University as a part-time tutor in the fields of gender, feminism and post-compulsory education.

Robin Usher   is a Reader in Education at the University of Southampton, and Head of School. He was the Faculty Research Co-ordinator. His current research interests include problem solving and discursive practice in the professions. He has recently published, with Ian Bryant, *Adult Education as Theory, Practice and Research: the Captive Triangle* and with Richard Edwards, *Postmodernism and Education*.

1   Introduction

David Scott and Robin Usher

The extensive and growing literature on research in education tends to be of two main types. First, there is a 'technical' literature where the concern is with practical issues and problems in conducting research in education. Second, there is a literature where the prime concern is to contribute to the ongoing debates about methodological issues and controversies in the social sciences. Both of these have problematic elements. The concentration on purely practical issues and problems leads to an excessive emphasis on methods and techniques, borrowed without examination from the social sciences. The consequence is a trivialisation and technicisation of educational research. On the other hand, the concentration on methodological controversies in the social sciences tends to downgrade the latter to a mere sub-species of social research and results in neglect of the specific problems of an educational research necessarily located in the practice of education.

Since educational research must of necessity be social in its orientation, it cannot entirely dissociate itself from the discourses of social research. However, this does not imply that it should be trapped in the latter's often sterile dichotomies and questionable paradigms. There is a need therefore to look anew at educational research paradigms and the epistemological contexts of educational research. This position, while recognising the contiguity of educational research and educational practice, does not commit educational-ists to technicising research. While accepting the need for educational researchers to possess appropriate research skills, there is also a need for educational practitioners to become critical 'readers' and 'writers' of research.

Accordingly, this book explores educational research in terms of the relationship between epistemology, methodology and practice. The various authors have considered these issues not in an abstract way but in relation to researching educational practice. At the same time, they have attempted to relate research to educational practice in terms of wider epistemological and methodological contexts. These frameworks, which underpin and legitimate methods used by researchers to investigate educational processes, systems and institutions are treated as problematic. Questions which are often taken for granted are brought to the surface and examined: what is legitimate knowledge in educational research? What is the relationship between 'educational theory' and the collection and analysis of data? How reliable and valid are conclusions drawn from particular collections of data about educational issues? How do research methods and techniques relate to current epistemological controversies about representation and reality in education?

This book therefore examines the philosophical and socio-cultural contexts of educational research and relates the latter to contemporary paradigm shifts such as feminism, critical theory and postmodernity. In the latter part of the book, a number of distinct, innovative and in some cases controversial approaches such as evaluation, action research, feminist research, ethnography and biographical research are critically examined. Each of the authors relates their approach to the framework presented here and in the first part of the book.

Robin Usher, in Chapter 2, refuses to treat educational research simply as a 'technology', a set of methods, skills and procedures to be implemented. Arguing that research should be seen as a social practice, he explores the implications of this position. This involves looking at traditional epistemological questions to do with what constitutes legitimate knowledge, models of explanation, theory-justification and acceptance, the nature of objectivity, probability and causality, and different traditions such as empiricism, rationalism and realism. Indeed, he argues that educational research is characterised by a diversity of purpose, a diversity closely related to the types of questions that historically have been asked in and about it. There is therefore a need to examine those historical, political and socio-economic contexts within which it operates, and the extent to which they constitute a paradigm shift or a dispersal of paradigms. Paradigms are not simply ways of looking at the world, but are imbued with the workings of power/knowledge (Foucault 1980). Strategies of educational research have therefore to be understood in relation to this.

In Chapter 3 he takes this argument one stage further and addresses the important issues of reflexivity and textuality. Having identified a repressed textual, and, it should be said, reflexive, dimension to most educational research, he argues that there is a need to bring these to the surface and inscribe them in the texts themselves. Authors frequently attempt to conceal their authorship, yet they rarely succeed. Whether it is possible to write without 'authority', to produce the 'writerly' text (Barthes 1975), is controversial. Much depends on whether the epistemological and ontological assumptions that researchers as writers make about the world are foregrounded or allowed to remain hidden. To some extent, this is also a question of power in the sense of a research community's power to exclude and repress.

David Scott in Chapter 4 examines the meaning of 'data' in the context of educational research and the relationship of these meanings to theory and practice in education. He focuses on the epistemological and ontological assumptions of experimental, survey, correlational, ethnographic and case study research, and in particular on political, ethical and reflexive problems. He argues that our knowledge of the social world, and in particular, the way we understand education, can only be secured if we take account of the views and perspectives of the social actors that are central to the activities we wish to describe. But this creates problems as to how we conceptualise the relationship between the researcher and the researched. The social actor always offers a view of the past mediated through their present understanding projected into the future (Ricoeur 1991). This leaves a gap between the text and what it refers to that is difficult to bridge.

In Chapter 5, David Scott looks at the various attempts that have been made to produce a set of specifications to judge quality in educational research. He considers a number of attempts by academic researchers from different traditions, all of whom have attempted to specify directly ways of differentiating 'good' from 'bad' research. Inevitably, he is concerned here with questions such as: if we abandon (for good reasons) correspondence versions of reality, do we then abandon the search for a coherent set of validity criteria? If the research text can only be retrospectively deconstructed rather than used to inform practice in a prescriptive manner, what sense is there in its production?

These questions have a particular relevance to educational evaluation, since its avowed purpose is to inform and improve practice. **Janet Harland** in Chapter 6 examines the theory and practice of evaluation research as it has come to be understood and practised over the past thirty years in different institutional, local and national policy contexts, and focuses on the politics and ethics of this type of research, methods of data collection and analysis, styles of reporting for different audiences, fieldwork ethics and skills, and contractual conditions for independent research. Again she poses questions about the relationship between educational theory and practice, which are taken up in the next chapter.

Ian Bryant in Chapter 7 conceptualises action research as a form of hermeneutical enquiry oriented to change as well as to understanding. Its primary concern is to widen understanding beyond, rather than develop knowledge within, the boundaries of academic disciplines on the one hand, and 'practical concerns' on the other. He examines the characteristics of action research, as revealed in action research projects, and in particular shows how action, understanding and change are mutually interactive. Action research has come to be associated with the notion of the reflective practitioner. This notion is examined in relation to the theory–practice problematic in educational research.

Another form of hermeneutic enquiry, albeit of a radical kind, is feminist research which addresses in particular the relationship between the researcher and what they are researching, and the value-impregnated nature of all such enquiry. **Pat Usher**, from a postmodernist vantage point, challenges in Chapter 8 the fundamental assumptions on which modernist thought is based, in particular the commitment to universal concepts of truth, objectivity, observer neutrality and methodologies believed to guarantee the 'truth'. Specifically, she challenges its gendered and weighted dualisms, for example, rational/irrational, subject/object, culture/nature, that structure thought and action, and argues that masculinity is always associated with the first element and privileged over the second which is always associated with femininity. In particular, she addresses the question of how participatory dialogue and reflexive approaches to research can be practised in empirical work.

In order to understand these reflexive approaches, relationships between researchers and the objects of their research need to be explored. David Scott in Chapter 9 assesses the relevance of ethnographic methods to the study of educational processes, institutions and texts. He identifies a number of important problems with a naive ethnographic approach: that the researcher can gain direct access to educational settings by close immersion in those activities which constitute them. He argues that understanding is always located within traditions, self-referencing and mutually incommensurable. This creates particular problems for the ethnographer seeking to bridge the gap between them.

Finally, **Michael Erben** discusses in his chapter the purposes and methods of biographical research. The purpose of biography or life-history research is to examine the manner in which social context and individual lives intersect. It then becomes an enterprise in which the strengths of both phenomenological and structuralist perspectives are utilised in the understanding of individual persons or selves. But this applies to the researcher as well as to the person or persons being researched. It is the tension between these two processes which gives the study of biography its particular importance, especially with regard to educational activities.

Robin Usher and David Scott close the book by drawing together the threads of the various arguments developed in the preceding chapters, while at the same time relating the theoretical framework developed in the first part to the various accounts of different educational research strategies in the second.

Finally, there is a need to stress that the authors do not write from the same perspective, and indeed, it would be surprising if they did. Social theory and epistemology are characterised by a theoretical pluralism and thus any one definition is inevitably controversial. The reader looking for consensus is bound to be disappointed. All the authors, however, have moved beyond advocacy of a naive form of positivism. Some argue from a modified hermeneutic position; others from a postmodernist stance, with its stress on the de-centred self, the separation of semantics from syntactics, and the questioning of universal notions of truth and objectivity; still others occupy more pragmatic ground and locate themselves within deliberative discourses (Walsh 1993).

However, what formally unites them is an interest in a number of funda-mental questions central to the study of education: how can we characterise the relationship between educational theory and practice? What is the role of values in educational enquiry? How should we understand the relationship between data-collection from educational settings and the development of educational theory? What sense can we make of educational theory? In short, this book explores the complex set of relations between epistemology, methodology and practice with particular reference to the study of education, and argues that these issues are frequently disguised and/or neglected. To surface and foreground them, as this book has attempted to do, is an important part of the process of better understanding.

REFERENCES

Barthes, R. (1975) *S/Z*, London: Jonathan Cape.

Foucault, M. (1980) *Power/Knowledge: Selected Interviews and other Writings 1972–1977*, C. Gordon (ed.), Brighton: Harvester.

Ricoeur, P. (1991) 'Life in Quest of Narrative' in D. Wood (ed.) *On Paul Ricoeur*, London: Routledge.

Walsh, P. (1993) *Education and Meaning: Philosophy in Practice*, London: Cassell.

Part I
Frameworks

2 A critique of the neglected epistemological assumptions of educational research

Robin Usher

> Science is a human activity. Therefore whatever we as scientists do as we do science has validity and meaning as any other human activity does only in the context of human co-existence in which it arises.
>
> (Maturana 1991: 30)

The focus of this chapter is a critical exploration of the philosophical under-pinnings of research, specifically the epistemological and ontological assumptions that underlie different research traditions – assumptions which have tended in the main to be largely unexamined in relation to the research process. It will be argued that it is the failure to examine these assumptions which leads to research normally being understood as a 'technology', as simply a set of methods, skills and procedures applied to a defined research problem. The quote from Maturana above alerts us to the fact that 'science takes place within the context of human co-existence' and I take this to mean that science (i.e. research) is a social practice, and that therefore what it says and what it does is significantly located within that context.

Having said this, however, it is certainly the case that until quite recently the dominant view has been that, although research investigates particular social contexts, its warrant, or the validity of its knowledge, must come from being located outside of any context. A feeling of strangeness is still evoked in the face of the claim that research is a social practice, yet it is only by making such a claim that it becomes possible both to examine the activity of research critically and to understand how research may itself be a critical activity.

Before proceeding further, however, I must emphasise that what follows is written from a personal perspective. Different research traditions are examined but it will be clear that I find it impossible to adopt the orthodox stance of complete neutrality and impartiality. Whether such a stance is possible anyway is a key issue to be discussed. Furthermore, having advocated the need for reflexivity I recognise that this is also applicable to my text (the question of reflexivity will be examined in more detail in the next chapter). I strongly hope that readers will also ask reflexive questions about this text and others they are bound to encounter as researchers, including, of course, their own.

SOME CHARACTERISTICS OF RESEARCH

In answer to the question: what are we doing when we do research? a common answer would be that we are systematically attempting to address and investigate certain pre-defined issues or problems. Of course, in a sense, 'addressing and investigating' educational questions, issues and problems is something that is likely also to be found in everyday practice. Does this mean therefore that practitioners are also always researchers? To some extent: yes. As practitioners we are also researchers more often than we think. Certainly, to be effective practitioners we ought to try and be researchers of our practice. But can we in our everyday practice also be researchers in the way in which 'research' is conventionally understood?

This raises the question of what characterises research and differentiates it from the kind of problem-solving or finding-out which occurs in everyday practice. In most text-books on research methods the main defining characteristic of research is taken to be its 'systematic' nature. Of course, once research is characterised as 'systematic' this also suggests related characteristics such as 'rigorous' and 'methodical'. There is no doubt that the correct use of appropriate method is accorded a significant place in all types of research and I shall return to this shortly. For example, empirical research, the most common research form, is commonly described as involving the collection, analysis and presentation of primary data in a rigorous, systematic and methodical way.

In empirical research, data on their own are not considered of much use per se. They assume significance only when used within descriptions, explanations or generalisations. *Descriptions* answer the question – what is happening? Or they can be more historical in orientation and answer the question – what has happened? *Explanations* answer the question – why is this happening? – and this 'why' generally tends to be answered in terms of a cause. *Generalisations* are the answer to 'why' questions which also utilise causes, but here the explanation always goes beyond a particular setting: for example, not why does X happen in this particular classroom but does it happen in all classrooms and if so is there an underlying and common cause Y? A generalisation is prized precisely because, in not being limited to a particular setting, it is seen as making application possible. Thus generalisations have traditionally been considered the highest level of research and very often as what research should always strive for. This is largely because research in the natural sciences, particularly in physics, aims for generalisations and such research is thought to be the model for all other forms of research. In the natural sciences generalisations are sought because they enable predictions to be made. Generalised explanation and prediction are not only two sides of the same coin but prediction makes control possible. Thus if it is known that X causes Y then it is possible to predict that where X is present Y will happen and if that is known then the presence of X can be controlled in order to make Y happen.

What I have been describing so far are some of the general characteristics of research in the 'scientific' mode. This is a powerful and influential way of understanding research, indeed one could argue that there is a 'discourse of science' which posits how research should be done not only in the natural sciences but in the human and social sciences also. In other words, it is a discourse characterised by a universalising thrust and a totalising aim and which therefore tends to be intolerant of difference. It produces a scientism which has the most profound consequences for research in the human and social sciences.

POSITIVIST/EMPIRICIST EPISTEMOLOGY AND RESEARCH

This discourse of science is implicated with philosophy's epistemological project and its most obvious manifestation – positivism and empiricism. *Epistemology* traditionally has been concerned with what distinguishes different kinds of knowledge claims – specifically with what the criteria are that allow distinctions between 'knowledge' and 'non-knowledge' to be made. *Ontology*, on the other hand, traditionally has been about what exists, what is the nature of the world, what is reality. Epistemological and ontological questions are related since claims about what exists in the world imply claims about how what exists may be known.

Historically, epistemology is the outcome of the Enlightenment's dismantling of tradition as the source of knowledge. With this dismantling came the question of how any given knowledge can be considered valid or indeed how it is possible to 'know' anything (as opposed to having a belief in or an opinion about it). The answer was to ground the validity of knowledge in scientific method in the form of measurement, testability and the right use of reason. Through empiricism, tradition was replaced by sense-experience gained through observation and experimentation as the source of knowledge. Epistemological issues came therefore to be seen in purely empiricist terms, with science as the privileged model of investigation – since it seemed to follow that only through this kind of investigation and the 'certainty' it provided could the resulting knowledge claims be considered valid.

Now any research, whether in the natural or social sciences, makes knowledge claims and for that reason alone is implicated in epistemological questions. It could be argued that all research is based on an epistemology even though this is not always made explicit – in fact most of the time the epistemology that underlies a particular piece of research is taken for granted. It is simply assumed that the research will be positivist/empiricist in its epistemology and therefore unproblematic as an epistemology.

Conventionally, epistemology argues that any claim to know must be justified on the basis of how the claim was arrived at. The argument is that since not all knowledge claims have the same status the determination of their status is the job of epistemology. Thus if the knowledge claim is based on observation and measurement, systematically and methodically carried out, and if logical rules of inference and confirmation have been used, then epistemologically this is taken as 'good grounds' for considering the knowledge claim to be valid or true.

One of the most important aspects of these epistemological 'good grounds' are that the researcher was 'objective', i.e. that he or she was unbiased, value neutral and took care to ensure that personal considerations did not intrude into the research process – in other words, that the researcher's subjectivity has been eliminated as a factor in the knowledge claim. The researcher then becomes the 'ideal universal knower', interchangeable with all other researchers. As I have already hinted, when we do research there is a tendency to take objectivity and the procedures for attaining objectivity, including the elimination of subjectivity, as a 'given', a taken for granted and necessary aspect of doing research. Consequently, we fail to see that in implicitly accepting objectivity in this form we are implicitly accepting a particular epistemology and all the commitments and assumptions which that contains.

The epistemology I have been discussing so far is usually referred to as *positivist/empiricist*. It contains the following assumptions:

1 The world is 'objective' in that it exists independently of knowers. This world consists of events or phenomena which are lawful and orderly. Through systematic observation and correct scientific methods, i.e. by *being* 'objective', it is possible to discover this lawfulness and to explain, predict and control events and phenomena.

2 There is a clear distinction or separation between subjects and objects, the 'subjective' knower and the 'objective' world. There is also a clear distinction between facts (which are to do with the world and therefore in the domain of the 'objective') and values (which are to do with the knower/ researcher and therefore in the domain of the 'subjective'). The researcher is concerned only with the former (except insofar as the latter is the object of the research). The subjective (the researcher's concerns and values) must not interfere with the discovery of 'objective' truth.

3 The validity of knowledge claims is a matter of whether these claims are based on the use of the senses, on observation enhanced by measurement. Different observers exposed to the same data (the underlying assumption here is that data are always the 'same') should be able to come to the same conclusions. This is intersubjective validation. Full agreement is therefore always in principle possible and it is this test of intersubjective replicability which is the most significant indicator of procedural objectivity.

4 The social world is very much like the natural world. Thus there is order and reason in the social world, social life is patterned and this pattern has a cause–effect form; things do not just happen randomly and arbitrarily. The goal of research, to develop general and universal laws that explain the world, is therefore common to both the natural and the social sciences.

5 All the sciences are based on the same method of finding out about the world. The natural and social sciences share a common logic and methodology of enquiry.
6 Epistemological enquiry and critique about the research process (such as we are doing now, for example) is a pointless exercise. So long as the right methodological procedures have been properly applied, questions of reflexivity need not be considered.

The assumptions of a positivist/empiricist epistemology lead to an approach to research that emphasises *determinacy* (that there is a certain truth that can be known), *rationality* (that there can be no contradictory explanations, that there must be convergence on a single explanation), *impersonality* (the more objective and the less subjective the better) and *prediction* (that research is the making of knowledge claims in the form of generalisations from which predictions can be made and events and phenomena controlled). Furthermore, it is an approach that is *unreflexive* because in focusing exclusively on methods and outcomes it fails to ask any questions about the research process itself.

Understanding research in this way involves accepting the claim of positivist/empiricist epistemology that it provides a set of logical rules of explanation, independent of the world and its social practices, which can distinguish between and judge *all* knowledge claims. It involves accepting that there is a logic of science which is more important than its historical or cultural locatedness, that research has a universal rather than an embedded rationality and a unitary and invariant method rather than a pragmatic diversity of methods.

All of these assumptions have been critiqued. It could be argued for instance that in making a knowledge claim it is not simply a matter of appealing to logical and universal rules because, since all knowledge claims involve justification, they all have a social dimension. Claims are *justified* within contexts of collectively held conceptions about the world, and how to relate to it and know it. It is these underlying conceptions that are embodied in particular epistemologies. Of course, some conceptions have more credibility and therefore more power than others. The most powerful conceptions are those of positivist/empiricist epistemology which holds up the methods and procedures of the natural sciences (scientific method) as the model for all research. One implication of this is that a positivist/empiricist epistemology is as much a matter of *politics*, i.e. power, than of mere logic. In other words, the rules are not themselves neutral.

What we can conclude from this is that methods are embedded in commitments to particular versions of the world (an ontology) and ways of knowing that world (an epistemology). These commitments are always held by the researcher, mostly tacitly. This means that no method is self-validating, separable from an epistemology and an ontology.

Furthermore, every ontology and epistemology is itself culturally specific, historically located and value-laden. 'Scientific method' is therefore not an abstract set of logical rules, 'made in heaven' and universal in their applicability, but a way of working specific to particular research paradigms (for a fuller discussion of this see below) and to particular disciplinary pursuits, and which has evolved historically with the growth of the natural sciences and of Western philosophy. It is because of the powerful tendency to think of scientific method as universal and 'made in heaven' that research is seen purely as a 'technology' or technical process.

The dominance of positivist/empiricist epistemology has had two main consequences. First, in the social sciences and in social research a pre-eminent place has been accorded to the production of knowledge based on discovering facts and formulating theory in terms of generalisations. Second, there has been an adoption of the language, methods and quantification of the natural sciences in social and educational research.

Prediction and the search for generalisations has not been realised in educational and social research. Two possible explanations can be given for this. The first is that generalisations are possible but they will tend either to be truisms or to be much too general. The second is that the search for generalisations is probably doomed to failure since it is questionable whether generalisable and predictive knowledge is possible in the social domain.

The problem with social and educational research based on a positivist/empiricist epistemology with its emphasis on the natural sciences as the model is that its ontological assumptions about the nature of the world, i.e. that it is orderly, lawful and hence predictable, are highly problematic. Social events, processes and phenomena are more usefully seen as open and indeterminate. Predictive generalisations are only possible if this openness is *closed*. Closure is only possible if a determinate world is assumed and so the closure that is necessary can only be *imposed*. But if it is imposed then the very status of the knowledge generated (the predictive generalisations) itself becomes questionable. Thus it is not so much that closure is impossible (since we do this all the time) but rather that if it is done then the imposed closure must inevitably raise questions of *power* which in turn raises questions about the 'objectivity' of the research process and the resulting knowledge claims.

KUHN'S CRITIQUE OF POSITIVIST/EMPIRICIST EPISTEMOLOGY

At this point, I want to highlight some aspects of the work of Thomas Kuhn, in particular his critique of positivist/empiricist epistemology. Kuhn's major work *The Structure of Scientific Revolutions* (1970) played a significant part in changing our understanding of science, research and scientific method by doing two things – first, focusing on the way scientists actually work i.e. on the practice of science rather than on scientific self-understandings, and second, showing that scientific discovery is located in the historical rather than the transcendental realm. He argued that the picture we have of scientific research is essentially *philosophical*, a projection of philosophy's understanding of science. Through a positivist/empiricist epistemology science has been reconfigured to the extent that what is supposedly done in scientific research bears no resemblance to what is actually done. Lyotard (1984) has argued that since science has never been a matter of simply observing and recording the regularities of the world but has always seen itself as discovering the 'truth' of the world, it has ben obliged to justify its project through a legitimating discourse which has to be philosophical.

Positivist/empiricist epistemology projects a picture of the natural sciences and generally of any research carried out in a 'scientific' way, as essentially an *individualistic* enterprise, as something carried out by individuals who can detach themselves from the world they are researching. Now on the face of it this seems a very plausible depiction and it is certainly the case that a great deal of research is done by individuals. But the 'individual' of positivist/empiricist research is unlike anyone recognisable in the real world. These are *abstracted* individuals with no history and unaffected by culture, values, discourses and social structures. Kuhn critiques this individualistic picture and instead presents science as a socio-historical practice carried out in research *communities* within which individual researchers are located. Sometimes the community is fairly invisible; very often (and this tends to be the case in social and educational research) it is fragmented and incoherent, which is probably why many researchers feel that they are on their own and that they do not belong to a research community.

Another tendency of positivist/empiricist epistemology is to present scientists and scientific research as *rationalistic*. Kuhn on the other hand presents rationality as mediated and shaped by factors such as socialisation, conformity, faith and processes very much akin to religious conversion.

Kuhn's key concept is the *paradigm*. A paradigm is, first, 'the entire constellation of beliefs, values, techniques shared by members of a given scientific community' (Kuhn 1970: 75) and second, it is an exemplar or exemplary way of working that functions as a model for what and how to do research, what problems to focus on and work on. Paradigms are frameworks that function as maps or guides for scientific communities, determining important problems or issues for its members to address and defining acceptable theories or explanations, methods and techniques to solve defined problems.

When a paradigm becomes settled and dominant within a scientific community, Kuhn calls the research carried out 'normal science'. This way of doing research is largely characterised by routine, problem-solving activity but from time to time it is interrupted by occasional breaks and discontinuities (which Kuhn calls 'scientific revolutions'). Here a paradigm shift occurs, dominant paradigms are overthrown and new paradigms take their place. A paradigm shift involves a new way of looking at the world and hence new ways of working (or new ways of doing 'normal science'). A shift comes about, first, through the awareness of anomalies by the scientific community – problems that cannot be solved, about which scientists become increasingly concerned – and second, because there exists an alternative paradigm that apparently accounts for the anomalies. At some point, this new paradigm comes to replace the old and in its turn becomes the dominant paradigm. The new paradigm is accepted when a sufficient number of scientists in a community are *converted* to it. This conversion occurs not because of the proofs or certainties which the new paradigm establishes but because it seems to offer a more fruitful way of pursuing normal science. The 'truth' of a new paradigm can never be known in advance.

Because of the powerful influence of positivist/empiricist epistemology and its abstracted model which emphasises the logic of scientific knowledge, we have tended to think of knowledge as proceeding in a linear, cumulative way where increasingly correct descriptions or 'truths' about the world are discovered. In other words, that scientific work is marked by an increasingly better 'fit' between scientific theories and an independent 'objective' world. Kuhn, however, by focusing on the *practice* rather than the logic of science, wants to critique this and argues instead that data and observations are theory-led, that theory is paradigm-led, and that paradigms are historically and culturally located. Theory or knowledge generation is therefore not dependent simply on how the world 'is' but on how the paradigm is developed through 'normal' science.

Not surprisingly, Kuhn's work challenged solidly entrenched orthodoxies based on positivist/empiricist assumptions. Knowledge claims, far from representing 'independent' universal knowledge of the world, are relative to paradigms. After a paradigm change 'scientists work in a different world' since what *counts* as 'objective' reality changes with the change of paradigm. Hence, the assumption of a fixed absolute reality against which theories about this reality can be tested is challenged. Furthermore, the criteria which are used to decide between competing theories are not just those of a theory's predictive accuracy, reliability, scope, etc. Consensus based on shared values and communal judgement is equally important. Precisely because it is promissory and exemplary, scientists have *faith* in the paradigm. Normal science provides a 'norm' of working, it enables order and regulation. At the same time, paradigms and their associated research communities provide boundaries which are inclusive but also exclude and silence. In other words, research communities exercise *power*. As we have noted earlier, research involves imposing a closure which is not purely epistemological.

Above all, through his work Kuhn showed that scientific research can be examined and critiqued in the same way as other social practices because research, contrary to dominant philosophical understandings, is a social not a logical process. Doing scientific research is a communitarian, culturally bound and culturally specific practice. The research process is therefore contingent rather than necessary and is itself researchable. Furthermore, Kuhn's work showed that there is a crucial hermeneutic/interpretive dimension to science. If practice is foregrounded, then science is not itself positivist/empiricist. This epistemology provides an idealised yet powerful picture of scientific research, made even more powerful because it is a picture which the natural sciences and other 'scientific' disciplines project. The hermeneutic dimension of science is repressed, perhaps because if it were acknowledged it would appear to make science too 'subjective'.

However, it is interesting to note that Kuhn's arguments are supported by developments within natural science itself. For example, quantum physics seems to show that Kuhn may be on to something in his argument that the physical world should not be seen as independent, mechanistic and orderly. A more apt way is to see it as holistic, indivisible and in flux. In quantum physics, events do not have well-defined causes since they occur spontaneously, their occurrence depending on the dynamics of the system rather than on a single cause/effect, part/whole interconnectedness. Furthermore, phenomena require an observer in order to be observed – so decisions about *how* to observe will determine *what* is observed. Hence the subject–object separation and the assumption of a knowable, independently existing world become harder to maintain.

Kuhn's view of science as it is actually practised – that theory or paradigm choice depends on normative consensus and commitment within scientific communities – means that the natural and social sciences are perhaps not that different. Certainly they are not different in the sense that the former is 'objective' while the latter is 'subjective'. Since any process of research has a hermeneutic/interpretive dimension, the natural sciences are just as 'subjective' in this sense as the social sciences. In both, data are not detachable from theory – facts do not 'speak for themselves', they do not lie around waiting to be 'discovered' – phenomena of all kinds are interpreted by 'scientists' through their paradigmatic frameworks. There are no 'brute data' which are givens and can speak for themselves. They cannot therefore function as the ultimate grounding for the validity of knowledge claims.

Furthermore, in both the natural and the social sciences there is no set of logical rules which are universally applied. Research is a social practice carried out by research communities and what constitutes 'knowledge', 'truth', 'objectivity' and 'correct method' is defined by the community and through the paradigm of normal science which shapes its work. This means that how the rules will be understood and applied will differ between communities and within communities particularly at times when the dominant paradigm is under threat. Research therefore is never simply a technical process involving the invariant application of universal rules of 'scientific method'. Above all, however, Kuhn shows that knowledge in both the natural and social sciences is an ongoing historical and social achievement characterised by disruption and discontinuity, i.e. it is neither linear nor teleological. In effect, we are forced to rethink the strong belief in the cumulative 'progress' of knowledge and of research as a matter of getting closer and closer to a single determinate 'truth'.

HERMENEUTIC/INTERPRETIVE EPISTEMOLOGY

Despite the sustained critique to which it has been subjected, the positivist/empiricist epistemology and its associated methodology still has an influential position in social and educational research. There is, however, another influential although not dominant epistemology in social and educational research which is usually referred to as 'hermeneutic/interpretive'. This argues that the model to follow should not be the idealised and universal logic of scientific research because this model is inappropriate. In social research, knowledge is concerned not with generalisation, prediction and control but with interpretation, meaning and illumination.

Hermeneutic/interpretive epistemology puts forward not so much a critique of science per se but of the philosophical reconfiguration of science. Above all, it takes aim at *scientism*, the view that the natural sciences are a 'supra-historic, neutral enterprise ... and the sole model of acquiring true knowledge' (Bleicher 1982: 3). Gadamer (1975) argues against the placing of science outside of history and human life generally. Above all, he disputes the powerfully held view that the natural sciences, because of their method, provide both the sole model of rationality and the only way of finding truth. For Gadamer, the main problem with scientism is the imperialistic claim it makes on behalf of the natural sciences. In opposition to this, he wants to argue that there is more to truth than scientific method and the natural sciences do not provide the one single model of rationality. There is a major problem with the scientistic model of rationality. In positing a universalistic, abstract model of rationality there is a forgetting of the conventionality of reason, how reason is forged in specific historical practices and thus operates through traditions rather than being an overcoming of tradition.

Hermeneutic/interpretive epistemology in social and educational research focuses on social practices. It assumes that all human action is meaningful and hence has to be interpreted and understood within the context of social practices. There is a questioning of the wholesale application of methods appropriate to the natural sciences since such methods, it is argued, cannot elucidate the meanings of human actions. If the concern rather is with *meaning* within *social interactions* then confining research to the observable or empirically 'given', as a positivist/empiricist epistemology does, is necessarily to miss out the most important dimension in social enquiry.

To explain the social world we need to understand it, to make sense of it, and hence we need to understand the meanings that construct and are constructed by interactive human behaviour. Human action is given meaning by interpretive schemes or frameworks. It follows from this that as researchers (engaged in the human action and social practice of research) we too seek to make sense of what we are researching and we too do so through interpretive schemes or frameworks. This process of double sense-making is referred to as the 'double hermeneutic'. In other words, unlike the situation in the natural sciences, in social research both the subject (the researcher) and object (other people) of research have the same characteristic of being interpreters or sense-seekers.

It follows also that since all sense-seeking is from an interpretive framework then all knowledge is perspective-bound and partial, i.e. relative to that framework. Knowledge therefore is always a matter of knowing *differently* rather than cumulative increase, identity or confirmation. Gadamer (1975) argues that it is impossible to separate oneself as a researcher from the historical and cultural context that defines one's interpretive framework. The 'subject' and the 'object' of research, commonly located in pre-understood worlds cannot therefore be separated. There is no object-in-itself independent of a context of knowing and of the knowing activities of subjects. The framework (or pre-understandings) constitutes 'the initial directedness of our whole ability to experience . . . it is the conditions whereby we experience something – whereby what we encounter says something to us' (ibid.: 173).

As well as being perspectival and partial, interpretations are always circular. The interpretation of part of something depends on interpreting the whole, but interpreting the whole depends on an interpretation of the parts. As an example, think of what happens when you read a book – the meaning of the book depends on the meaning of each of its chapters (the parts), yet each chapter's meaning depends on the meaning of the whole book. This determination of meaning in the interaction of part and whole is called the *hermeneutic circle* of interpretation. Knowledge-formation is therefore conceived as circular, iterative, spiral – not linear and cumulative as portrayed in positivist/empiricist epistemology.

An important characteristic of the hermeneutic circularity of interpretation is that it always takes place against a background of assumptions and presuppositions, beliefs and practices, of which the subjects and objects of research are never fully aware and which can never be fully specified. Gadamer calls this 'tradition'. Let us take some examples to illustrate this. First, an example of an apparently simple action such as raising my arm. How are we to interpret or make sense of this? Obviously a mere physical description would not be enough since it would tell us nothing about the meaning of this action. A fuller interpretation would require an account of my intentions, for example, that I wished to leave the room. Yet this in itself would still not be enough. There would have to be some description of the context in which the action took place since arm-raising might mean different things in different contexts (in a classroom or in an athletics contest), so the meaning of the action is not exhausted by pointing to its 'underlying' intention. But we could go even further than this. We might want to specify how arm-raising is culturally understood as a form of signalling, how it is associated with practices such as turn-taking and so on. We could then go even further and compare the meaning of arm-raising in other societies.

Another more complex example might be that of the act of negotiating. Again, this cannot be understood simply at a descriptive level, for example, of exchanging offers, because this itself presupposes a whole set of beliefs such as the autonomy and distinct identity of human beings, cultural values such as conflict and self-interest, other practices such as the drawing up of contracts and a number of different and related actions such as bargaining which are part of negotiating. It is clear that none of these individually can be understood in isolation from the whole practice of negotiating. Furthermore, the act of negotiation again only has meaning in relation to a background (or tradition) of which those negotiating are 'unconscious' – in other words, the background is necessary to the act of negotiating even though the actors are not aware of it as they negotiate.

The point is therefore that in order to understand the meaning of an apparently simple action such as arm-raising or even more complex ones such as negotiating, it is necessary to understand how these are immersed and inseparable from a network of culturally-conditioned beliefs and practices, assumptions and pre-suppositions. Furthermore, while actors may be conscious of intentions they are not conscious of the background or 'tradition' wherein this action has meaning. This implies, as I have already noted, that meanings are not co-terminous with intentions.

Thus no matter how full, the interpretations we as researchers give of arm-raising and negotiating can never be complete. Certainly, it would not be complete if we merely provided a description of intentions. Human actions are interpretable only within the hermeneutic circle, hence any knowledge of them is indeterminate – that is why a positivist/empiricist methodology is inappropriate. As we have seen, such a methodology requires a closure and any understanding of human actions based on closure would necessarily be incomplete. To refer back to our example, closure would result in understanding the action of raising my arm only in terms of the physical movements or of my stated intentions.

The existence of a background or 'tradition' means that there is no 'fact of the matter' or empirical 'given' which could be appealed to in deciding between different interpretations. The kind of understanding required is circular because it is already an interpretation. Research involves interpreting the actions of those who are themselves interpreters: it involves interpretations of interpretations – the double hermeneutic at work.

Several questions now arise for the researcher. Presumably, given that research is a human action then are researchers themselves not part of a background or 'tradition' which gives meaning to their actions as researchers yet of which they are largely unaware? The answer is of course that they are and as we have seen earlier when discussing Kuhn this is the case even with researchers in the natural sciences (in a sense paradigms can be seen as 'traditions'). Given this, the notion of the individual researcher standing outside the world in order to understand it properly, seems highly questionable. (That is what I meant earlier when I argued that the 'individual' researcher of positivist/empiricist epistemology bears no relationship to real people.) Caught within the hermeneutic circle, it would seem impossible for researchers to take such a stance.

Gadamer argues that within the social sciences knowledge cannot be objective in a positivist/empiricist sense. Understanding an object is always 'prejudiced' in the sense that it can only be approached through an initial projection of meaning. This initial projection is from the subject's situatedness, from the subject's standpoint in history, society and culture. Any methodical enquiry has as its starting-point the pre-understandings which subjects have of objects through sharing the world with them. Thus the purpose which motivates and animates enquiry, the carving out of a field of study, the emergence of criteria and standards by which scientific study is evaluated – all this is dependent on the historical situatedness of scientific activity and therefore on the pre-understandings (or that which we consider worthwhile knowing) of researchers. This now immediately poses the problem of how as researchers, as interpreters, as meaning producers, we can be objective about the meanings produced by those we are researching. One answer to this problem is that although we must recognise our situatedness we must also 'bracket', i.e. temporarily set aside, our meanings, suspend our subjectivity, and assume the attitude of a disinterested observer.

A moment's thought shows that this position is not altogether satisfactory. An alternative suggested by Gadamer shows why. He argues that it is impossible to escape from our 'pre-understandings' even temporarily. But at the same time, it is precisely through the interplay between one's interpretive framework or pre-understandings and the elements of the actions one is trying to understand that knowledge is developed. In other words, one's pre-understandings, far from being closed prejudices or biases (as they are thought of in positivist/empiricist epistemology), actually make one more open-minded because, in the process of interpretation and understanding, they are put at risk, tested and modified through the encounter with what one is trying to understand. So rather than bracketing or 'suspending' them we should use them as the essential starting-point for acquiring knowledge. To know, one must be aware of one's pre-understandings even though one cannot transcend them.

Gadamer characterises research within the hermeneutic circle as a *fusion of horizons*. 'Horizon' refers to one's standpoint or situatedness (in time, place, culture, gender, ethnicity, etc.). The fusion results from seeking knowledge while grounded in a perspective arising from one's situatedness, a perspective which cannot be bracketed (or put aside) during the process of enquiry. Because it is situated, this horizon is inevitably limited but it is open to connecting with other horizons (perspectives, standpoints). The resulting fusion is an enlargement or broadening of one's own horizon.

The fusion of horizons constitutes a standard of objectivity which can function as an alternative to the objectivity of positivist/empiricist epistemology. A fusion of horizons is the outcome of intersubjective agreement where different and conflicting interpretations are harmonised. By comparing and contrasting various interpretations, a consensus can be achieved despite differences – indeed *because* of differences. Hermeneutic understanding is therefore a learning experience involving 'dialogue' between ourselves as researchers and that which we are trying to understand.

THE CRITICAL THEORY TRADITION

Critical Theory is 'critical' in the sense that it challenges both the positivist/empiricist and hermeneutic/interpretive traditions of social research – although it is fair to say that it is much more critical of the former than of the latter.

The term 'critical' refers here to the detecting and unmasking of beliefs and practices that limit human freedom, justice and democracy. Habermas (1972) argues that different knowledge/research traditions are linked with particular *social* interests. (I am emphasising 'social' because it is important to distinguish this from the interest in knowing of any particular individual.) According to him, the natural sciences and dominant tendencies in the social sciences employ a technical/instrumental reasoning where ends are pre-given and achieved by following known rules and pre-given means. Because of its instrumental means/ends character, Habermas described this kind of knowledge as guided by a technical interest. The hermeneutic sciences such as history and other human sciences as well as some forms of the social sciences employ practical modes of reasoning. Here neither ends nor means are pre-given and known rules of method are not followed. What is involved here is the making of right and appropriate decisions and judgements in the light of the circumstances of the situation.

Empirical/analytic science or knowledge is linked with the positivist/empiricist research tradition and with prediction and control; hermeneutic science or knowledge with the hermeneutic/interpretive research tradition and with enlightenment, understanding and communication. Neither, however, has an interest in research that changes the world in the direction of freedom, justice and democracy.

Habermas therefore isolates a third type of 'knowledge-constitutive interest' which he links with critical science or theory. The knowledge interest involved in Critical Theory is *emancipatory* – the unmasking of ideologies that maintain the status quo by restricting the access of groups to the means of gaining knowledge and the raising of consciousness or awareness about the material conditions that oppress or restrict them. It is important to note here that empowerment does not mean individual self-assertion and upward mobility, even less the psychological experience of feeling powerful and self-realised. What it means is understanding the causes of powerlessness, recognising systemic oppressive forces and acting individually and collectively to change the conditions of life. The main approach of Critical Theory is therefore *ideology critique*. However, in the Critical Theory tradition research is not confined to unmasking or consciousness-raising but is also about taking action to change situations. Habermas calls this the *organisation of enlightenment*.

In Critical Theory there is a rejection of the assumption that there can be 'objective' knowledge. There is no neutral or disinterested perspective because everyone is socially located and thus the knowledge that is produced will be influenced always by a social interest. Knowledge is always socially constructed and, as I have pointed out, always related to either a technical 'making' interest, a communicative 'practical' interest or a critical 'emancipatory' interest. The question that follows from this therefore is – if everyone's knowledge is grounded in history and social structure, then whose knowledge is 'best'? And what are the criteria that define 'best'?

It is Habermas who is most commonly associated with Critical Theory. In *Knowledge and Human Interests* (1972) he writes about 'systematically distorted communication' and how this can be overcome. Two arguments of his are crucial here. The first is the idea of *validity claims* – that all human communication involves speakers implicitly making such claims. What this means is that in any communicative transaction when one person says something to another that person implicitly makes the following claims:

- that what is being said is intelligible or meaningful;
- that the propositional content of what is being said is true;
- that the speaker is justified in saying what he or she is saying;
- that the speaker is speaking sincerely.

On the basis of this, Habermas concludes that undistorted communication is language use where speakers can defend all four validity claims – where what is said can be shown to be meaningful, true, justified and sincere. The implication then is that transactions should be of such a nature for it to be possible for the parties involved to make successful validity claims. The task therefore is to create conditions which remove limitations to the successful validation of claims.

The second argument Habermas puts forward is that of the *ideal speech situation*. This is bound up with Habermas' conception of truth. For him, truth is not correspondence with the world. Truth can only be understood in relation to processes of argumentation. When we say something is 'true' we mean we can back it up – that we can 'warrant' what we are claiming. Truth therefore refers to agreement or consensus reached by such warrants. For Habermas, truth is *rational agreement reached through critical discussion* and it is possible to distinguish an agreement of this kind from a consensus based on custom, faith or coercion.

This means that a claim to truth can only be acceptable if it is based on situations where, first, all the relevant evidence has been brought into play, and second, where nothing apart from logical, reasoned argument is involved in reaching a consensus. This is what Habermas means by an 'ideal speech situation'. It is one where there are no external or extraneous constraints, where each participant has an equal and open chance of participating and where all validity claims therefore are successful. He argues that truth reached in this way is the condition of human emancipation. Referring back to the question asked earlier, this also means that the 'best' knowledge is that which emerges in the ideal speech situation where all validity claims can be fully met.

Although most actual conditions of social interaction and communication are not like this, the notion of an ideal speech situation can function as a *regulative ideal* insofar as it supplies a critical measure of the inadequacies of existing forms of interaction and social institutions. Actual situations can therefore be analysed to find out the degree to which they deviate from an ideal speech situation; this knowledge then becomes an important means for changing the situation to bring it closer to the ideal of one where successful validity claims can be made.

Both the hermeneutic/interpretive and Critical Theory traditions would argue that being 'objective' is not a matter of having the 'right' methods but of having the 'right' arguments and of being prepared and able to subject them to the scrutiny of critical dialogue. This requires a dialogic situation, one where researchers are able to bring their pre-understandings into contact, through dialogue, with the pre-understandings of the researched and other researchers. But the condition for this is that dialogue must be free and unconstrained by structural/ideological inequalities. It is only in this context that a 'fusion of horizons' or an 'ideal speech situation' can be achieved and it is in the failure to incorporate these structural/ideological constraints and distortions that Critical Theory finds itself most at odds with the hermeneutic/interpretive tradition.

But if this condition is not present then the question arises: should we as researchers try to do something to bring it about? This is the question with which Critical Theory is particularly concerned. In other words, if research is not to be either an instrument simply for the further dominance of technical-rationality or for the furtherance of human understanding and communication, then it has to involve *praxis* (informed, committed action). Dialogue then is only a condition of emancipatory action since praxis encompasses dialogue and action. This poses the question of whether researchers need, at the very least, to take action to ensure that the right conditions for dialogue are present? What action is necessary? Furthermore, if dialogue is not enough, what further action is required if the purpose of research is truly emancipatory? If research, in other words, is not merely to be a matter of 'finding out' about the world but of changing it in the name of justice and democracy.

A major problem with Critical Theory is its self-proclaimed commitment to an emancipatory project posited as a universal value. Foucault's argument that everything is dangerous is a salutary reminder that universalising emancipatory discourses may not always have the effect intended. Gore (1993: 61) deploys Foucault's notion of a 'regime of truth' to argue that Critical Theory has its own 'power–knowledge nexus which, in particular contexts and in particular historical moments, will operate in ways that are oppressive and repressive to people within and/or outside'.

POSTMODERN APPROACHES TO RESEARCH

The questioning of what 'scientific', 'rigorous' research is and what its effects are, is part of a contemporary condition which Habermas has called a 'crisis of legitimation', and Lyotard 'a scepticism about the grand narratives of the European Enlightenment', an aspect of what is now generally referred to as 'postmodernity'.

Postmodernism, the cultural and intellectual aspect of postmodernity, questions formerly secure foundations of knowledge and understanding. The quest for a 'God's eye view', a disembodied and disembedded timeless perspective that can know the world by transcending it is no longer readily accepted. What has taken its place, and what the postmodern expresses, is a loss of certainty in what is known and in ways of knowing. What we have now is not an alternative and more secure foundation but an awareness of the complexity and socio-historical contingency of the practices through which knowledge is constructed about ourselves and the world. All approaches to research are a reflection of cultural beliefs about the world we live in and want to live in. Postmodernism reflects the contemporary decline of absolutes and a questioning of the belief that following the correct method guarantees true results. It is not anti-science but instead emphasises the need for science to be self-reflexive about its limitations.

We have seen how social and educational phenomena are more aptly understood as indeterminate and open-ended. Postmodernism challenges the powerful view that there is a determinate world which can be definitively known and explained. It views the social sciences as sciences of indeterminacy where theories do not succeed because they predict unique and determinate outcomes.

As I have already argued, to see social and educational research as consisting of a technology, a set of invariant procedures, leads to a failure to recognise it as a social practice, the product of one of many social, historically-located practices. What this points to is the *conventionality* of research, its constructed quality and the fact that it could be other than a technology. If we see all research (including research in the natural sciences) as a social product, this foregrounds the possibility of critiquing the *process* of research.

Postmodernism displays a scepticism about epistemology's traditional aim of distinguishing true, certain knowledge through a general account of the nature and limits of knowledge. Epistemology came to be equated solely with empiricism and positivism and thus privileged scientific method as the methodological guarantee of a true and certain knowledge. Universal rules were formulated as to what could be counted as scientific knowledge. These were considered to be a set of universal characteristics which, when present, qualified a practice as 'scientific', a theory or explanation as adequate.

Postmodernism therefore displaces epistemology as a philosophical enterprise by questioning the dominant epistemology's positivist/empiricist conception of scientific knowledge which traditionally set the standard and provided the model for all knowledge claiming to be scientific. In particular, it challenges the leading assumptions of the positivist/empiricist research tradition that:

- observation is value-neutral and atheoretical;
- experience is a 'given';
- a univocal and transparent language is possible;
- data are independent of their interpretations;
- there are universal conditions of knowledge and criteria for deciding between theories.

In the postmodern, there is a questioning of whether knowledge is established through systematic empirical observation and experiment or whether a necessary first step requires a shifting of the way the world is seen and the construction of a new world to investigate. In other words, an epistemology must be preceded by an ontology.

On the other hand, a postmodern approach does not simply embrace the alternative hermeneutic/interpretive research tradition since it sees this as still implicitly operating within the terms and discourse of the positivist/empiricist tradition – in other words, the emphasis on the 'subjective' instead of the 'objective' is merely a reversal which still works within a framework of 'objective–subjective' as polar opposites. Instead, a postmodern approach seeks to subvert this dichotomy and suggest alternatives which radically challenge and critique the dominant epistemological discourse in all its various forms.

One of these alternatives is to turn to the actual historically located practices of the various sciences, natural as well as social. This historical approach, that for example informs the work of Kuhn (1970), displaces the essentialist and transcendental view of science which is to be found in both the positivist/empiricist and hermeneutic/interpretive traditions and instead argues that all sciences are social practices. This emphasis on the actual practice of a science highlights its specificity and situatedness and the practice-constituted criteria for judging the validity of knowledge claims and theory choice. This approach is informed by an anti-essentialist view of what counts as scientific knowledge, that denies any single set of features qualifying a practice as scientific or an explanation as adequate. Instead the emphasis is on knowledge as contingent and perspectival and on the situational features of research practices.

Another postmodern alternative arises as a consequence of this displacement of epistemology and the consequent foregrounding of ontology. This has two important aspects. The first is to do with 'world-making' through language, discourses and texts. All research is both a socio-cultural construct and is itself constructive or 'world-making'. This occurs because of the implication of research with language, discourse and texts.

Postmodernism sees knowledge-generation as a practice of 'languaging', a practice of textual production. Here, language is not conceived as a mirror held up to the world, as simply a transparent vehicle for conveying the meaning of an independent external reality. Since there is always an already existing structure of significations which gives rather than reflects meaning, referents are an effect of language. Language is both the carrier and creator of a culture's epistemological codes, the way we as researchers know and the way we are located within culture. No form of knowledge can therefore be separated from language, discourses and texts at work within culture. The structures, conceptuality and conventions of language, embodied in discourses and texts – language as a meaning-constituting system – govern what can be known and what can be communicated.

One consequence of this is that knowledge, being relative to discourses, is always partial and perspectival. Thought and experience, the positivist/empiricist bedrock, are not independent of socio-cultural contexts and practices. Epistemological research traditions are coded by language and discourse in terms of binary and hierarchical oppositions, for example, masculine–feminine, subject–object, rational–irrational. One effect of these hierarchies is to constitute the identity of both researchers and researched in particular ways.

Science's claim to authority has been premised on its appeal to experience mediated by purportedly value-neutral, logical–empirical method which promised the growth of rational control over ourselves and our world. Practices of control and prediction were rooted in unreconcilable binary opposites, for example: linearity – chaos; teleology – historical contingency; representational language – constitutive language; 'innocent' knowledge – power/knowledge; facts as given – facts as constructed by the questions asked.

In every case, as we have already seen, one pole of the opposites is privileged over the other, for example, linearity over chaos, facts as given over facts constructed. What this means, however, is that these polar opposites are not 'natural', existing in reality, but are themselves social constructs, organised in hierarchical forms, functioning as cultural codes, and possessing normative power precisely because they are thought to be 'natural'.

The second aspect of the postmodern is a decentring of the knowing subject, the epistemological subject with a universal and essential human nature – unitary, rational, consciousness-centred and the originary point of thought and action. This essential nature is conceived as allowing subjects to be autonomous of the world and to occupy an Archimedean point that transcends their own subjectivity, history and socio-cultural location. This stance of 'objectivity', where the subject is a pure experiencer and reasoner transcending particularity, partiality and contingency, is the condition for the interchange-ability of knowing subjects and hence the public verifiability of scientific knowledge (Code 1993).

Postmodernism challenges and displaces this abstract, transcendental subject, arguing instead that subjects cannot be separated from their sub-jectivity, history and socio-cultural location. In the postmodern, there are no Archimedean points, the subject is instead decentred, enmeshed in the 'text' of the world, constituted in intersubjectivity, discourse and language. Equally, the separation of subject and object, objectivity and subjectivity, is itself a position maintainable only so long as the knower is posited as abstract and decontextualised and the known object posited as the 'other' unable to reflect back on and affect the knower (Acker *et al.* 1991).

The need to take account of the status of knowers/researchers and their socio-cultural contexts, the intimate inseparability of knower and known, the known and the means of knowing, the impossibility of separating the subjects and objects of research challenges the empiricist and positivist epistemological assumption of an 'objective' world and the foundational systems of thought which secure, legitimate and privilege 'objective' ways of knowing that world. Science, formed in its self-understandings by this epistemology, has tradition-ally assumed a knowing subject, a known object and an unambiguous knowledge. None of these can any longer be taken for granted.

As I have noted earlier, the notion of an absolute and universal knowledge is questionable. In the postmodern, there is a foregrounding of complexity, uncertainty, heterogeneity and difference. There is a questioning of the power-ful notion that there is 'one true reality', stable and ordered, that exists independently of knowers, which can be experienced 'as it really is' and which is best represented in scientific models of research. Instead, postmodernists argue that the 'real' is unstable, in flux and contingent. Although we can sense the real, knowing it is only possible by representing it through a signifying system. But in representation, the real is not simply being reflected 'as it really is' but is being constructed or shaped in a way particular to the codings of the signifying system. As we have seen, these codings take the form of binary, hierarchical and oppressive oppositions.

What this implies is that social events, processes and phenomena are indeterminate. As I have already argued, knowledge in the form of predictive generalisations requires a closure which itself pre-supposes a determinate, orderly 'real'. Hence the closure that is necessary can only be *imposed* – it is not something that exists naturally in the real and is simply reflected in the form of predictive generalisations. Closure involves violence and therefore raises questions of power which are not supposed to be relevant in 'scientific' research. Once questions of power do become relevant, however, then the 'objectivity' of the research process becomes highly problematic.

The need to take account of the dimension of power challenges the possibility of 'disinterested' research and value-free knowledge. Science is both constituted by a particular set of values and itself is value-constituting, yet the scientific attitude is one that continually attempts to suppress the place of values and conceal the workings of power. The postmodernist would argue that it is impossible to escape the value-ladenness of research since ways of knowing are inherently culture-bound and will therefore reflect the dominant values of the particular culture in which they are located. The striving for value-neutrality and the striving for detachment from the world is itself a value position located in the particular culture of Western society as it has developed since the European Enlightenment. One thing that this implies therefore is the need to be reflexive, to be aware of how values permeate research both in its methods and outcomes.

By denying the place of values and power, by ignoring the question of how research is an enactment of power relations, science becomes a form of mystification and a source of oppression. As Foucault has argued, power is always present in any attempt to know, indeed power works its effects through its intimate interconnection with knowledge and with 'regimes of truth'. It is for this reason that a postmodern approach to research highlights the need to consider not only outcomes and methods but also the implication of research with power and unspoken values. It is not enough to adopt the unquestioning position that research is simply the disinterested pursuit of truth. Research must always, of necessity, seek the truth, or perhaps more accurately *a* truth (out of many possible truths), but to place all the stress on this leads to a failure to consider the workings of power within the research process.

The dependence of knowledge on socio-cultural practices and contexts, unacknowledged values, tacit discourses and interpretive traditions means that research is embedded in unconscious fore-structures of understanding, the 'unsaid' and 'unsayable' – that is, the condition of any methodical knowing. All knowledge of the real is textual, i.e. always already signified, interpreted or 'written' and therefore a 'reading' which can be 're-written' and 're-read'. Hence there is neither an originary point of knowledge nor a final interpretation. However, as I have just noted, some readings are more powerful than others. The most powerful readings are those imposed by the violence of closure and the 'metaphysics of presence' – the claim to a direct and unmediated knowledge of the real that can only be provided by scientific method. Yet given that all readings are subject to contingency and the historical moment in which they are read, and given that the object of scientific research is always open to contest, then all claims to presence, to unmediated knowledgeability, are always problematic.

Postmodernism challenges foundationalism, the position that knowledge is founded in disciplines, and the consequent boundary-defining and maintenance that is characteristic of disciplinary knowledge. There are two aspects to this. The first is that social scientists, located as they are in the modernist epistemological project, want to give 'reasoned', connected and totalising accounts. But as we have seen, the world they investigate and seek to explain is not one that can readily be *reflected* in their theories and accounts. It is, in other words, not organised naturally into disciplinary compartments. They are therefore always, as Acker *et al.* (1991: 149) point out, in the business of attempting to systematically 'reconstruct social reality and to put these reconstructions into the form of a social theory'.

The social sciences conceive of themselves as representing the real whereas what they are actually doing is 'writing' it. Social reality does not exist as an extra-discursive context, rather the real and the discursive are intimately interwoven: 'the social is written ... there is no extra-discursive real outside cultural [i.e. meaning] systems ... the social world does not consist of ready-made objects that are put into representation' (Game 1991: 4). If disciplinary theorising is itself a practice of writing then theory cannot be tested against the real. The question then becomes: by what discursive strategies does a discipline maintain its claims to the status of knowledge? In the case of the social sciences, this is done through a privileged representation of social reality based on the binary opposition 'real–representation' and the consequent repression of the fictionality or textuality of the social sciences.

Research practices inscribe certain kinds of legitimation. When we think of research as a practice rather than a technology we can see more readily how research becomes authoritative *because* it is embodied in particular kinds of text. Although research is always an attempt to represent the world, it is also an example of the productivity of language within a framing authorial context. The author is also an 'author-ity'. For the postmodernist therefore, objectivity is a textual construction, where the use of certain textual devices, for example narrative realism, constructs the 'scientific self' of the 'objective' researcher. Hence, as well as stressing outcomes and methodology we also need to be aware of research as a text, the way in which research is *written*.

As an example of a postmodern approach to research I will now briefly describe a piece of research carried out by Patti Lather and reported in *Staying Dumb: Student Resistance to Liberatory Curriculum* (Lather 1991). Here, what is provided is not only a description of the research, its purpose, methods and outcomes but also an exploration of what it means to do research in a postmodern way.

The research was a three-year enquiry into student resistance to a liberatory curriculum in an introductory women's studies course. This course attracts a significant percentage of mature students (mainly women), minority groups and alternative lifestylers. On the face of it, the research is conventionally empiricist. Data are collected from interviews, research reports and entries from her own reflective diary. However, Lather's aims in doing the research were rather different from most empiricist educational research. As she herself states she sought:

1 to make a space from which the voices of those not normally heard could be heard;
2 to move outside conventional research texts, outside the textual devices which help to construct research as 'scientific';
3 to ask questions about the way she as the 'author' constructs her research text and organises meaning, and in this way to highlight the performativity or constructive nature of language;
4 to challenge the myth of a found or already existing world in research and its communication outside the intrusion of language and an embodied researcher;
5 to explore a complex and heterogeneous reality which does not fit neatly into pre-established categories;
6 to be concerned with the politics of research, in particular to examine how any categorising is an act of power which always marginalises;
7 to put the researcher back into the picture, given that the researcher is a social subject in relation with others. The specificity of the researcher, for example, Patti Lather's interest in emancipatory pedagogy, shapes the process and product of her enquiry.

A postmodern approach to research questions and displaces the orthodox consensus about how to do research scientifically. As we have seen, there are many research traditions each with its own epistemology and each exercising a differential power. Postmodernism, however, is not an alternative tradition although it does foreground and critique the epistemological commitments which are implicit in all research traditions, and for this reason cannot itself become a research tradition since it must remain reflexively critical.

To do research in a postmodern way is to take a critical stance towards the practice of sense-making and sense-taking which we call research. What it focuses on however is not the *world* which is constructed and investigated by research but the way in which that world is written, inscribed or textualised in the research *text*.

This is an unfamiliar process because generally what we think we are doing as researchers is producing a text which accurately represents the world that has been researched. We also assume that the appropriate and correct use of methods ensures that the representation is accurate. Furthermore, we tend to believe that once we have done this then no more questions need be asked about the text itself.

To take a postmodern approach to research involves more than generating accurate representations. It involves focusing on the text (both in the wide and narrow sense) and asking certain questions about it. This is an essentially *reflexive* or self-referential task. We ask: Why do we do research? How has our research been constructed? What is it silent about? What gives our text its narrative authority? What are the gender, race and class relations that produce the research and how does the text reproduce these relations? To what extent does research empower (and disempower) those involved in it?

These are all reflexive questions. They are partly autobiographical but even then not in a purely individualistic sense. As researchers we all have an individual trajectory which shapes the research we do, the questions we ask and the way we do it. But as researchers we are also socio-culturally located, we have a social autobiography, and this has an equally if not more important part to play in shaping our research and directing the kinds of reflexive questions which need to be asked but rarely are. These are some of the questions which will be taken up in the next chapter.

REFERENCES

Acker, J., Barry, K. and Esseveld, J. (1991) 'Objectivity and Truth: Problems in doing Feminist Research', in M. Fonow and J. Cook (eds) *Beyond Methodology*, Bloomington: Indiana University Press.

Bleicher, J. (1982) *The Hermeneutic Imagination: Outline of a Positive Critique of Scientism and Sociology*, London: Routledge.

Code, L. (1993) 'Taking Subjectivity into Account', in L. Alcoff and E. Potter (eds) *Feminist Epistemologies,* London: Routledge.

Foucault, M. (1980) *Power/Knowledge*, Brighton: Harvester Press.

Gadamer, H-G. (1975) *Truth and Method*, London: Sheed & Ward.

Game, A. (1991) *Undoing the Social*, Milton Keynes: Open University Press.

Gore, J. (1993) *The Struggle for Pedagogies*, London: Routledge.

Habermas, J. (1972) *Knowledge and Human Interests,* London: Heinemann.

Kuhn, T. (1970) *The Structure of Scientific Revolutions*, Chicago: University of Chicago Press.

Lather, P. (1991) *Feminist Research in Education*, Geelong: Deakin University Press.

Lyotard, J. (1984) *The Postmodern Condition*, Manchester: Manchester University Press.

Maturana, H. (1991) 'Science and Daily Life: the Ontology of Scientific Explanations', in F. Steier (ed.) *Research and Reflexivity*, London: Sage.

3 Textuality and reflexivity in educational research

Robin Usher

> Why do research if you cannot say anything about what is out there and all research is self-reflexive? Why do research for which you must deny responsibility for what *you* have 'found'.
>
> (Steier 1991: 10)

Writing is not a set of abstract transcendental marks but rather a concrete, material activity located within particular textual practices each with its own characteristics and therefore its own form and content of writing, its own unique texts. Education writes in its own way – it has, in other words, its own textual practices. For example, because in education there is always an intertwining of theory and practice, its writing cannot slip free from practice to live within a timeless, decontextualised world of general theoretical knowledge.

Of course, the textual practice of education produces a varied range of writing and, indeed, one of its strengths is that no particular kind of writing predominates. Yet there is a strong tendency for the research text not to draw attention to itself as a text. Decisions about how the text is to be written and the criteria for evaluating a 'good' piece of writing are determined by the need to convey a subject-matter transparently. In this kind of text, writing is seen as simply a neutral vehicle for transporting the 'truth'. Thus the *textuality* of research 'falls away' with writing appearing as simply an unmediating means for communicating a reality that is 'outside' the text. Underlying this is an implicit opposition or dualism of 'reality' and its 'representation' (the research text) which works to repress the very textuality of educational research, its 'reality' as a practice of writing, and to ignore the question of *how* educational research as a practice of writing 'constructs' reality.

REFLEXIVITY AND RESEARCH

Having foregrounded the significance of this 'repressed' textual dimension I want to argue that the need to surface and recognise this dimension becomes more urgent. In research writing becomes unavoidable and the very productivity of writing makes questions of textuality, and of reflexivity, unavoidable.

Educational research is located in a knowledge-producing *community*. Following Kuhn (1970) I would argue that the production of any kind of theoretical knowledge always takes place within such a community. Of course, communities will display a great deal of variation in their cohesiveness, the strength of their 'disciplinary matrix', and the flexibility of the procedures by which they validate knowledge claims. Education as a field of research and theorising is not firmly rooted in any single disciplinary matrix and therefore probably lies at the 'weak' end of the spectrum, although I think this need not in itself be seen as a weakness.

To say that educational research is located in a community is significant because it is to recognise that it, like all research, is a social practice. I have already commented on this in an earlier chapter but here I want to emphasise both the 'social' aspect and the 'practice': the former as a necessary antidote to the powerful view that research is always individualistic, the latter because it shifts us away from seeing research as a procedure, a way of 'seeing' which undoubtedly has a certain heuristic value but which is also very limiting insofar as it portrays research as mechanistic and algorithmic. The problem with this is that it implies that research is both disembedded – an essentially ahistorical, apolitical technical process, a transcendental, contextless procedure – and disembodied – carried out by isolated, asocial, genderless individuals without a history.

Seeing research as a social practice forces us to recognise certain things. First, that research is not a matter of applying a set of transcendental methods or of following an algorithmic procedure. Rather it is a set of activities legitimated by a relevant community – that is one of the reasons why it is social. One consequence of this is that some activities will be considered appropriate and will function as criteria for validating knowledge outcomes, others will be ruled 'out of order' and excluded. Communities define rules of exclusion, set boundaries, and impose closures. Consequently, this narrows what can be done and what will count as legitimate research and valid knowledge outcomes. In educational research, falling at the 'weak' end of the spectrum, what is communally sanctioned is fairly flexible and changing – rules are not so rigid, boundaries not so firmly set, and the closures not so complete. Yet despite this there are boundaries and consequently exclusions. It is still impossible, for example, to present one's research as a literary text.

Now on the face of it this may seem a 'wild' example but it demonstrates an important point through its very extremeness. I want to argue that if research is a social practice, a practice of producing certain kinds of knowledge that are socially validated, then as such it is a set of activities that constructs a world to be researched. When we delineate what we intend to study, when we adopt a particular theoretical position, when we ask certain kinds of questions rather than others, when we analyse and make sense of findings in one way rather than another, when we present our findings in a particular kind of text: all this is part of constructing a researchable world. In other words, research is not simply a matter of representing, reflecting or reporting the world but of 'creating' it through a representation.

But literature as a textual practice is also in the business of 'creating' worlds. Once we get out of the habit of simplistically counterposing 'fact' to fiction and once we stop unproblematically equating fiction with 'untruth' then we can begin to see that research is just as 'fictional' as literature. If we were to conduct our research in a literary mode and present our 'findings' in the form of a literary text then we would have created a world, albeit a very different one, just as much as if we had faithfully followed the linear model. It is just that the communal paradigm in which our research is located is likely to approve of the latter and disapprove of the former. This is not to say that social and educational research is the same as literature but both are practices and, more specifically, textual practices. Writing dissolves the opposition of fact and fiction and reverses the privileging of the former over the latter. Both research and literature as practices of writing construct worlds and are therefore 'fictional'. Thus, in both, reflexivity becomes an issue and both have the means from within their own practice to conceal its significance.

In one sense, the reflexivity issue is not new. It could be said to be as old as Western philosophy itself, where traditionally it has tended to be seen as a problem. Indeed, that it can be seen as a problem is itself a product of that philosophy, although that does not make it any the less powerful. At one level, the 'problem' is deceptively simple; that the activity of the knower influences what is known since nothing can be known apart from these activities. The question that then follows from this reflexive 'problem' is that if research, the making of knowledge claims, is dependent upon the activity of the researcher, do we then as researchers simply research ourselves? Is research merely a subtle form of writing the self – a different, non-literary way of writing one's autobiography? Are we really finding out about ourselves rather than about the subject of our research? Indeed, what is the 'subject' of research? Who, for that matter, are 'ourselves'?

Furthermore, what kind of problem is reflexivity, indeed is it a problem at all? In a framework of postmodern theory which argues for a foregrounding of how we construct what we are researching, reflexivity is no longer seen as a problem but as a resource. It helps us to recognise that we ourselves are a part of rather than apart from the world constructed through research. More than this, however, by becoming aware of the operation of reflexivity in the practice of research, the place of power, discourse and text, that which in a sense goes 'beyond' the personal, is revealed.

This is the other important thing we are forced to recognise when we start seeing research as a social practice. Research may be carried out by individuals but it is not individualistic. Indeed, it could be said that the very notion of the 'individual' is a *subject position* produced by a certain kind of discourse (see Foucault 1982 and Game 1991). It is to a fuller consideration of what 'going beyond the personal' implies in relation to research and reflexivity that I now turn.

THE PERSONAL AND THE SOCIAL IN RESEARCH

Of course, foregrounding reflexivity is not without its problems. The foremost of these is that it can lead to a 'personalisation' of research, encapsulated in the notion that research is 'finding out about oneself'. There is a personal element in research in the sense that doing research is moved by a desire to explain and understand that always points back to self-understandings and self-construc- tions. We are reminded by Foucault (1980: 109–33) that the will to truth is also a will to power. Even when our research is moved by an emancipatory desire we are still 'writing the self' – and not in a purely autobiographical sense either – but more significantly fulfilling a desire for mastery, self-affirmation and maintaining self-sameness. Whatever its forms, desire is not something which merely starts off the research process and provides the energy to keep it going, but rather is a structuring element in every aspect of the research act. Its very existence makes problematic the scientistic notion of researchers as decontex- tualised and disembodied 'pure reasoners'.

Nowadays, there is a general scepticism about the very possibility of value- neutrality and a 'disinterested' stance. It is a scepticism found in certain tendencies in the social sciences, in educational theorising and research to a certain degree and, above all, in feminist and postmodern research. It is in effect a recognition that reflexivity, even if only to a limited degree, is always present in the practice of research. Being aware of reflexivity in this limited sense is considered no bad thing since it is seen as enabling researchers to be more 'upfront' about the 'subjective' elements, including the values of the researcher, that cannot simply be ignored or banished from research.

This kind of reflexivity, often known as 'personal' reflexivity, refers to 'the researcher's own identity as an individual, a woman, and a feminist. For the individual his or her research is often an expression of personal interests and values ... Thus the topics one chooses to study are likely to derive from personal concerns' (Wilkinson 1988: 494). The value of this notion of personal reflexivity is that it points to the importance of the 'autobiography' of the researcher's lived experience and in so doing clearly shows the influence of the researcher's values and standpoints, not only in the choice of subject or topic researched but also in how the research is carried out, how 'data' is generated and how its significance is evaluated.

However, 'autobiography' and 'lived experience' are themselves terms that need to be problematised. Not to do so is to see lived experience as 'presence', a pure, unmediated and authentic knowledgeability, and autobiography as a kind of true and direct 'speech' of the autonomous, self-present person. But again, autobiography is written, it is a text and therefore constructed through textual genres, conventions and strategies, while lived experience is mediated by language and discourses – as Connor (1989: 3) argues, experience is always 'interpreted in advance by the various structures of understanding and interpretation which hold at particular moments in particular societies'. The question that arises therefore is of the relationship between autobiography and the lived experience of which it is an 'account'. The relationship is a complex one but at the very least it is impossible to argue that the autobiography simply and transparently reports 'lived experience'; that it somehow merely 'translates' this experience into a publicly communicable form.

At the same time, reflexivity is not confined to the 'personal'. Reflexivity does not simply direct our attention to the problematics of the researcher's identity but also to the 'identity' of the research. Here, the question highlighted is: what is going on in this research? What kind of world or 'reality' and what kind of knowledge is being constructed by the questions I am asking and the methods I am using? What is involved, therefore, is a 'continuous, critical examination of the practice/process of research to reveal its assumptions, values and biases' (Wilkinson 1988: 495).

I may think, for example, that my research is simply a neutral 'finding out', but the kinds of questions I ask and the methods I use may mean that it functions oppressively. Much research in the social sciences and in education, operating as it does through a positivist/empiricist paradigm, tends to have this effect, despite its 'neutrality' and the best intentions of the researcher. Equally, I may want my research to be emancipatory and I may as a researcher be very conscious of the need to act in an emancipatory way, but the kind of methods I use and the implicit values I hold may result in a completely opposite effect. Most action research, for example, tends to be like this (Kosmidou and Usher 1991): a kind of mechanistic, 'going through the stages' activity which works to negate any empowering intent.

There is also an epistemic or disciplinary reflexivity where having moved from the researcher to the research act the focus switches to the communities within which research as a practice is located. I referred earlier to the significance of seeing research as located in a community and, in particular, following Kuhn, the effect this has on the way research is organised through a community's disciplinary matrix. Here the term 'discipline' has a double meaning as, on the one hand, a body of systematic knowledge progressively added to through research, and on the other, a system of regulation and control. As Foucault (1977, 1986: 169–256) points out, this double meaning is no coincidence but, on the contrary, marks the effect of power/knowledge formations, the co-implication of disciplinary knowledge and regulatory power.

Disciplinary or epistemic reflexivity recognises that because research is communally located and sanctioned it always carries within itself an epistemology, a theory about knowledge and truth and their relationship to the world or 'reality'. A great deal of social science research, for example, carries an epistemology of an independently existing or 'objective' reality that can only be truthfully known through the use of 'scientific' method. This epistemology is not 'innocent', however, but contains within itself a set of values which privilege the interests of individualism, capitalism and patriarchy. There is therefore a 'politics' of research, an implication of research with power relations. Thus epistemic reflexivity, in making us aware of the necessary place of research communities, also makes us aware of their power of exclusion and closure and provides us with the means to interrogate and problematise our immersion within them as researchers. In practical terms, this means that we should not and need not take our epistemology for granted.

The discussion of the significance of reflexivity in research has a number of implications. First, I hope I have shown that in doing research there is always a reflexive understanding potentially present: 'in our action is our knowing' (Lather 1991: xv). Second, that we need to see this reflexive understanding as a *resource* rather than as a source of bias and one way we can do this is by subjecting ourselves as researchers to critical self-scrutiny, in other words by being reflexive. Third, reflexivity has more than one form and this in itself has implications for the very notion of 'being reflexive'. In particular, it implies that reflexivity is not simply a matter of becoming aware of one's personality and temperament. Reflexivity is not simply a bringing into the open, through some kind of self-revealing introspection, one's psychological make-up.

Of course, as we have seen, personal reflexivity is a reminder of the place of the 'psychological' subjective. But as we have also seen even personal reflexivity involves much more than this. It is rather the 'social' subjective in the sense of the embodied and the embedded self that is being foregrounded. What personal reflexivity draws attention to is that the self that researches has an autobiography marked by the significations of gender, sexuality, ethnicity, class, etc. In other words, that these significations are socio-cultural products that are part of the practice of writing and which have *effects* upon both the form and the outcomes of research.

By understanding the 'personal' in terms of the social, the cultural and indeed the political, we can begin to make sense of the notion that all research requires and operates through a set of pre-understandings. Research is always approached with something 'in mind' in the sense that without pre-understandings, without knowing what questions to ask, we could not even get research off the ground. But these pre-understandings are not simply 'mine', a product of my psychological make-up. Research as knowledge production is ongoing; there is always an 'always already' as Derrida (1982) puts it, outside the control of individual researchers, so that the knowledge produced by any piece of research is always relative to and conditional upon that which is already known. Gadamer (1975) reminds us that our individual pre-understandings are also part of a 'tradition', an interpretive culture, which defines what is 'worth' knowing and therefore points research in certain 'worthwhile' directions. In practical terms then, being reflexive involves surfacing the pre-understandings which inform research and being aware of how these change in the course of the research. This need not just be a 'before' or 'after' exercise but something that is on-going *during* the course of the research.

Reflexivity does therefore involve finding out about ourselves but primarily in the sense of our immersion in the historical and the social, the inscription or the 'writing' of the self that researches through language, discourses and interpretive cultures in the practice of research. Research is a practice of knowing that constructs a reality to know about – 'we as researchers construct that which we claim to find' (Steier 1991: 1). The way we as researchers come to know reality constructs the reality we come to know. But, as Steier (1991: 5) goes on to point out, 'constructing is a social process, rooted in language, not located inside our heads'. This means that accepting reflexivity does not force us to adopt an idealist or subjectivist position whereby reality is conceived as a purely personal and 'mental' construction. Reflexivity foregrounds the implication of the personal within what is 'beyond' the personal; it is as much about the inscribed ('written') I as the inscribing I (the 'I' that writes) – the I that is a subject constituted in research as a practice of writing by the language, discourses and interpretive culture, as against the I that is the author of writing, the self-present, autonomous and author-itative I of scientific *and* humanistic discourses, positivist-empiricist *and* interpretive paradigms of research.

RESEARCH AS A REPRESENTATIONAL PRACTICE

Research is generally thought of as a process of 'finding out' about the world. Reflexivity, on the other hand, is 'finding out' about how meanings, including the meanings given to and generated by research, are discursively constructed within the practice of research, and therefore how all understanding, including the understanding which precedes and accompanies research, is bound up with language and its work of constructing a world to be researched. To say that research is a practice 'in' language rather than a transcendent process 'outside' it is to claim that research is a discursive practice of 'languaging' or making 'moves' both through and within language. Such a claim immediately makes problematic the idea of research as a process whose procedures and methods are designed to guarantee 'true' representations of the world. Here, the outcomes of research, what is found out, are supposed to represent the 'reality' investigated, a representation which the research text is supposed to convey. When research is seen as a process the key questions are always concerned with the extent to which research outcomes, as reported, are adequate, correspond to, or truly represent the reality investigated. The effect of this concern is therefore an emphasis in research on outcomes and method.

Reflexivity has traditionally been seen as a 'problem' that must be avoided or overcome because it interferes with or 'contaminates' outcomes as truthful representation. Methodology, or the correct and systematic use of methods, is seen as the answer because it supposedly banishes the reflexive 'problem'.

Methodology works through decontextualisation where methods separate or distance subject and object, the researcher and the researched. The researcher is taken out of her/his social and cultural context and made into the 'pure reasoner'; the researched are taken out of their context and made into 'objects' with natural rather than social attributes, in other words, constituted as the 'other'. Through decontextualisation both are taken out of language and the shared socio-cultural context to which they 'belong'. This process works to maintain the notion ('fiction'?) of an independently existing yet independently knowable reality. Thus methodology is taken to be the guarantee that the knowing activities of the researcher will not leave a 'dirty footprint' on what is known. Only then can the knowledge claims of the researcher be accepted as an adequate or truthful representation.

The separation of subject and object or, to put it another way, the positing of difference between subject and object by making the object 'other', is thus the condition of truthful representation. At the same time, however, the representation and that which it represents cannot be *too* different because otherwise the former could not be deemed to be *about* the latter. For example, knowledge of quarks that truthfully represents the reality of quarks must be about quarks but must not itself be a quark. The result of this is that methodology must work to construct a representation that combines both sameness and difference.

Now when we think of method we do so in terms of a powerful natural science paradigm where it is a set of transcendental rules which, when properly applied, generates a truthful representation. I want to argue, following Kuhn (1970), that there are concrete *methods* rather than transcendental Method. I also want to argue that representation is a representational *work*, something that is achieved within research as a practice of writing. Concrete methods therefore do their work within specific representational practices which discursively define the kind and degree of separation of subject and object, the combination of sameness and difference, that are appropriate and necessary to different kinds of research. That is why an 'adequate' or 'truthful' representation is not, therefore, a function of transcendental Method but a practical *achievement*.

The natural sciences understand themselves as marking and maintaining a strict separation or difference between subject and object, between quarks and those who research quarks. There is nature, the realm of reality, on the one hand, and culture, the realm of the researcher, on the other. Nature is cast as both radically different to, yet knowable through, culture and thus any representation of nature can be both sufficiently different and sufficiently the same to make 'truthful' representation possible. The radical difference takes the form of the object of research being constituted as 'other' by being denied qualities and characteristics supposedly possessed by the subject – for example, that the object does not have a mental life or that it does not itself engage in representational practices. In this way the 'problem', indeed the existence, of reflexivity can be wished away, yet, and this is what I want to emphasise, the 'wishing away' is itself a function of the natural sciences' own representational practices which depend on constructing the subject that researches and the object researched in particular ways as radically other to each other.

Social research, insofar as it aspires to be scientific, insofar as it locates itself within a positivist-empiricist paradigm, adopts the self-understandings of the natural sciences and with it their representational practices. Psychology, for example, which models itself most on the natural sciences, goes furthest in this direction. Where social research adopts the self-understandings and practices of the natural sciences, reflexivity is considered to have been methodologically removed. But social research in the 'scientific' mode faces a problem which, unlike the natural sciences, cannot be circumvented. The problem is that of the double hermeneutic and its effects (Giddens 1976). Put at its simplest, social researchers are engaging in representational practices whose outcomes purport to be truthful representations of a social reality whose members themselves engage in representational practices.

The double hermeneutic means that reflexivity is present at the very heart of the practice of research. Thus a constructed difference can no longer function unproblematically as the guarantee of a truthful representation. Researchers cannot separate themselves from the objects of their research, indeed they can no longer define them negatively as 'objects', lacking the qualities which they as subjects possess. Even in positivist-empiricist terms, if they set themselves apart from the reality they study they run the risk of not knowing it properly, of generating inadequate representations. In effect, they can only hope to know the reality they investigate by being part of it. But to accept that they are part of it is to accept the workings of reflexivity and to accept this is to accept that reality is known through their practices of knowing, and that therefore these practices are themselves researchable. As Aldridge (1993: 53–54) argues, there is a need 'to reveal, understand and analyse not only the *product* of knowledge but its *production* and therefore, its *producer*'.

This 'problem' of reflexivity in the social sciences is 'resolved' in a number of different ways. One option is to explain it away by saying that although researcher and researched engage in representational practices the representations of the former are at a 'higher' or meta-level than those they are researching, and hence exempt from the workings of reflexivity. Another option, commonly used in ethnographical and 'grounded' research, is to accept reflexivity but attenuate its consequences. Woolgar (1991: 22) refers to this as a 'benign introspection' which involves 'thinking about what you are doing' and usually takes the form of 'addenda to research reports, sometimes in the form of "fieldwork confessions", which provide the "inside story" on how the research was done'. Woolgar argues, rightly in my view, that benign introspection is a form of reflexivity which appears to question 'scientific' or positivist representationality but actually works to strengthen it. By presenting the 'inside story' of research it appears to bridge the separation of subject and researched object, but by seeing reflexivity as something to be accounted for subsequently rather than as something always present, it merely serves to reinforce the separation.

Ethnomethodology and critical ethnography go furthest in accepting reflexivity in its full rigour. In ethnomethodology, reflexivity is constitutive rather than something 'added on' because, as Garfinkel (1967) argues, the accounts of the researched constitute the reality that is researched. Research therefore can only be understood as an activity of discursive construction where the representation and what is represented cannot be separated because they are mutually interactive. Since the practice of research is reality constructing, research is always reflexively problematic. Researching others must therefore necessarily involve researching researchers so reflexivity, rather than being a 'problem', is, on the contrary, the key to the research act. In critical ethnography, there is an emphasis on research as a practice of writing and a problematising of 'representation' in the sense of the researcher-ethnographer's claims to author-itatively represent (speak for) the researched. The argument is that ethnography does not 'represent' (in either sense) the 'objective' reality of the researched, since the ethnographic text, as text, is a construction rather than a reflection or translation of socio-cultural reality. Clifford and Marcus (1986) argue that both researchers and researched are the 'authors' of socio-cultural representations (see also Woolgar 1991: 14–34). Once again, then, reflexivity becomes the central issue in posing questions about how 'authors' (whether researchers or researched) come to be authors.

REFLEXIVITY AND WRITING

I want at this point to return to my original problematic of research as writing and textuality. I have argued that the representational practices of research are inextricably bound up with writing and the production of texts. What is achieved through these practices, for example the decontextualisation and separation into subject and object, the constitution of subjects as authoritative and of objects as 'other', is all made possible through writing. As Barthes (1977: 201) argues, method is 'a spectacle mounted in the text'.

Research is necessarily embodied in the production of a written text but, as I hinted earlier when discussing the possibility of a literary text, not any text will do. In most cases, a particular kind of text, the academic text, is needed. As Parker and Shotter (1990) point out, academic texts

by the use of certain strategies and devices, as well as pre-determined meanings, [are] able to construct a text which can be understood (by those who are party to such 'moves') in a way divorced from any reference to any local and immediate contexts. Textual communication can be relatively decontextualised.

(Parker and Shotter 1990: 2)

Academic texts, therefore, work in ways which make them appear as if they are located in no particular context. I say 'appear' because their context is actually the research practices of the relevant community. Reading such texts requires initiation into the community and having command of its shared 'pre-determined meanings'. It requires, as Parker and Shotter emphasise, being 'party to the necessary moves'. For those who are not, the text is meaningless, they literally do not have the means to enable them to read it.

Academic texts are about 'reality' but the reality in which they are situated, from which they are produced and through which they can be read, falls out of view. They can thus deny their own being as textual practices and therefore by 'truly' representing what they are about, become an ideal vehicle for the dissemination of decontextualised knowledge .

Specifically, two things fall out of view. One is that research is writing and the production of a text. The other is the significance (and significatory power) of the representational means or system, the context of language, writing and its textual 'strategies and devices'. Since the representation is itself affected by the form of the representational system, the research text cannot be simply a faithful representation of a reality outside the text. Once texts are seen as constructed and constitutive, the distinction between text and reality becomes blurred or, at least, the conventional dualism of text and its 'outside' becomes questionable. As Parker (1989) points out, research in both the positivist-empiricist and interpretive paradigms assumes that this dualism is itself 'real'. From this it seems to follow that we can check out the truth of the text, the adequacy of its representations, by going back to the reality it is about and independently sampling it. But to do this would be simply to end up with another text. This is what Derrida (1987) means with his claim that there is no 'outside' of the text. Whatever is 'outside' can only be made knowable by being already 'inside'. In appealing to truth, by arguing for the adequacy of representations, we are not appealing to something that is outside the text but doing something within and through writing – and indeed doing some-thing which can *only* be done within and through writing.

That academic texts are not 'innocent' in this sense does not mean that the knowledge claims they convey are worthless. The fact that texts are con-structed and constructing, that truth depends on truth-producing textual practices, does not imply that they are arbitrary or 'subjective' and therefore false. As we have already noted, writing points away from individuals towards their inscription in textual practices. This itself undermines the powerful idea of the researcher as 'sovereign' author – the individual researcher not only writes but is also *written*. In an academic text one cannot, beyond a certain point, say what one wants in any way one wants. Research is 'objective', not in spite of, but because of its textuality. Equally, the fact that texts construct rather than discover a reality does not make them false. Thinking this way is a product of the science–myth dualism which is itself an 'unconscious' textual construction. Texts can speak *a* truth even though they cannot speak *the* truth.

It is the power of the science–myth dualism which makes us theorise truth as correspondence with reality. But if we stop seeing language as doing a purely referential job and start seeing our knowledge-producing activities as 'languaging' then it is possible to see truth as having many dwellings. What this means is that truth is not a matter of epistemology, of satisfying a correspondence *theory* of truth, but the outcome of many different social practices. Thus no one practice, for example the practice of natural science, has the monopoly of truth nor does its criteria of what constitutes truth have a monopoly over all others.

What is significant about writing is that it makes possible the use of certain textual strategies, which in the case of the academic text is that of narrative realism. Realism emphasises certain and singular meaning and the reporting rather than the construction of reality. The realist text does not draw attention to itself as a text and as Woolgar (1991: 28) points out, it has the status of 'a neutral medium for conveying pre-existing facts about the world … [its] neutrality exempts it from consideration as a species of social/cultural activity'. The text operates at a different or meta-level from that which it is about, it does not appear to help *create* the 'about' because it is not supposed to be productive. Thus it is through a realist textual strategy that the 'problem' of reflexivity can be most effectively banished.

The academic texts in which research is so often embodied are therefore 'writerly' texts which point away from their 'writerliness'. Through the textual strategy of realism they direct attention away from themselves as texts to that which they purport to be about. What this means is that it is only through writing that the constitutive effects of writing can be *denied*. The most important effect of writing is to conceal its own being as writing. As Derrida (1976) has pointed out, writing can only be disprivileged through writing i.e. by the use of metaphors of inscription (see also Payne 1993). Although writing is a necessary condition of claims to knowledge it is also the means by which the constitution of such claims in a textual production can be denied. It is only through writing, therefore, that the focus can be shifted from writing to that which the writing is about. To put it simply, it is writing that makes realism possible.

In the academic text it is precisely what is 'outside' the text that has to be privileged if the text is to do its work. It must not draw attention to itself as a text but to the reality outside the text which it both represents and re-presents. The meanings which the academic text 'transport' must be expressed clearly and univocally, i.e. in a transparent language. They must be seen to be pitching themselves against reality and not against other texts because 'reality' is what the text is supposed to be about. The realist form is one that is most appropriate for the representationalism by which most research is structured and methodology privileged. With the realist form of academic texts the world in which they are located, the interests and values which animate them, the very processes by which they came to be texts *about* something fall out of view. It is writing therefore which makes possible the 'becoming invisible' of textuality.

I want to argue therefore that researchers need to be aware of the *textuality* of any form of writing and beyond this they need to have the means to interrogate it. Furthermore, I want to argue that while all educational practitioners need not always be researchers, they are increasingly faced with the need not only to 'write' research texts but to be able to 'read' them too. By foregrounding the textuality of research and the reflexivity inherent in this textual staging of knowledge we can develop a critical awareness of the place of textual strategies such as narrative realism and we are then better able to problematise their assumptions, directionality and effects. In this way we can 'subvert' dominant forms and become critical writers and readers with alternative strategies of our own.

I want now to put forward a possible alternative in the hope that it can provide critical conceptual resources for interrogating textuality and foregrounding reflexivity in the production (writing) and consumption (reading) of research texts. This involves understanding, from the start, that texts are not simply what is written on the page or what they represent 'outside' the text. Instead, the work that their textuality does can only be understood by becoming aware of and using certain features that they have in common as the basis for reflexive analysis.

Con-text

If research is a textual practice, a textualising of the world through the production and consumption of authoritative knowledge claims in the form of texts, then these always have a 'con-text', in the sense of that which is *with* the text. What is 'with' the text in this sense is the situated autobiography of the researcher/reader.

Here, what is being highlighted is the socio-cultural subjective, the contextual self or, to put it another way, the embodied and embedded self. By asking reflexive questions about con-text we can scrutinise the 'knowledging' effects of the self that researches (writes) and the self that 'reads' research, a self with an autobiography marked by the significations of gender, sexuality, ethnicity, class, etc. These significations are socio-cultural products that effect, through writing, the very forms, outcomes and consequences of research and the way in which research is 'read'. They are not simply biases which can be eliminated by first admitting them and then placing ourselves under methodological control. These are 'biases', ineliminably part of us, which can be recognised but not willed away. They are the marks of the trajectory of our desires and emotional investments in the research act.

Pre-text

If research is a textual practice, then language as a signifying system assumes a central place. Here language needs to be seen not simply as a neutral vehicle for conveying representations but as an activity of 'languaging', the means through which the representational work of research is carried out. Consequently, research texts have a 'pre-text' in the sense of that which is *before* the text: language as the repository of meaning, discourses as particular ways of organising meanings, the textual strategies, literary conventions and rhetorical devices of writing. As Shotter (1990) points out:

> It is by the use of such rhetorical devices – as reference to 'special methods of investigation', 'objective evidence', 'special methods of proof', 'independent witnesses', etc. – that those with competence in such procedures can construct their 'factual statements' and claim authority for them as revealing a special 'true' reality behind appearances . . .
>
> (Shotter 199: 25)

This is an aspect of research to which we pay little attention. We focus on methods and outcomes and do not ask how meanings are created and received. As Game (1991: 28) points out 'if research is understood as writing, critical attention is drawn to the process of textual production which *is* research, as opposed to a final writing-up of research results'. As I have argued, this is due to the academic form that most research reports take, which function to conceal their own textuality: the pre-text repressed by the form itself.

However, it is by asking reflexive questions about pre-text that we can better understand that the self as researcher writes within prescribed forms (and this is why, to answer an earlier question, research cannot be presented as a literary text) that create the meanings of the textualised world that is researched, and of the texts that make knowledge claims about that world.

Sub-text

I referred earlier to research as a practice of 'presencing', of the making of authoritative claims to unmediated knowledgeability in the form of truthful representations of the world. What this implies is that claims to presence are implicated with the operation of power, the ability to claim and establish presence. Thus research texts have a 'sub-text' in the sense of that which is *beneath* the text: the operation of research paradigms and traditions and the power/knowledge discourses through which they are expressed and have their effects (Foucault 1980). The research act is constituted by power relations between researcher and researched, the outcome of which is the production and consumption of 'powerful' texts, texts which frequently become part of regulatory mechanisms in the domain of governmentality.

This is something we often find difficult to accept, since, given the traditional separation of knowledge from power, we tend to think of research, particularly our personal research, as innocent, 'powerless', perhaps even useful and emancipatory. A reflexive questioning of the sub-text enables us better to interrogate the implication of our practice within discourses of power, and how it becomes part of oppressive and dominant discourses through a 'reflexive', in the sense of a taken for granted acceptance of the neutrality of research, its pragmatic usefulness or its emancipatory potential – and how as writers and readers of research we become part of such discourses despite our best intentions.

Inter-text

Research in the scientific mode generally takes the form of decontextualised knowledge claims which are made through and against other textually-embodied claims. To paraphrase Kuhn, researchers do not match up their claims against an independently existing objective reality, but against other claims. Thus research texts have an 'inter-text' in the sense of that which is *between* texts. Intertextuality refers to the inhabiting of any particular text by 'the structure of the trace . . . the interlacings and resonances with other texts' (Wood 1990: 47), and which works both at the conscious and unconscious levels. In effect, intertextuality points to the place of history in textual production – the way in which history is inserted into the text and particular texts into history.

At the conscious level, intertextuality works through citations that are actually 'present'. Unconsciously, intertextual traces are always present both between the researcher's own 'different' texts and between the researcher's texts and other texts. As Barthes (1977) puts it:

> a text is not a line of words releasing a single theological meaning [the author's meaning] but a multidimensional space in which a variety of writings, none of them original, blend and clash. The text is a tissue of quotations drawn from the innumerable centres of culture.
>
> (Barthes 1977: 146)

These traces, the 'tissue of quotations', are citations which, although not physically present, are present as 'absences'. They speak *through* the text in an endless referability and are potent in their effects even though they are not spoken about *in* the text.

Intertextuality means, first, that texts have a referability, they can be cited author-itatively without the 'presence' of their author. Second, it means that texts are productive in the sense that they both transform prior texts (texts can be 're-read' through new texts) and make possible new texts (a text can only be written if there is a culture of writing and discourses which 'reveal' a world to be researched). However, this productivity is bounded, socially and culturally constrained and subject to relations of power (Fairclough 1992). Researchers are never fully the 'authors' of their texts.

In terms of reflexivity then, the centrality of writing creates an ambiguous situation. At one level, writing, by making the realist text possible, both enshrines reflexivity and at the same time appears to deal effectively with it. On the face of it, therefore, we could simply continue with our realist writing, research reality and come up with outcomes that appear to 'work'. Why then worry about reflexivity? At the very most, is it not just an unnecessary self-indulgence? Do we really want to fall into an endless regress of reflection and meta-reflection?

These are reasonable questions and they do warn of the danger of thinking too much about research rather than actually getting on and doing it. However, I also think that it would not be right to conclude that reflexivity is something we need not bother about. Steier (1991) reminds us that 'reflexivity' can also mean acting in a habitualised, perhaps even in a 'knee-jerk' way. I think this usefully points to the possibility that if we are not reflexive we can easily become 'reflexive' in this other sense. In particular, by taking textuality for granted, by taking writing 'at its own word', we blind ourselves to the *effects* of textuality.

When we talk about texts and textual practices we should not have in our minds some paradigm of 'harmless' and 'unworldly' literature. Texts, after all, are the means by which power-knowledge discourses are disseminated and with 'real' effects. Writing in general has power effects because the weighted dualisms of thought and their consequent hierarchies are produced through it. These dualisms and hierarchies are not mere abstractions but have, as feminist research has shown only too clearly, concrete exclusionary and disempowering effects. Reflexivity therefore is not dealt with by the realist text, rather the workings and effects of power through texts are merely hidden. It still has a part to play in helping us consider, as researchers, the way in which our dualisms, frameworks and categories, all the basic intellectual 'tools' of research, are implicated with power.

REFLEXIVITY AND EDUCATIONAL RESEARCH

Reflexivity as a 'bending back on itself' thus raises the question of whether we can avoid researching our research, including ourselves as researchers. As I have tried to show, there are textual practices and strategies for avoiding this question and in the actual doing of research we very often do avoid it, even when our research is self-consciously not located in a positivist paradigm. In a sense, the research paradigm does not really matter since reflexivity is present regardless of the nature of the paradigm. This means that the question of what the effects of such an avoidance are is relevant to any kind of research. Furthermore, I think this question is particularly important in educational research.

In educational research the need to problematise the practice of research is not unfamiliar. As I pointed out earlier, this is now fairly common practice, particularly in the emphasis on action research and practitioner-based enquiry. To some extent, therefore, there is a certain awareness of the significance of the working of reflexivity. Increasingly, we are careful not only about our methods but about their consequences. We certainly recognise, for example, that we as researchers, as well as those whom we research, have values and that the very attempt simplistically to eliminate all values from research in favour of the 'facts' and in the cause of objectivity, is in itself a value position.

But what I think we do not pay any attention to is the textuality of our research and its reflexive effects. Of course, in a sense we do not pay much attention because writing itself conceals this reflexivity from us. So effectively does it do this that our 'natural' attitude is simply to want to get on with our research and not bother too much with the 'meta' questions raised by reflexivity. We still think it is much more important to know how we should best go about our research rather than what effects it might have. Even those who explicitly want their research to be beneficial or 'useful' fall into this 'natural' attitude as a matter of second nature.

In education, we need to be aware of reflexivity because even when we think our research is useful or even emancipatory we are still 'objectifying', still speaking for others, and education is full of people who speak for others in the name of doing good by them. Thus an awareness of reflexivity enables us to interrogate our own practice of research, in terms of how it can become part of dominant and oppressive discourses through a 'reflexive' acceptance either of the neutrality of research, of its 'pragmatic' usefulness or its 'emancipatory' potential, and in terms of how we contribute to such discourses despite our best intentions. As long as we keep on taking textuality for granted, as long as we keep on seeing writing as merely a neutral vehicle for describing and theorising an outside world, for capturing 'reality' clearly and transparently, we will just keep on doing this.

It could reasonably be argued that the emphasis on writing and textuality is all very well but what has it really to do with education? Yet it is particularly important that textuality is not taken for granted in educational research. First, education is not itself a discipline. Insofar as it is located in any kind of disciplinary matrix it is that of the social sciences, but they have little in common as far as that is concerned. The only thing they do have in common, and here education can also be included, is the double hermeneutic, although not everyone in the social sciences recognises its effects. Thus educational research is itself a representational practice and hence can either 'wish away' the consequent reflexivity in research or recognise and 'work' with it.

Since in education worlds are always being created and their meanings and significance are always being contested, it is impossible to stand outside of the constructive process and its outcomes. In educational research there is a need to recognise the place of writing because it is only through writing that the capacity for questioning and subverting the tendency both of its own and of other social practices and discourses to become power-knowledge formations can be maintained.

CONCLUSION

Reflexivity and critique, critique through reflexivity, are skills which research-ers in education need to develop. But as Wood (1990) points out, it is not always the case that reflexivity is best secured by the use of a reflexive strategy. Neither is it the case that a didactic exposition of reflexivity would be appropriate. Reflexivity, given its elusiveness, can only be approached allu-sively. Yet because reflexivity is an integral and constitutive part of any research practice it need not be imposed in a direct and obvious way. The purpose of the framework outlined above is that it suggests the kinds of questions and issues that researchers seeking to be reflexive would want to pose about their practice. I would want to argue that being reflexive in this sense is just as, if not more, important than those aspects of research that are conventionally highlighted and which are used to 'justify' it.

If the truth-producing practices of a research community preclude the production of 'writerly' texts, texts which foreground their own textuality, there can at least be an awareness that research and the production and consumption of texts are inseparable. This awareness can be unsettling and what I hope has been achieved in this text is precisely that – a making strange of something that more often than not parades around in a taken for granted way. It is not simply that all research understands the limits of its methodology – there is nothing particularly unsettling in saying that and that is why I have deliberately not said it. Rather, I think there are two things in what I have said that may be unsettling. First, that research is always writing, a practice of textual production, and that therefore reflexivity is at the very heart of its being. And second, that with some kinds of research, textuality and reflexivity cannot but be denied and repressed. It is impossible to do research in the positivist-empiricist paradigm (and all its variants and mutations) *and* at the same time recognise the place of textuality and reflexivity in the research activity itself. Ultimately, what I hope I have shown is that this is potentially the case for virtually every kind of research whatever its locating paradigm. In other words, research is always more than just 'finding out' about the 'world'.

Finally, there is no doubt that the kind of framework I have suggested as a critical resource in the writing and reading of research could equally apply to this text. Why, for example, have I written it? Am I trying to 'enlighten', am I simply writing my 'autobiography' (clearly in one sense I am), am I engaging in some kind of power play, or is this an example of writing led by career imperatives? Although it is obviously all these and more, the limits placed upon the writing of this text (its 'otherness') precludes me from fully addres-sing these questions. Of course, it is open to others to subject my text to deconstructive scrutiny, for example, by using the framework I have suggested against it. Such a reflexive exercise is, however, best carried out by others. Meanings, after all, are realised not through individual intention but through intersubjective transactions.

REFERENCES

Aldridge, J. (1993) 'The Textual Disembodiment of Knowledge in Research Account Writing', *Sociology* 27, 1: 53–66.
Barthes, R. (1977) *Image–Music–Text*, New York: Hill and Wang.
Clifford, J. and Marcus, G. E. (eds) (1986) *Writing Culture: The Poetics and Politics of Ethnography*, Berkeley: University of California Press.
Connor, S. (1989) *Postmodernist Culture*, Oxford: Basil Blackwell.
Derrida, J. (1976) *Of Grammatology*, Baltimore: Johns Hopkins University Press.
—— (1982) *Margins of Philosophy*, Chicago: University of Chicago Press.
—— (1987) *Positions*, London: Athlone Press.
Fairclough, N. (1992) *Discourse and Social Change*, Oxford: Polity Press.
Foucault, M. (1977) *Discipline and Punish*, London: Penguin Books.
—— (1980) *Power/Knowledge*, Brighton: Harvester Press.
—— (1982) 'The Subject and Power', in H. L. Dreyfus and P. Rabinow (eds) *Beyond Structuralism and Hermeneutics*, Chicago: University of Chicago Press.
—— (1986) *The Foucault Reader*, P. Rabinow (ed.), London: Peregrine Books.
Gadamer, H-G. (1975) *Truth and Method*, London: Sheed & Ward.
Game, A. (1991) *Undoing the Social*, Milton Keynes: Open University Press.
Garfinkel, H. (1967) *Studies in Ethnomethodology*, Englewood Cliffs, NJ: Prentice-Hall.
Giddens, A. (1976) *New Rules of Sociological Method*, London: Hutchinson.
Kosmidou, C. and Usher, R. (1991) 'Facilitation in Action Research', *Interchange* 22, 4: 24–40.
Kuhn, T. S. (1970) *The Structure of Scientific Revolutions*, Chicago: University of Chicago Press.
Lather, P. (1991) *Getting Smart*, London: Routledge.
Parker, I. (1989) *The Crisis in Modern Social Psychology*, London: Routledge.
—— and Shotter, J. (eds) (1990) *Deconstructing Social Psychology*, London: Routledge.
Payne, M. (1993) *Reading Theory*, Oxford: Basil Blackwell.
Shotter, J. (1990) 'Social Individuality versus Possessive Individualism: The Sounds of Silence', in I. Parker and J. Shotter (eds) *Deconstructing Social Psychology*, London: Routledge.
Steier, F. (1991) 'Introduction: Research as Self-reflexivity, Self-reflexivity as Social Process', in F. Steier (ed.) *Research and Reflexivity*, London: Sage.
Wilkinson, S. (1988) 'The Role of Reflexivity in Feminist Psychology', *Women's Studies International Forum* 11, 5: 493–502.
Wood, D. (1990) *Philosophy at the Limit*, London: Unwin Hyman.
Woolgar, S. (1991) 'Reflexivity is the Ethnographer of the Text', in S. Woolgar (ed.) *Knowledge and Reflexivity*, London: Sage.

4 Methods and data in educational research

David Scott

This chapter examines the meaning of 'data' in the context of educational research and its relationship to theory and practice in education. It focuses on three research strategies and analyses their different ways of understanding data and method, the different implications of these for theory-building and the different relationships they assume between the researcher and the subjects of their research. Experimental researchers adopting positivist frameworks[1] carefully separate out their values from the data they collect and argue that theory-building is always nomological in character, based as it is on the hypothetico-deductive method.[2] Survey researchers operating with positivist or post-positivist perspectives (Guba and Lincoln 1994) understand relationships between phenomena as having only a high probability of application in other contexts.

Both of these can be contrasted with hermeneutic/interpretive approaches,[3] proponents of which assert that educational settings cannot be examined properly without referring to the meanings participants give to their activities. Whereas those educational researchers who would place themselves within the positivist camp pay little attention to political, ethical and reflexive concerns, those who would locate themselves within the hermeneutic/interpretive camp argue that the research enterprise is empty without explicit reference being made to these issues.

EXPERIMENTAL METHODS

The experimental researcher (e.g. Ingham 1981, Harvey and Cooper 1978) attempts to discover causal relationships between phenomena by intervening in the natural setting and controlling all the relevant variables. Three approaches have been developed. The least complicated version is the single-group,[4] pre-test and post-test design. If a comparison between the scores on these two tests shows a change, it is possible to conclude that the educational intervention has had an effect. A variation on this is where a control group is added so that comparisons can be made between it and the experimental group. Both groups are constructed with similar characteristics, and this can in some cases be achieved by the process of random sampling. If two groups are picked randomly (the one to act as the experimental group and the other as the control), then it is possible to be confident that internal characteristics of the two groups will be similar.

However, it is rarely possible to pick groups randomly in a tightly structured setting such as a school. Furthermore, it is difficult to ensure that the interventions given to the two groups are standardised. Experimental research methods in educational settings involve manipulation of a large number of variables and thus are not easy to put into effect. The third approach is where the researcher accepts that more than one variable may be influential, arguing that a particular variable affects behaviour in one context, but not in another. In order to take account of this, the researcher studies a number of groups, each of which has different characteristics, and each of which is subjected to different types of interventions. These methods are essentially deductive, and involve the testing of hypotheses. As a result, experimental researchers are able to argue that such methods allow replication, and ultimately the development of general propositions about educational activities (cf. Chaplin 1947, Boring 1953, Barratt 1971).

An example of an experimental design in educational research is provided by Adey *et al.* (1989). They were interested in discovering whether formal operational thinking could be promoted among 11–14 year olds. They devised a two-year set of interventions based on Piaget's maturational schema. Students were tested before the interventions, immediately after and one year later. The results of the tests pointed to significant differences between the experimental group and the control group, with the former outperforming the latter. Furthermore, they discovered different gender effects at different ages and in different subjects. In trying to make sense of their findings, they generated two explanations. The first was that boys and girls have different intellectual development patterns, and this explanation is therefore partially located within a biological model of maturation. The second explanation sought to prioritise the social over the biological, and, particularly with reference to science and mathematics, suggested that the results could be explained in terms of the different learning experiences of boys and girls in these domains. Though the authors of this research report were confident about the enhancement they observed as a result of their interventions, they expressed less confidence in providing convincing explanations for these effects.

The strengths of this method are well-known, and much debated in the literature on research methodology (cf. Cohen and Manion 1989). Testing hypotheses by experiment yields useful information, even if these hypotheses are in the end falsified. Since the purpose of such research is to establish the validity of relations between phenomena, this method of controlling variables makes it possible to eliminate extraneous causal factors. It can then be claimed with some certainty that x causes y. This allows the development of a set of law-like generalisations about social activity, and it allows prediction. However, advocates of the experimental method have been disappointed because uncontested and secure propositions about the way society works are rarely forthcoming.

The reasons for this are complicated. In essence, they are fourfold. First, many things are not easy to test for. Effects may be more subtle or difficult to conceptualise than experiment allows. Second, the experimental researcher studies human interaction in artificial settings, and as a result it may be difficult to draw valid conclusions which relate to real-life situations; that is, experiments may be ecologically invalid. Third, the experimental method may not be appropriate when the researcher seeks to understand the culture of the setting. Indeed, critics (Giddens 1984, and others) would go further, and suggest that social phenomena cannot be properly understood without referring to the accounts given by participants in those social settings.

However, a more conclusive reason for doubting the claims made by experimental researchers is that human beings both generate and are in turn influenced by social scientific descriptions of social processes. As Giddens (1984) argues this 'introduces an instability' into social research which immediately renders experimental data and those findings produced by experimental methods problematic:

> the Social Sciences operate within a double hermeneutic, involving two-way ties with the actions and institutions of those they study. Socio-logical observers depend upon lay concepts to generate accurate descriptions of social processes; and agents regularly appropriate theories and concepts of social science within their behaviour, thus potentially changing its character. This ... inevitably takes it some distance from the 'cumulative and uncontested' model that naturalistically-inclined sociologists have in mind.
>
> (Giddens 1984: 31)

Finally, experimental researchers may involve themselves in complicated ethical dilemmas which their method leaves them ill equipped to resolve. Interpretive researchers (cf. Hammersley and Atkinson 1983) refuse to draw such a clear distinction between ethical and epistemological issues, arguing that data collection methods, and thus by implication the data themselves, are never free of political and ethical concerns.

Experimental researchers therefore conceptualise data, methods and theory, and the relationships between them in distinctive ways. Data are separate from their collection and the values of their collector. They represent reality in an objective sense. Conclusions drawn from experimental settings can be transposed to other settings with essentially similar characteristics. These relations between phenomena are causal. Method is a neutral means of collecting data and thus is not implicated in the theory that eventually emerges.

In short, these propositions relate to Denzin's (1989) list of five characteristics by which he sought to distinguish positivist from interpretive and meaning-based research strategies. They are: objective reality can be grasped; researchers can remain neutral with their values separate from the descriptions of reality they provide; observations and generalisations are a-situational and a-temporal; causality is linear; and inquiry is an objective activity.

SURVEY METHODS

Survey researchers (e.g. Boulton and Coldron 1989, Adler *et al.* 1989) attempt to collect data about larger populations than is usual with experimental research. Surveys may lead to simple frequency counts or to more complicated relational analysis. In educational research there are two important versions of the latter. The first is correlational research (e.g. Mortimore *et al.* 1988) in which, through the use of various statistical devices, relationships between phenomena are identified, and a determinant of the probability of those relationships holding firm in other settings adduced. The second is ex post-facto research (e.g. Christie and Oliver 1969, Cox 1987) in which the researcher searches for causal relationships among phenomena by retrospectively reconstructing what happened. Data are collected in a number of ways, but their collection typically involves structured interviews, postal questionnaires, standardised tests of performance or the use of attitude inventories. Though it may be possible to sample all the cases in a particular population, more usually a selection has to be made. Cohen and Manion (1989) refer to two general methods of sampling. The first is probability sampling in which the criteria for selecting respondents are known. The second, non-probability sampling, refers to criteria which are unknown. In the first instance, sampling may be systematic, or stratified. In the second instance, sampling is less systematic, with the result that researchers can be less sure that their sample of respondents represents the larger whole about which they want to draw conclusions.

An example of this type of educational research is provided by Smith and Tomlinson (1989). This was a longitudinal study of eighteen schools in four Local Education Authorities in England. Data were collected in two ways, the first of which was the use of standardised tests. These were norm-referenced: that is they were designed to differentiate between pupils in terms of pre-determined norms or quotas, those norms having been determined by reference to characteristics of a sample of the relevant national population. Those tests, the authors argue, had a high degree of reliability for two reasons. They were conducted in controlled settings, and they had been pre-tested with pupils who had recorded scores of a similar nature when they re-sat them at a later point in time. These 'mental capacities develop in a relatively predictable way, and having developed they tend strongly to persist' (Smith and Tomlinson 1989: 12). They thus measure actual competencies and have a high level of predictive validity. The second set of data was collected by using pre-coded questionnaires.

A sample of pupils in each of the schools took these standardised tests at the beginning and end of their first two years. At the same time, information was collected about their family and socio-economic backgrounds. Predicted results from the second set of tests were calculated using a mathematical model (Goldstein 1987) which combined the first test results and these socio-economic factors. The prediction was then compared with the actual score obtained and the progress made by each pupil was measured. Pupil data in each school were then aggregated to give a school effect. Meanwhile, using other types of data-collection methods, information was collected about structures, organisations, styles of management and curricula. These data were correlated with pupil achievements, and this allowed conclusions to be drawn about the type of schooling which contributes most effectively to the progress made by pupils in schools.

Eight sets of information were collected by the researchers involved in the project: attitude scores to act as an indication of behavioural problems; attainment scores for the pupils at entry in mathematics, English, comprehension, writing, verbal reasoning and numerical reasoning; attainment scores at the end of the second year in English, mathematics and verbal reasoning; absences (measured in half days) per pupil for the first two years; attitude scores as they relate to rewards and punishments, participation in curricular and extra-curricular activities, and friendship patterns; socio-economic data (ethnicity, family structure, religion, employment, attitudes towards schooling); data about option choices; and public examination results (GCE 'O' levels and CSEs) for each pupil.

In order for the data to be processed statistically, each socio-economic subgroup was divided into a number of manageable categories. For example, the country of origin of both parents was divided into four categories: 'UK/Eire', 'South Asians', 'West Indians and Others', 'mixed origins'. Again, each pupil was placed in one of six categories to indicate the family's socio-economic grouping: 'parents unemployed for 5 years', 'unskilled manual labour', 'semi-skilled manual labour', 'skilled manual', 'white collar' and 'professional or managerial'. Equally, measures of pupil, teacher and parent behaviours were categorised in a number of discrete groupings. Thus expressions of dissatisfaction by parents were itemised as: 'bad behaviour', 'not enough discipline'; 'too strict or inconsistent'; 'low academic standards'; 'not enough remedial, too much homework'; 'general criticism of teachers'; 'lack of consultation or communication'; 'poor facilities or buildings'; 'other answers'.

It was concluded from the study that there were 'very important differences between urban comprehensive schools' in terms of the progress made by their pupils: 'The findings show that the same child would get a CSE grade 3 in English at one school, but an 'O' level grade B in English at another. There are equally large differences in maths and in exam results in total across all subjects' (Smith and Tomlinson 1989: 301). This piece of research is vulnerable to a general critique of this methodology.

Advocates of such methods make a number of assumptions, the first of which is that a valid account of social interaction can be obtained, and the agenda for the investigation set, without reference being made to the way participants in the research understand and interpret their world. Research into race issues highlights this particular problem, since in much of the literature words such as 'race', 'immigrant', 'ethnic', 'black' and 'coloured' are employed as though they are neutral descriptive terms (cf. Smith and Tomlinson 1989). Race categories, it has been suggested, always incorporate a self-referential element. Those researchers who use pre-coded questionnaires necessarily make a number of assumptions about respondents which cannot be openly contested except by a refusal to take part in the exercise.

A second assumption that proponents of survey methods make is that method can be decided upon without reference to the emerging data and precedes fieldwork. Inductive qualitative researchers (e.g. Glaser and Strauss 1967),[5] by way of contrast, have developed the idea of progressive focusing to explain the complicated relationship, as they understand it, between the methods they use to collect data and the analysis of those data. A dialectical relationship is said to exist between theory building and data collection (Hammersley and Atkinson 1983). As fieldwork proceeds, the researcher's initial hunches, hypotheses and conjectures are gradually refined and refor-mulated, and this acts progressively to focus analysis and reorganise data collection.

A third assumption made is that if researchers get too close to the subjects of their research, they may 'contaminate' it, and thus render its conclusions unreliable. A number of methodological frameworks have been developed to illuminate the relationship between the researcher and what is being re-searched. They come from different research traditions, and therefore denote a different understanding of this important relationship. The notion of contamination, for example, may be used to suggest that researchers' presence in the research setting and the way they behave, are likely to change in some significant way what is being researched. Descriptions of educational settings are liable to be less than complete, less than adequate, because of the distortions engendered by the presence and activities of the researchers. They have literally 'contaminated' that slice of reality. The metaphor is of course borrowed from research in the natural sciences, and in particular medicine, where inadequate laboratory techniques can render experiments invalid because standardising procedures are not adhered to. A less pejorative term is that of reactivity, in which the researcher's actions condition and structure the type of data that is collected. Participants in the project react to the researcher and this constitutes distortion or bias, when what is being sought is an accurate and valid account of what is happening.

The fourth assumption made is that data are a-theoretical: educational settings can be described and analysed without referring to any theoretical framework or a priori way of understanding. There are two opposing positions. First, it is argued that educational events cannot be recognised and described because language is wholly inadequate to the task of defining and categorising those events. Second, there is a weaker version, which is that data are always to be understood as theory-impregnated (Harris 1979); that even the most commonplace categories used to describe the world imply a particular way of understanding, and thus cannot be free of theory under some description. These two positions are frequently conflated.

A fifth assumption is that if a correlation can be established between two variables, it is possible to assert that the one caused the other to happen in an unproblematic way. Unlike experimental researchers, survey researchers do not attempt to control all the relevant variables, even if they could identify them. Though they may observe a relationship between x and y, they cannot be certain that the one caused the other. There is always the possibility of a third variable causing variance in both. Furthermore, they cannot be sure as to which variable is prior to the other. Sanday (1990), for example, examines the first finding of a study by Mortimore *et al.* (1988) into effectiveness criteria in primary schools. He asks three questions: does the observed correlation between the effective school (as it is identified by a battery of achievement tests conducted on its pupils) and purposeful leadership by the head teacher indicate that an effective school has to have this characteristic? Can a school function effectively without such leadership? Even if the head teacher does show purposeful leadership, could the school still be ineffective? Correlations identified in survey research are literally no more than this and need to be distinguished from causal relationships.

These five notions may be located within research traditions or paradigms which are characterised in the following way. Values can be separated from facts, with the researcher's task designated as uncovering and reporting those facts. Researchers operate as neutral conduits between research setting and audience. They are not considered to be a part of the research and their presence is not expected to affect the quality or type of data that is gathered. The values of the researcher, it is argued, are irrelevant therefore to the scene being surveyed.

There are no meaningful differences between natural and social science methodologies. Bhaskar (1979) in fact develops this argument, though his solution is radically different from other social theorists in the research tradition under discussion. He suggests that both social scientific and scientific methodologies should be understood as one: 'both the dominant naturalist tradition, positivism, and its anti-naturalist hermeneutical foil rest on an ontology rendered obsolete by these developments' (new collateral theories of philosophy and ideology). 'The time is therefore overdue for a "sublation" of their historic confrontation' (Bhaskar 1979: ix). Without a solution of this sort, social scientists who introduce reflexive and interpretive elements into their methodologies are deemed to have acted unscientifically and therefore without objectivity.

The textual account that eventually emerges is thus objective, separate from the value positions of the researcher and representative of an intransitive reality. Researchers working within this tradition would thus seek to privilege their accounts by ignoring the problem of reflexivity, by denying that those accounts are essentially constructed, and by minimising through the use of certain textual and methodological devices the place of the researcher in that construction.

However, seeking to decontaminate the research experience by separating researchers from the object of their study involves the adoption of a particular value position, principally that data which are collected in this way effectively and adequately represent reality. Furthermore, it is difficult to imagine that those decontaminating devices do in fact separate off the researcher from what is being researched. All types of research involve selective and thus value-laden interventions of different types during their conduct. In particular, research methods are structured by perceptual and conceptual maps of reality which determine both method and analysis. It is in this sense that data are value-impregnated. The researchers, tacitly or overtly, have already mapped the areas which they are studying, based on experience and knowledge. But within that process of conceptual mapping, there is a place for change, realignment and modification. The researcher finds out things during the course of the research which he or she did not know. Since reflexive processes are considered essential elements in research, this process of realignment relates both to examination of the researcher's own conceptual and affective maps, the way those maps mediate and structure reality for the researcher, and equally to examination of what is being researched.

THE QUALITATIVE/QUANTITATIVE DIVIDE

Traditionally, some methodological strategies (experimental, ex post-facto, correlational and survey) have been designated as quantitative and others (ethnography and condensed case study) as qualitative. In a similar way, some methods (structured interviews, postal questionnaires, standardised tests of performance and attitude inventories) have been categorised as quantitative, while others (unstructured interviews, participant observation, diary-keeping) have been categorised as qualitative. More recently various attempts have been made to sublate the divide between the two strategies and sets of methods (Rist 1977, Smith and Heshusius 1986, Bryman 1988, Hammersley 1992). The assumption that they represent two distinct and opposed approaches to the study of the social world is being challenged. This is not to deny that differences exist; but it is to suggest that the two methods do not belong within separate research paradigms and thus can sensibly be used within the same investigation. Hammersley (1992) in his defence of this position identifies seven ways by which qualitative methods have been distinguished from quantitative methods, and seeks to show that drawing a distinction between the two is of limited use and in some cases leads to misleading conclusions.

He first argues that both quantitative and qualitative researchers employ terms which relate to number and that anyway precision or accuracy may not best be expressed numerically. He then goes on to suggest that the claims made by qualitative researchers about the ecological invalidity of much quantitative research are misleading for two reasons: first, that valid and representative data can be collected in artificial settings; second, that even participant observers affect the setting which they are studying thus rendering it to a greater or lesser extent artificial.

The third assertion that Hammersley seeks to challenge is that qualitative researchers focus on meaning while their quantitative associates concentrate on behaviour. Again, he presents two counter-arguments: first, he denies that qualitative researchers necessarily focus on the meanings of participants in social settings to the exclusion of behaviours; and second, he suggests that methods which traditionally have fallen within the quantitative camp, such as surveys, frequently focus on meanings.

Hammersley is next concerned with two epistemological issues. The first is the natural science/social science divide. He claims in response to this that many educational researchers who would place themselves within research traditions which stress the interpretive and meaning-making capacity of the social actor would also in various ways subscribe to a model of natural science method. He further suggests that the deductive/inductive divide is false. Ethnographers[6] of various sorts argue that their craft is not purely descriptive but may also involve the testing of previously formulated hypotheses. Furthermore, there are inductive and deductive elements involved in all types of data analysis. Researchers may differ about when or at what stage of their research they should employ deductive or inductive techniques, but this does not amount to a major difference between the two approaches.

Hammersley discusses two other arguments that have been proposed for distinguishing between qualitative and quantitative research. The first is that the former is used to identify cultural patterns, while the latter is understood as primarily nomological. Again Hammersley suggests that the contrast between these two positions has been too sharply drawn: that ethnography is not purely descriptive and that survey methods frequently focus on cultural patterns. Finally, he argues that the distinction that is sometimes drawn between the two in terms of realism and idealism is false, as he claims that frequently what are compared are extreme versions: relativistic idealists and representational realists. It is more common to find that researchers from both camps accept that their accounts are constructed but that as researchers they do not invent reality. Their descriptions relate in some way to phenomena which operate outside the direct remit of the researcher.

I first want to draw a distinction between method and methodological framework. Method frequently refers to the instruments by which data are collected. Thus interviews, observation schedules, questionnaires and attitude tests are methods. Items in a questionnaire, for example, may be located along three continua: factual/opinion, open/closed and structured/unstructured. Thus a questionnaire, a data-collection device which has traditionally been placed in the quantitative camp, may embrace questions which are closed ended, factual and pre-set as well as questions which are open, allow the respondent to set the agenda and are primarily about the perspectives and views of social actors. If this is compared with an interview, a data collection device which has traditionally been located in the qualitative camp, it can be seen that it may be used in a number of ways, from the collection of factual data to the itemising of opinions and views of respondents. The former is of course written and the latter spoken. However, though the interview may allow more flexibility, neither method by virtue of what it is can be located firmly within one or other of the two camps. It is therefore difficult to locate differences of a substantive kind in the research instrument itself.

On the other hand instruments are generic titles for a range of practices, and it is perhaps more fruitful to try and locate any differences here. The traditional qualitative interview, it has been suggested, is unstructured, allows the agenda to be set by the interviewee and is primarily concerned with the interviewee's views and opinions on a range of phenomena that relate to past and present events. A number of epistemological assumptions are being made: first, that data as they are captured in a formal or semi-formal setting relate to how that social actor actually behaves and has behaved in the past. In other words, that data collected in settings which are not natural are ecologically valid and allow us to draw conclusions about reality. Second, that the collection of these data is essential to the research enterprise if we conceive of this as being the development of understandings about social relations and activities, and we define this as inclusive of the reasons social actors give for their behaviours. In short, the way we conceive of the purposes of our research will determine how we go about collecting data, and what methods we use. Thus our search for real or imagined differences between quantitative and qualitative methodologies must at some stage address these epistemological questions. Indeed we cannot avoid them.

In contrast to method, methodological framework or research paradigm (Guba and Lincoln 1994)[7] may be defined as a distinct way of approaching research with particular understandings of purposes, foci, data, analysis and more fundamentally, the relationship between data and what they refer to. Thus different and contrasting methodological frameworks may embrace the same data collection method, but because that method is used to collect data in different types of ways and thus different data, it is possible to distinguish between them.

We are now in a position to address some of the issues raised by Hammersley. Though the word/number contrast he discusses would seem to be central to the quantitative/qualitative divide, we can now see that, though Hammersley argues that it may not be important at the level of method, it is important at the level of framework. If human activities are reduced to data sets expressed in numerical terms and if these fixed categories are deemed to represent properties of human beings and do not need to be interpreted, then there very well may be a meaningful difference between this methodological framework and another, proponents of which understand the commonplace categories we use to describe the world as inevitably the consequence of interpretive activity, and thus not amenable to precise quantification. It is not so much that those who use quantitative methods necessarily adopt a-theoretical stances, but that the reduction involved in quantification always produces intensionality (Wilson 1987) and thus some measure of distortion.

The second distinction Hammersley makes is between natural and artificial settings, and he argues that it is not possible to draw a clear and unbroken line between those methods which are artificial in some way (the researcher draws conclusions from this about 'uncontaminated' reality) and those which are used to collect data in the field about the way human actors behave in real life. There are degrees of artificiality both about unstructured interviews conducted in the field and experiments. If on the other hand these issues are addressed at the level of framework, then a clearer distinction can in fact be drawn.

As we have seen, Denzin (1989) characterises a positivist framework in five ways. Objective reality can be captured at the levels of data and description. The observer can be separated from what is being observed. Observations and generalisations are a-temporal and a-contextual. Causality is linear and inquiry is value-free. This can be contrasted with an alternative framework, proponents of which deny that data are or can be free of theory under some description; argue that the values of the researcher are centrally implicated in the production of the data and thus of any conclusions drawn from them; and assert that, fundamentally, the more that researchers try to avoid reactivity, the less they are able to bridge the gap between researcher and researched. In short, that the more artificial the data collection method is, the less valid it is.

Hammersley next argues that qualitative and quantitative approaches, though portrayed in the first case as being about meaning and in the second about behaviour, in fact both focus in different ways on meaning and behaviour. We have already conceded that at the level of method, questionnaire data can refer to the meaning frames of participants in the research and that participant observers, though they stress the primacy of actors' accounts, are also concerned with observing behaviour in natural settings. However, we should, once again, not be so concerned with the data-collection method as with the methodological framework within which the research activity is located. Ethnographers (e.g. Hammersley and Atkinson 1983, Burgess 1984) argue that understanding is a developmental and social process. Thus the experimental researcher operating within a positivist framework may collect data about the meanings actors attribute to their behaviours, but because their view of causality is linear, they are bound to give them less importance than a symbolic interactionist, for example, who would understand social reality as the construction of meanings in interaction. If the concern of the experimental researcher is merely with causal relations between phenomena, then they are doing something which is different and therefore can be said to operate within a different methodological framework.

Hammersley's fourth and fifth areas of discussion focus on issues directly relevant to frameworks as opposed to methods. Indeed, the differences, as they have been identified by Hammersley, have frequently been exaggerated. Ethnographers and other qualitative researchers have sought to adopt aspects of the 'scientific method' and few now argue that qualitative approaches are exclusively inductive. Bhaskar (1989), for instance, has suggested that it is time to sublate the historical confrontation between positivist approaches and those methods which are hermeneutic in orientation. He goes further and in the process refers to Hammersley's last concern – that is the division between realism and idealism. For Bhaskar, reality is ontologically stable and thus any description we make of it does refer to an intransitive phenomenon, but epistemologically unstable. Thus our knowing of reality is always subject to social and political arrangements which are transitive.

The trouble is that even given the desire for a way out of the dilemma, it is not clear how in fact it can be resolved. Bhaskar for instance is unable to provide a rationale for supporting a central tenet of positivist thought, which is that research is conducted in order to establish law-like descriptions of social reality and is thus nomological in character. Second, the positivist researcher understands the relationship between researcher and researched in a different way from the hermeneutic researcher, and this has profound implications for the status of the data that are collected, for the relationship between those data and what they relate to and for the way the researcher conceptualises the method used to shape them to produce the research text. These epistemological distinctions are fundamental to the conduct of research and Hammersley's concentration on them at the level of method has obscured real and profound differences.

Two further questions need to be addressed: first, do these distinctions refer to what is or to what ought to be? Second, is there one correct approach or are different approaches and strategies appropriate for different tasks? The first question refers to the link between epistemology and data collection method, the argument being that no necessary linkage has been established between the two (Bryman 1988). That many researchers have not discussed the epistemological bases of their research or written from a paradigmatic perspective are almost truisms. However, what researchers have done in the past cannot be a guide as to what they will do or should do in the future. Bryman (1987: 125), arguing from an a-paradigmatic perspective, claims that: 'the problem with the "ought" view is that it fails to recognise that a whole cluster of considerations are likely to impinge on decisions about methods of data collection'. Empirical research is a social activity, and is therefore never likely to be completely coherent, reliable or valid (however these are defined). The researcher may choose to use a questionnaire to collect data about the opinions of a group of respondents for practical rather than theory-driven reasons, but such practices tell us little about which method ought to be used.

The second question refers to the debate about whether the study of the social world can accommodate different but complementary approaches. If the researcher wants to investigate structural arrangements in society, then survey methods are usually considered to be the most appropriate. If that same researcher now wants to investigate a cultural setting, then he or she is more likely to use ethnographic methods. However, this gives a false picture. Giddens (1984), for example, suggests that social structures only have substance, and then only fleetingly, in the reasons actors have for their behaviours. He is therefore arguing that data which refer to the knowledgeability of agents are essential elements in social research, whether such study is of a macro-, meso- or micro-type. Methods which prevent the researcher from gathering reliable and valid data about this are not, therefore, appropriate or useful.

Paradoxically, here a-paradigmatic and uni-paradigmatic theorists find common ground. On the one hand, Bryman (1988) seeks to sublate the divide between quantitative and qualitative methods and methodologies on the grounds that the identification of epistemological paradigms artificially restricts the means by which researchers can come to understandings of social reality. On the other hand, uni-paradigmatic theorists (cf. Bhaskar 1989) seek to show that there is only one correct approach to the study of the social world (because what it is demands a unified strategy), which by necessity places limits on the types of methods that should be employed to capture it. Hammersley (1992) has argued that a multi-paradigmatic perspective involves a set of semantic and linguistic confusions, the unravelling of which will solve the paradigm problem. This, I have argued, can be contrasted with an approach which suggests that a multi-paradigmatic perspective is false because one of those paradigms is more appropriate to the study of the social world than the others. These two approaches are not the same.

PHENOMENOLOGICAL APPROACHES[8]

If this argument is accepted, then we have to acknowledge that the hermeneutic researcher will understand data, method and theory and the relations between them in different ways from the researcher operating from within a positivist framework (at the same time we can still subscribe to the view that the latter is conceptually flawed). One version of the hermeneutic approach is phenomenology (Schutz 1967). Here, priority is given to actors' accounts of social reality.

An example of this type of research is provided by Scott (1990). In examining the introduction of a new type of examination in schools, he developed a typology of attitudes, the data having been collected exclusively from interviews with teachers. Six approaches were identified from these data, and these were typified as: conformist, adaptive, oppositional, ritualistic, transformative and non-conformist. This piece of research is vulnerable to the following general critique of its methodology.

Interview data are the result of a series of selections made by the researcher both before and during the fieldwork. The researcher makes a number of decisions about which setting to conduct their research in, who to interview, where and when those interviews should take place, and, even more fundamentally, which instruments to use. In short the data-set is a selection from all the other possible data-sets that could have been made. The researcher's account, as a consequence, is positioned.

Interview data are also the result of a series of social activities, which incorporate an asymmetrical relationship between interviewer and interviewee. The researcher's time-bound concerns serve to structure the interviews and impose an agenda on them. The role they are perceived as playing shapes the data which are collected. Furthermore, method operates in a dialectical fashion with analysis, and is thus constantly changing. Different themes and different areas of interest are pinpointed at different phases of the fieldwork. Above all, interviewer and interviewee do not operate on a level plain, as Ball (1983) argues:

> the interviewee is asked to elaborate, illustrate, reiterate, define, summarise, exemplify and confirm matters in his talk in ways that would be unacceptable in other talk situations. The interviewer controls the specification of topics and maintains a verbal monitoring of the speech situation ... The rules of conversational discourse are flagrantly disregarded in the name of social science ... The interviewer comes to 'know' his subjects without ever necessarily having to engage in a reciprocal process of personal 'social striptease'.
>
> (Ball 1983: 93–5)

The data that emerge are the direct consequences of the method used to collect them, and have therefore been structured by the social activity which constitutes that method.

Having so far concentrated on sampling procedures and the internal relations that make up an interview, it is important to discuss the nature of the data themselves and what they represent. Burgess (1984) offers three reasons for choosing interviewing as the principal method of data collection. First, interviews can allow the researcher access to past events. Second, they can allow access to situations at which the researcher is not able to be present. Third, they can allow access to situations where permission is refused for the researcher to be present. There is thus a gap between the events referred to by the interviewee and the account given to the researcher. What the researcher is doing is retrospective analysis. He or she is not examining the phenomenological perspective that preceded the series of activities that form the subject matter of the interview. Actors' perspectives are not descriptions or formulations of intentions. They are actors giving accounts of how they feel they should have behaved as well as how they feel they did behave. It is therefore not possible to argue that their accounts of their intentions relate precisely to what caused those actors to behave in the way they did, because first, the chronological sequence of events makes this impossible; and second, since they are likely to be post-hoc rationalisations, they do not co-exist in a simple, naming relationship with the actions they seek to describe. This refers to Ricoeur's (1991) notion of 'narrativity' in which social actors, embedded in time, give new meaning to their past, but always in terms of the present.

This rationalising process may be deliberate or unintended, distant or near in time to the activities being described, and transparent or opaque. In the latter case it allows many or few clues as to what really happened, and employs or fails to employ devices to protect its status as a definitive account. Interviewees may deliberately set out to deceive in order to protect their own interests, other interests, or to place in the public domain an account of proceedings which they judge advances a particular political project more effectively. Indeed, they may be encouraged to make considerable changes to their first account if they feel that the latter provides a better and more adequate re-presentation of their previous behaviours. The negotiation of the release of data in non-democratic research situations serves to generate more data, whereas for democratic researchers it serves to reconstruct the reality of the situation. No deceit may be involved, since as G. H. Mead (1934) argues, the self is forever evolving and thus both reconstitutes itself at different moments and, more importantly, reconstitutes reality, both past and present.

Indeed, though Mead and symbolic interactionist researchers (Blumer 1969, Rock 1979) would argue that the only real purchase we can have on knowledge is through the perspectives and viewpoints of those actors that are central to the setting we wish to study, it has been suggested that such a research strategy can never fully provide us with the tools to unlock understandings of social reality. Phenomenological analysis gives priority to people's accounts of intentionality and subjective meanings. This is the phenomenological researcher's first and only point of reference. Those who dispute the adequacy of this seek to go beyond subjective meanings and argue that there is an important difference between 'things seeming to be the case to the actor and things being the case' (Sharp and Green 1975: 21). In other words, they fail to come to terms with those structures that underpin and position actors' intentional behaviours.

Society, as far as Bhaskar (1989: 4) is concerned, 'is the ensemble of positioned practices and networked inter-relationships which individuals never create but in their practical activity always presuppose, and in doing so everywhere reproduce and transform'. Bhaskar argues here that social behaviour or activity may depend on or involve four conditions which are outside the consciousness of the individual actor. They are: unacknowledged conditions, unintended consequences, the exercise of tacit skills, and unconscious motivation. Social practices therefore are never reducible to the content of human consciousness, but must always incorporate a material dimension. As a consequence, it is possible to identify three gaps: between interviewer and interviewee, between the interviewee's account and those perspectives and intentions which preceded the activities being described, and fundamentally between the interviewer's account in whatever form, and what really happened.

Finally, it is important to place interview data within the double hermeneutic framework that Giddens (1984) argues characterises all interpretive research. We have already identified one form this might take. Human beings both generate and are in turn influenced by social scientific descriptions of social processes and this introduces an instability into social research which renders the production of law-like propositions about social activity problematic. There is, though, a second and more fundamental sense given to the notion of the double hermeneutic. Human beings, as reflexive and intentional actors, are engaged in interpretive activity throughout their lives. Symbolic interactionists argue that it takes a particular form: social actors come to see the world as other see it and to see themselves as others see them. They are thus able to reflect on, and reflexively monitor, their own actions. However, the presence of a researcher, and the researcher's desire to investigate social reality by focusing on the perceptions and behaviours of social actors requires a further level of interpretation. Thus researchers interpret through their own conceptual and perceptual lens the interpretations made by those being studied. The double hermeneutic involved in this renders problematic the validity of data collected in this way.

However, without taking account of the way actors interpret and thus understand their worlds, sociological explanation is left empty and devoid of meaning. By adopting research methods which preclude the collection of data of this sort, researchers are doing more than simply excluding vital evidence from their studies. They are also assuming a particular view of social activity and of social actors, which asserts that reasons for actions cannot be causes and that research should be concerned above all with those phenomena that compel social actors to behave in certain ways regardless of their intentions and understandings. They are thus assuming a way of seeing which reduces human beings to the role of 'unwitting dupes' of structural forces beyond their comprehension and influence.

Giddens (1984) attempts a reconciliation between these two positions. His structuration theory synthesises structural and agential perspectives. Human beings are neither the subjects of external and overwhelmingly influential forces nor free unconstrained agents, neither controlled nor influenced by those sets of relations and conjunctions which constitute society. Actors continually draw upon sets of 'rules and resources' which, once substantiated, allow social life to continue as they become routinised. Archer (1982: 458) adopts a similar approach with her morphogenetic schema, though she disputes the necessity of tying structure and agency so closely together: 'structuration, by contrast, treats the ligatures binding structure, practice and system as indissoluble, hence the necessity of duality and the need to gain a more indirect analytical purchase on the elements involved'.

She also questions whether every human action, every facet of the particular human being, is involved in the ongoing moulding and remoulding of society that is implied by structuration cycles. She writes: 'there are a good many things about human beings and their doings (things biological, psychological and spiritual) which have a precious independence from society's moulding and may have precious little to do with re-modelling society' (Archer 1982: 455). Both Archer and Giddens argue that human beings play an active and intentional role in the construction of their world, though that building activity is subject to structural constraints. Human beings make their world in the context of previous attempts, and at the same time transform these structures and change the conditions which influence subsequent moves to make the world. It is also important to recognise that while agency is responsible for structural transformation, in the process it simultaneously transforms itself (Archer 1982). Structures only then have substance, and then only fleetingly, in the reasons actors have for their behaviours: 'study of the structural properties of social systems cannot be successfully carried on, or its results interpreted, without reference to the knowledgeability of the relevant agents' (Giddens 1984: 329). Data that refer to the knowledgeability of agents are therefore essential elements in the research enterprise, and their collection, as I have argued, is a social and ethical affair.

ETHICS AND EPISTEMOLOGY

As a consequence, we need to examine the relationship between ethics and epistemology in educational research. Hermeneutic/interpretive researchers argue that data collection is a social activity, with the researcher in the field confronted by a series of methodological dilemmas, the solutions to which determine the data that are collected. Those fieldwork dilemmas involve researchers in making decisions about how they should conduct themselves, and are therefore concerned with the rights and responsibilities of both researcher and researched. Three models have been suggested. Proponents of the first, covert research, emphasise the need to conceal from respondents the aims and purposes of the research and for the researcher to act in a clandestine way. Those who support the second, open democratic research, stress the rights of participants to control which data are collected and which are included in the research report. Proponents of the third, open autocratic research, argue the case against allowing respondents these rights of veto. This therefore obligates the researcher to protect the interests of those who have agreed to take part in the project.

The ethical dilemmas associated with covert research point to the central problem in fieldwork relations. The researcher, as an outsider, seeks to collect data about a group or groups of people with the intention of producing a coherent account of their lives. Gathering information bestows certain obligations on the gatherer and yet they are motivated by conflicting impulses. Their account needs to be credible: that is, it must reflect, refer to, or in some sense illustrate what is happening or has happened, and yet fieldwork is a social activity which demands a level of trust between researcher and researched. At times these two impulses conflict, and researchers either have to modify their views of reality (the epistemological dimension), or modify participants' rights to construct and reconstruct reality as accounts of it are placed in the public arena (the ethical dimension). This also points to the inevitable interlocking of the epistemological and ethical dimensions. The way researchers choose to manage the data which they collect, and interact with those participants in the research project who provide them with those data, determines the epistemological status of those data.

Democratic researchers seek to allow participants in their projects rights of veto over what is considered germane to the study and what is included in the final report (whether it be an evaluation, research report, or sociological study). Simons (1984) has suggested, in relation to evaluation, that democratic ethical procedures should take five forms:[9] first, it is incumbent on the researcher/evaluator to act impartially, that is 'withhold their judgements' or suspend their own value positions in deciding on important matters concerning the research design and use of data. They should thus represent a range of views. Second, participants should have control over the release of data at every stage of the proceedings: after each data collection session (the right to read and amend interview transcripts); after each report-writing session (the right to change, either by including or excluding, information in the report); and at the dissemination stage (the right to control the release of the data either in its raw or organised form). Third, the control mechanism should be a series of negotiations between the researcher/evaluator and participants in the project. The implicit assumption here is that negotiations can take place on an equal basis and would thus be concerned with the fairness, accuracy and relevancy of what is going to be reported: both researcher and researched have sufficient understanding of the dissemination process to act from an equal base and together to decide on what should be included in the research report when it is placed in the public domain. Fourth, research and evaluation are not activities which should compel participation. Fifth, the researcher/evaluator is accountable not just to participants in the project, but also to other bodies with an interest in the information that has been collected.

Autocratic researchers point to a number of problems with this approach. Because the needs of different participants may not be known at the beginning of the research, there are bound to be initial decisions made about method which will structure the type of data that are collected. Furthermore, there is a temptation on the part of researchers to present their negotiated accounts as neat and coherent views of reality because they are operating in the public domain. Stenhouse (1982: 32) writes that, 'our minds are beguiled by systematic tidiness and by comprehensive breadth'. But more importantly, negotiating with participants (especially with children) can never be between equals. The researcher understands the consequences of release and publication better than the participant. Finally, the manner of negotiation is determined by the structures of the institution. Burgess (1984: 32) reminds us that 'people respond to the structured situations in which they are located'.

If data are to be construed as information which is subject to review, either as a consequence of a re-evaluation brought about by increased understanding of the events to which they refer, or increased knowledge of how that information would be received in the public domain, then this has certain consequences. The account that emerges can now be said to be constructed through the mediating efforts of the researcher/evaluator and constitutes a political programme which has as its raison d'être the desire to effect change in that institution or educational setting. It is thus normative and prescriptive.

We have already made reference to the role of participants' accounts in research. There it was noted that persuasive arguments have been put forward which stress that a reliance on the perspectives of participants to the exclusion of an understanding of the context within which they lead their lives or the conditions under which they were persuaded to give their accounts, would give an incomplete picture. However, it was also argued that ignoring such data renders the methodology bereft of its most compelling and useful ingredient. The researcher therefore has to make a judgement about two matters: first, about the emphasis they would place on the descriptive as opposed to advocative purpose of collecting the data in the first place, second, about how they should behave towards participants in their research project during the data-collection phase. The argument that has been developed here is that the issues involved in providing answers to these two questions cannot be separated in any meaningful sense. Ethics and epistemology are thus two sides of the same coin.

CONCLUDING REMARKS

In this chapter I have sought to distinguish the way proponents of three different methodological strategies conceptualise data, methods and theory and the relationships between them. At this level there are clear and explicit differences which point to important epistemological distinctions between positivist and hermeneutic/interpretive frameworks. I have also suggested that our knowing of social reality and in particular our developing of understandings about education can only be secured if we take into consideration those views and perspectives of social actors which are central to the activities we wish to describe. Even here, there are still immense problems and these relate to the inability of the researcher to represent precisely those views and expressions. There is thus always a gap between different accounts, regardless of the sophistication of the representational devices we use. It is in this sense that our claims to knowledge about educational matters must always be approximate.[10]

NOTES

1   Positivism has a complicated history, though most commentators accept that its most important advocate was Auguste Comte, as he sought to transpose the methods of the natural sciences to the social sciences.

2   The hypothetico-deductive method consists of a series of steps: (i) an hypothesis is constructed; (ii) its implications are deduced; (iii) the relation expressed by the hypothesis is tested empirically; (iv) the hypothesis is accepted, rejected or modified in the light of this testing.

3   Various interpretive sociologies have been developed, and these range from existential phenomenology, ethnomethodology, post-Wittgensteinian philosophy to critical versions.

4   Experimental researchers may substitute individuals for groups. Here, pairs of subjects are matched in terms of a specific characteristic, i.e. IQ. A comparison is then made between performance or behaviour of the individuals involved, using an experimental design.

5   What Glaser and Strauss (1967) have done is to use the principle of induction as a criteria for validating research findings. This highly controversial move is discussed in Chapter 5.

6   For Hammersley (1992: 8) ethnography can be equated with qualitative method: 'Throughout this book I use the term "ethnography" in a general sense, that is broadly equivalent to "qualitative research".'

7   Guba and Lincoln (1994) take up a similar position by clearly separating method and research paradigm. They define the latter as that basic belief system or worldview which is central to the research strategy and which incorporates its ontological and epistemological orientation.

8   To use the word 'phenomenology' is not to refer to a single unified body of thought, though its origins can be traced back to Edmund Husserl.

9   Norris (1990) argues that for all practical purposes evaluation and research are not distinct activities. My argument is based on this same presupposition.

10   This has specific implications for the practice of education. I address these issues in Chapter 9.

REFERENCES

Adey, P., Shayer, M. and Yates, C. (1989) *Thinking Science: the Curriculum Material of the CASE Project*, Basingstoke: Macmillan.

Adler, M., Petch, A. and Tweedie, J. (1989) *Parental Choice and Educational Policy*, Edinburgh: Edinburgh University Press.

Archer, M. (1982) 'Morphogenesis versus Structuration', *British Journal of Sociology* 33, 4: 455–83.

Ball, S. J. (1983) 'Case Study Research in Education: Some Notes and Problems', in M. Hammersley (ed.) *The Ethnography of Schooling*, Driffield: Nuffield.

Barratt, P. (1971) *Basis of Psychological Methods*, Queensland: John Wiley and Sons.

Bhaskar, R. (1979) *The Possibility of Naturalism*, Brighton: Harvester Press.

—— (1989) *Reclaiming Reality*, London: Verso.

Blumer, H. (1969) *Symbolic Interactionism: Perspective and Method*, Englewood Cliffs, NJ: Prentice-Hall.

Boring, E. (1953) 'The Role of Theory in Experimental Psychology', *American Journal of Psychology* 66: 169–84.

Boulton, P. and Coldron, J. (1989) *The Pattern and Process of Parental Choice*, Sheffield: Sheffield City Polytechnic.

Bryman, A. (1988) *Quality and Quantity in Social Research*, London: Unwin Hyman.

Burgess, R. G. (1984) *In the Field,* London: Allen & Unwin.

Chaplin, F. (1947) *Experimental Designs in Sociological Research*, London and New York: Harper & Row.

Christie, T. and Oliver, R. (1969) 'Academic Performance at Age 18+ as Related to School Organisation', *Research in Education* 2: 13–31.

Cohen, L. and Manion, L. (1989, third edn) *Research Methods in Education*, London: Routledge.

Cox, T. (1987) 'Slow Starters versus Long Term Backward Readers', *British Journal of Educational Psychology* 57: 73–86.

Denzin, N. (1989) *Interpretive Interactionism, Vol 16, Applied Social Research Methods*, London: Sage.

Giddens, A. (1984) *The Constitution of Society*, Cambridge: Polity Press.

Glaser, B. G. and Strauss, A. L. (1967) *The Discovery of Grounded Theory: Strategies for Qualitative Research*, Chicago: Aldine.

Goldstein, H. (1987) *Multilevel Models in Education and Social Research*, Oxford: Clarendon Press.

Guba, E. and Lincoln, Y. (1994) 'Competing Paradigms in Qualitative Research', in N. Denzin and Y. Lincoln (eds) *Handbook of Qualitative Research*, London: Sage.

Hammersley, M. (1992) *What's Wrong with Ethnography?*, London: Routledge.

—— and Atkinson, P. (1983) *Ethnography, Principles in Practice*, London and New York: Tavistock Publications.

Harris, K. (1979) *Education and Knowledge*, London: Routledge and Kegan Paul.

Harvey, T. and Cooper, C. (1978) 'An Investigation into Some Possible Factors Affecting Children's Understanding of the Concept of an Electric Circuit in the Age Range 8–11 Years Old', *Educational Studies* 4, 2: 149–55.

Ingham, J. (1981) *Books and Reading Development*, London: Heinemann Educational Books.

Mead, G. H. (1934) *Mind, Self and Society*, Chicago: Chicago University Press.

Mortimore, P., Sammons, P., Stoll, L., Lewis, D. and Ecob, R. (1988) *School Matters*, London: Open Books.

Norris, N. (1990) *Understanding Educational Evaluation*, London: Kogan Page.

Ricoeur, P. (1991) 'Life in Quest of a Narrative', in D. Wood (ed.) *On Paul Ricoeur: Narrative and Interpretation*, London: Routledge.

Rist, R. (1977) 'On the Relations among Educational Research Paradigms: from Disdain to Detente', *Anthropology and Education Quarterly* 8, 2: 42–49.

Rock, P. (1979) *The Making of Symbolic Interactionism*, London: Macmillan.

Sanday, A. (1990) *Making Schools more Effective (CEDAR Papers 2)*, Centre for Educational Development, Appraisal and Research, Coventry: University of Warwick.

Schutz, A. (1967) M. Natanson (ed.) *Collected Papers (Vol.1),* The Hague: Martinus Nijhoff.

Scott, D. (1990) *Coursework and Coursework Assessment in the GCSE*, Centre for

Educational Development, Appraisal and Research, Coventry: University of Warwick.

Sharp, R. and Green, A. (1975) *Education and Social Control*, London: Routledge & Kegan Paul.

Simons, H. (1984) 'Negotiating Conditions for Independent Evaluations' in C. Adelman (ed.) *The Politics and Ethics of Evaluation,* London: Croom Helm.

Smith, D. and Tomlinson, S. (1989) *The School Effect: A Study of Multiracial Comprehensives*, London: Policy Studies Institute.

Smith, J. K. and Heshusius, L. (1986) 'Closing Down the Conversation: the End of the Quantitative–Qualitative Debate among Educational Inquirers', *Educational Researcher* 15, 1: 4–12.

Stenhouse, L. (1982) 'The Conduct, Analysis and Reporting of Case Study in Educational Research and Evaluation' in R. McCormick (ed.) *Calling Education to Account*, London: Heinemann.

Wilson, T. (1987) 'Sociology and the Mathematical Method' in A. Giddens and J. Turner (eds) *Social Theory Today*, London: Polity Press.

5 Making judgements about educational research

David Scott

This chapter will examine how educationalists make judgements about their research activities, whether such judgements are legitimate, and whether the nature of the social world (in particular those activities and behaviours which have come to be known as educational) can support a clear set of specifications as to how it should be understood. In addressing these questions, ontological and epistemological concerns will be to the fore. Indeed, an assumption will be made that empirical research method cannot be divorced from social theory. How we understand the social world will determine how we know it and this in turn will influence how we collect data about it. These moments, therefore, are interconnected, with answers to the one delimiting and excluding possible answers to the other two. They refer specifically to ontology, epistemology and methodology (Guba and Lincoln 1994); and though at some points they are only loosely coupled (see the argument about the relationship between method and methodological framework in Chapter 4), the connections are strong enough for it to be possible to organise them in research paradigms. A research paradigm can be identified by its ontological, epistemological and methodological stances and by the relations between them. It can further be distinguished by the types of evaluative criteria which practitioners develop to judge quality in research.

The natural science model[1] has served as a prototype for social scientists, and in some cases has been uncritically appropriated to provide justification for their methods and procedures. Hammersley (1992) takes this as his starting point, and suggests that social scientists (including those concerned with the study of education) can choose between three alternative positions. The first is that they should not distinguish between methods or paradigms. There are no fundamental differences between the study of the social and natural worlds, and therefore they should use the same evaluative criteria for both. Those forms of internal and external validity (Campbell and Stanley 1963, Bracht and Glass 1968) which experimental researchers use to evaluate their work should apply to all types of research. Hammersley's second position is that the study of the social world is substantively different from that of the natural world, and therefore different methods and evaluative criteria should be employed to capture these different activities. His third position is that it is not possible to develop criteria which underpin the study of the social world, because what it is renders such an activity meaningless. Denzin and Lincoln (1994) suggest a different typology which includes a fourth position: positivist methods are inappropriate for the study of natural as well as social phenomena. This points to the need for a new research paradigm which will embrace all forms of enquiry (Bhaskar 1989).

Denzin and Lincoln's four positions are:

1 positivist: natural science criteria are equally appropriate for the study of the social world (this is an a-paradigmatic perspective);
2 post-positivist: study of the natural and social worlds are such that different criteria are appropriate for each (this is a di-paradigmatic perspective);
3 post-modernist: no criteria are appropriate for the study of the social world (this is a multi-paradigmatic perspective);
4 post-structuralist: new criteria need to be developed which are appropriate for all forms of research (this is a uni-paradigmatic perspective).[2]

While these four alternative stances represent typifications and should not exclude positions which do not fit easily into one or the other, they do point to a source of tension in social theory.

POSITIVIST CRITERIA

Advocates (Campbell and Stanley 1963) of traditional a-paradigmatic approaches (in particular, the experimental method) have identified two types of invalidity. The first is internal, and this involves the researcher in ascertaining whether the effects they ascribe to the interventions in their experiments are in fact caused by those interventions and not by other factors. Threats to the internal validity of an experiment may involve other factors: its history – participants have other experiences during the timespan of the research, and the researcher may mistakenly attribute such effects to the intervention; the maturation of participants – changes which the researcher suggests have occurred because of the intervention may have happened anyway due to natural processes; and pre-test sensitisation – this refers to the ability of the test to cause participants to behave in abnormal or artificial ways because they were being tested.

They also involve the reliability of the tests. Theorists (Wood 1987, for example) have argued that tests are imperfect instruments for measuring capability. Wood and Power (1987) identify a gap between competence and performance, and suggest two forms it might take: false negative and false positive, as shown in Table 5.1.

In the first place, due to anxiety, test nerves and a host of other reasons, test takers under-perform. In the second place, the test over-rates the capabilities of participants. False negative cases are more common than false positive ones.

Table 5.1 Error types in relating performance to competence

	Success on task	*Failure on task*
Child has underlying compentence (in suffi-cient degree)	Performance correlated with competence	False negative error: failure due to factor other than lack of com-petence
Child does not have un-derlying competence (in sufficient degree)	False positive error: suc-cess due to factor other than competence	Performance correlated with competence

Source: (Wood and Power 1987)

Furthermore, test indicators have to be precisely formulated. If the test is unreliable, it is difficult to be sure about the findings of the experiment. Finally, experimental researchers who operate with control groups have to be certain that the experimental and control groups are as alike as they possibly can be. Both groups must remain intact during the project, especially if they have been chosen randomly. The tendency for members of the different groups to drop out is known as experimental mortality. Both of these – selection problems and experimental mortality – have the effect of decreasing the researchers' sense of certainty about the validity of their findings.

In contrast to internal validity, external validity refers to sampling proce-dures and to whether findings can be generalised to larger populations. Bracht and Glass (1968) have identified four difficulties with generalising findings. They are: the researcher's need to conceptualise performance indicators so that other researchers can replicate the experiment; the researcher's need to ensure that experimental and control groups are representative of larger populations; the researcher's need to be confident that the way he or she operationalises variables in the experimental setting can be replicated in real-life situations; and the researcher's need to be certain that internal validity variables such as history, maturation, pre-test sensitisation, test reliability and selection will not damage the external validity of the experiment. If the former threaten the internal validity of the findings, then equally they threaten the ability to generalise to larger populations and other settings.

These two sets of criteria are underpinned by a number of assumptions about research. First, the behaviour of the researcher must be carefully controlled so that it does not affect the activities being investigated. Only then can theory, which has been developed from observations of behaviours, be generalised from sample to population, across time and from one setting to another. If researchers cannot be certain of this, their data are purely localised and have no special significance. Second, there is an objective reality, separate from the activities and behaviours of the researcher, which can be captured. The term 'representational realism' has been coined to describe this position. Third, researchers are primarily concerned with causal relations between phenomena. In developing theory the researcher identifies those necessary and sufficient conditions which structure social activity. Fourth, experimental activity is public and can be reproduced at a different point in time. This is the principle of replicability. Fifth, researchers can infer properties of human beings from the study of cases. In short, four criteria can be identified which allow researchers to make judgements about the effectiveness of their research: representational value, applicability, consistency and neutrality.

GROUNDED THEORY

In comparison, a number of data analysis techniques[3] have been developed specifically to deal with the study of the social world. Grounded theorists for example, 'share a conviction with many other qualitative researchers that the usual canons of 'good science' should be retained, but require redefinition in order to fit the realities of qualitative research and the complexities of social phenomena'. These they identify as 'significance, theory-observation compatibility, generalisability, consistency, reproducibility, precision and verification' (Strauss and Corbin 1990: 4). This method of data analysis proceeds in a series of steps. Bartlett and Payne (1995) suggest ten phases: collecting data, transcribing data, developing categories, saturating categories, providing abstract definitions, theoretical sampling, axial coding (this involves developing and testing relationships between categories), integrating theory, grounding theory, and filling in the gaps. Others (e.g. Charmaz 1983) have suggested similar ways of proceeding, though all seek to represent heuristically the principles of grounded theory as they were originally articulated (Glaser and Strauss 1967, Glaser 1978, Strauss 1987, Strauss and Corbin 1990). It was never intended that these steps should be understood as rigidly prescriptive, since the researcher may choose to go backwards or forwards, or to spend more time on some rather than others. But they were intended as a possible model for delivering the method.

Grounded theory has generated a number of methodological debates and these need to be addressed. Malinowski (1922) identified an early stage of research, which he called 'foreshadowing the problem'. This involved the clarification and development of ideas about the area of research before fieldwork began. Glaser and Strauss (1967), in their original development of grounded theory, specifically recommended that the researcher should avoid presuppositions, hypotheses and previous research studies. This tabula rasa approach has been criticised (cf. Bulmer 1979) on the grounds that it is difficult to achieve and it ignores the way researchers actually conceptualise research problems. It was further argued that all data collectors make a number of theoretical assumptions, the adoption of which occurs prior to fieldwork (cf. Harris 1979).[4]

Strauss and Corbin (1994: 227) have since accepted that 'they [Glaser and Strauss] greatly underplayed ... the unquestionable fact (and advantage) that trained researchers are theoretically sensitised'. Undoubtedly, they intended their method to be primarily inductive, and thus they were and are opposed to the exclusive use of deductive techniques more commonly adopted by natural scientists. They were concerned that their analysis of the data should not be contaminated by a priori theoretical conceptualisations and understandings (Glaser 1978), though they were prepared to accept that deductive processes were appropriate at later stages of the analysis as the emergent theory was tested against new data. Their validity criterion is whether the analysis is inductively grounded in the data: that is, monosemically formed from it. This implies three tests: comprehensiveness (the theory takes account of all the data), logical inference (the one correct way of organising and representing the data is identified and applied), and phenomenological bracketing (the analyst is able to put to one side his or her own preconceptions and prejudices during the analysis).

In pursuit of this, they suggest a number of processes which, if properly carried out, allow researchers to be more confident about their analysis and the conclusions they draw from it. The two most important are theoretical sensitisation and saturation. The first, theoretical sensitisation, allows the researcher to gain an insight into the data, to realise intuitively what they signify. Sensitised researchers are able to go beyond the technical literature and their own personal experience, and discover properties which belong to those data (Strauss and Corbin 1990). Saturation is a companionate concept, in which further analysis and sorting of the data become redundant, because they only add 'bulk to the coded data and nothing to the theory' (Glaser and Strauss 1967: 111). These activities are not just closure devices employed for practical reasons, but they represent techniques for establishing validity: the claim can now be made that when the categorisation phase is complete, those categories are valid.

These processes for establishing validity therefore are second-order operations. They refer exclusively to the analysis of data. They do not refer to how the data were collected in the first place, and therefore cannot address ontological questions about what they represent, or refer to, even though all forms of data collection implicitly or explicitly make claims about their ostensive or denotative purposes. This is confirmed by Strauss and Corbin (1994: 278) when they argue that 'theories are interpretations made from given perspectives as adopted or researched by researchers'. The data, and theory subsequently developed from them, are only valid in as much as the way those data were collected in the first place was valid. Again, they suggest that 'multiple voices are attended to, but note that these are also interpreted conceptually by the researcher who follows our methodology' (Strauss and Corbin 1994: 280). Though data may be collected from a number of different sources, and though the research text is intended to be multi-vocal, the research project is still idiographic, dependent as it is on the way the data were collected in the first place. The emergent account is therefore always positioned. Grounded theorists make truth claims about those findings which have been produced by the adoption of their method. I have argued here that such truth claims should be of a restricted nature and apply to later stages of the research process. In order to go further, we need to address questions about the original status of the data which are collected and the meaning of such activity, and to do this, we need to develop an understanding of ontological as well as epistemological issues, which grounded theory does not allow us to do. Grounded theory offers one approach to the study of the social world, naturalistic enquiry another.

NATURALISTIC INQUIRY

Guba and Lincoln (1985) in their advocacy of naturalistic research[5] have sought to substitute different criteria for judging research, which complement but do not replace traditional criteria (internal validity, external validity, reliability and objectivity). They want to substitute credibility for internal validity, transferability for external validity, dependability for reliability and confirmability for objectivity. They are attempting to adapt criteria thought appropriate for the study of the social world, as it was conceived from within a positivist framework. As a result, they are implicitly adopting a number of epistemological and ontological positions, the effect of which is to reinforce the idea that research is nomological, objective, capable of replication and directly represents reality. If it can be shown that it is inappropriate to represent the social world in this way, then equally it is inappropriate to transpose the one set to the other, while at the same time making small adjustments to meet new demands. This model has also been criticised as internally incoherent. Hammersley (1992) for example has suggested that the distinction between internal and external validity is superfluous because the one implies the other. If the original model is misguided, then to base another model on it, albeit for a different purpose, is to compound the original difficulty.

The first of these, internal validity, refers to the research's truth value and the accuracy with which it is related to reality. Its ontological orientation is therefore representational realism: some accounts are better than others because they are better representations. Guba and Lincoln (1985: 296) contrast this position of naive realism with one that takes account of multiple realities, and they suggest that: 'the naturalist must show that he or she has represented those multiple constructions adequately, that is, that the reconstructions ... that have been arrived at via the enquiry are credible to the constructors of the original multiple realities'. A piece of research therefore, is credible in terms of its method of enquiry and as to whether participants in the research recognise their contributions and affirm that they are valid. They propose a number of procedures to establish and maintain credibility. Researchers should engage in prolonged fieldwork, persistent observation and triangulation. They should use other researchers to confirm judgements that are made during the research. They should use negative case analysis, continuously refining hypotheses until they can account for all known cases. They should during fieldwork use other recorded material, such as video tapes, to check later analysis of the data, and they should employ systems of respondent validation.

These various tests of reliability are familiar and work by comparing different data collection episodes: these data 'moments' having occurred at different points in time, in different places, and with different participants. For example, the last of Guba and Lincoln's tests is respondent validation. Here, judgements made by participants at different times in the research project are compared. If the later judgements confirm the validity of early ones, the researcher can be more sure about their conclusions. This debate has been polarised between those who argue that respondents have a right of veto over what is included in the research text at every point in the proceedings, or whether, if they are allowed this right, their desire to present a public face overrides their commitment to give an authentic account of what happened. There is thus a trade-off between the rights of participants to control the research agenda and the authenticity of their accounts.

External validity refers to the ability of a piece of research to relate to other contexts and environments. There is a relationship of inverse proportionality between internal and external validity. If the setting is controlled as in an experiment, then it is harder to be sure about its ecological validity, that is, whether its findings can be transposed to other settings. In addition, there is a problem with the notion of a sample representing a population because it implies that there are real characteristics in nature which conform to this way of representing it. In its place, Guba and Lincoln (1985: 316) propose that 'the naturalist cannot specify the external validity of an enquiry; he or she can provide only the thick description necessary to enable someone interested in making a transfer to reach a conclusion about whether the transfer can be contemplated as a possibility'. The burden of proof is therefore placed firmly on the reader or receiver, and by definition, this provides no guidance as to how they should judge the piece of research. Its one specification is that the description should be 'thick' (Geertz 1973), but this is too general to allow confidence in its use.

The third way of judging research was in terms of its reliability. Guba and Lincoln want to substitute a notion of dependability. They make a number of points about this. First, it is implicit in the idea of credibility. If a piece of research is credible, it will also be dependable. Second, given the nature of naturalistic research, traditional means of establishing reliability are inappropriate. The design is likely to be emergent, and thus research teams conducting enquiries independently are not likely to come to the same conclusions. Indeed, if the role of the researcher is seen as integral to the data which are collected, then replicating an enquiry is unlikely to succeed. Guba and Lincoln develop the notion of an auditor to determine both its dependability and their fourth criterion, confirmability (this is designed to replace the traditional notion of objectivity). The auditor would have a number of tasks, chief of which would be to 'ascertain whether the findings are grounded in the data . . . whether inferences based on the data are logical', whether 'the utility of the category system: its clarity, explanatory power and fit to the data' are realistic, and finally 'the degree and incidence of inquirer bias' (Guba and Lincoln 1985: 318).

Guba and Lincoln are also committed to the idea that researchers are able to identify the effects of their methods on the data and thus separate out those effects. This would result in an unadulterated, and thus, by implication, valid account of proceedings. Qualitative researchers adopt methods which emphasise progressive focusing whereby the shape of the research is not determined before fieldwork begins, but is responsive to the initial data collected, and in turn has an influence on subsequent methods that are used. If this is accepted as legitimate, it is hard to see how researchers could in any meaningful way separate out their effects from the data, since data and method in this sense are indistinguishable. Finally, Guba and Lincoln's fourth criterion can only operate in a limited way as a measure of validity, because it is a second order concept. It may be useful as a way of reminding researchers that their conclusions should always relate to the data that have been collected, but it cannot refer to the collection of data itself, and therefore cannot act as a bridging concept between description and reality.

AUTHENTICITY CRITERIA

Guba and Lincoln (1989) were aware of some of the faults implicit in their approach, principally that it was too closely associated with positivist perspectives, and too concerned with method, rather than epistemology or ontology. They therefore developed a second set of criteria which did not have roots or origins in a positivist perspective.[6] They described these as authenticity criteria. The first is fairness, and here they argue that equal consideration should be given to all the various perspectives of participants in the research. The second is educative authenticity: a piece of research is valid when individual respondents' understanding of other viewpoints is enhanced. The third, catalytic authenticity, refers to whether the research process has stimulated activity and decision making. Finally, they suggest no evaluative schema is complete without an acknowledgement that research is designed to empower participants to act. Before I address some of these issues, we need to examine one other attempt at developing a set of evaluative criteria.

Hammersley (1992) develops a three-item schema which has some similarities. His three criteria for establishing validity are plausibility or credibility, coherence and intention.[7] The first concerns the issues of plausibility and credibility, and he accepts that, since such notions depend on audience, they will be subject to changing fashions and evolving political and social arrangements. It is worth reminding ourselves of the importance now attached to ethnographically-based research studies in the field of education and elsewhere, in comparison with, and as a reaction to, the dominance of quantitative methods after the second world war. The second criterion Hammersley suggests should be used to judge the validity of qualitative studies is that the kind of evidence presented should be central to the arguments of the research. He thus makes a case for the need to be coherent, that is, evidence and argument should logically cohere. Finally, Hammersley argues that qualitative studies should be judged in terms of their intentions. A descriptive study should not be judged to have failed because it did not test in any meaningful way a developing theory. He therefore argues that: 'from my point of view ... the assessment of validity involves identifying the main claims made by a study, noting the types of claims these represent, and comparing the evidence provided for each claim with what is judged to be necessary, given the claim's plausibility and credibility' (Hammersley 1992: 72). He also develops a notion of relevance to complement his validity criteria.

Hammersley's more concise version avoids some of the problems discussed above, though it does have problems of its own. First, if plausibility or credibility are defined in terms of their public applicability, then they are subject to social and political arrangements which are stratified. Thus 'truth' is controlled by those in positions of power. Second, in the same way that Guba and Lincoln's criterion of confirmability is a second-order concept, so too is coherence, which means that it can be subjected to the same type of critique. Finally, Hammersley's injunction that qualitative studies should be judged in terms of their intentions is problematic in two ways: authors of such studies may not know how to describe them and even if they do, may not believe that such categorisations are meaningful and coherent.

THE PRACTICE OF EDUCATION

These different sets of criteria have been developed to allow judgements to be made about research. They are, in essence, validity claims, and range from simple representations of reality, so long as a number of conditions are met (cf. Campbell and Stanley 1963, Bracht and Glass 1968), methodological approaches which stress correct procedures (cf. Glaser and Strauss 1967), comparisons between different data-collection episodes (Guba and Lincoln 1985) to an emphasis on relevance as well as validity (Hammersley 1992). This last places research firmly in the political sphere.

In order to develop criteria for making judgements about educational research, researchers need to address the relationship between educational theory and what it refers to. In other words, they need to address validity questions, or the relations between text and reality. If we take the effect of class sizes on the quality of learning in schools (Mortimore and Blatchford 1993) for example, we have to be in a position to judge the quality of evidence produced to support the thesis that smaller class sizes lead to improvements.[8] In doing this, we need to assess the relationship between the data and what they refer to, the role the researchers assume in the collection of those data, the way sampling and other fieldwork decisions are made, and more importantly, the epistemological status of the claims made by the research team.

Such an assessment may provide straightforward answers to these various questions. On the other hand, it may provide answers which refer to the complicated nature of the representational act in research. Reality is always textually mediated, with authors producing realist (Usher 1993), confessional (Van Maanan 1988), transparent, opaque, monologic or dialogic (Hammersley and Atkinson 1994) texts. It is also mediated in other ways. These sets of criteria which we use to judge the quality of research determine what is considered good or bad research; and in so doing, they always assume epistemological and ontological positions. They are, therefore, never neutral. What counts as evidence, what logical relations are deemed appropriate, what is considered relevant to the thesis argued for in the research report, are all ways in which 'good research' is constructed. By sanctioning a set of criteria, certain types of truths are excluded.

These sets of criteria are different because they make different epistemological claims. If research is understood as the development of propositions about educational activities which reflect the world as it is, allow predictions about future educational states, and can be replicated by other educational researchers, then this provides support for the technical–rationality model of the relationship between theory and practice.[9] Here we refer to a model which understands the practitioner as a technician whose role is to implement 'objective' educational truths, and therefore has a passive role in the implementation process. If it is possible to identify such 'truths' about education, the practitioner who chooses to ignore them is likely to make inadequate judgements about how they should proceed in practice. This is regardless of the need for practitioners to own or incorporate such findings into their own understandings to inform their practice (Rudduck 1991). If theory about education can be developed which transcends context, then practice is better if informed by it.

On the other hand, if we are not prepared to accept that research should be understood in this way, this relationship between theory and practice needs to be rethought. The difficulty with this is to conceptualise the new relationship without resorting to theory or timeless truths about education. Operating in a non-technicist way demands that practitioners do not behave as objective theory says they should. But this reconceptualisation of the relationship between theory and practice is itself theoretical and, moreover, theoretical in a normative sense. This can only be resolved by accepting the need for theoretical knowledge, which means that we also have to accept that it refers to something. Rahkonen (1991), among others, has argued that because knowledge is always textually mediated, it follows that there is nothing outside the text (this position, in essence, is postmodernist, and one of its implications is that there is no need to develop evaluative criteria to judge research because the social world expressed in texts can never be captured in this way). One of the problems with this is that deliberative action becomes empty, derived as it is of a psychology, sociology or philosophy.

Walsh (1993) identifies four educational discourses: the utopian, the deliberative, the evaluative and the scientific. The utopian is 'directly committed to the flourishing of education' (Walsh 1993: 53) and is concerned with ideal representations. The deliberative is defined as those behaviours which lead to wise actions. It is therefore concerned with practice and is idiographic in orientation. It is closely associated with practical theorising, and can only be judged to have succeeded by whether it has contributed to improved practice. The evaluative discourse 'describes, analyses and judges educational practices and contexts with a view to their maintenance and development, and educational proposals with a view to their adoption' (Walsh 1993: 56–57). Finally, the scientific discourse is concerned with explanations of educational activities and behaviours. Walsh reminds us that it is important to understand the way these discourses can be distinguished as well as the connections between them.

These connections, however, are never straightforward. The technical–rationality model prioritises the scientific over the deliberative by giving precedence to 'objective' theory about education. Deliberative discourses are more closely tied to practice and activities associated with those practices. They are concerned with action and change, and can only be judged in terms of their effects. They are, as a result, embedded within ethical frameworks and are problem-solving activities (Schwab 1978). Above all, though, they understand the social world as praxis, continually in flux and always being worked on.

NOTES

1   There is some doubt about what constitutes the natural science model. For example, the hypothetico-deductive approach is increasingly being seen as an inadequate way of describing how natural scientists actually operate because it ignores inductive, serendipitous and intuitive forms of discovery (cf. Gillies 1993).

2   Each position has an ontological, epistemological and methodological orientation. So, a positivist researcher is likely to adopt a naive realist ontology, a dualist/objectivist epistemology and an experimental/quantitative methodology. A post-positivist researcher is more likely to adopt a critical realist ontology, a modified dualist/objectivist epistemology and a methodology which embraces both qualitative and quantitative methods. Post-modernists or post-structuralists, on the other hand, are more likely to adopt historical realist and relativist ontologies, critical and constructivist epistemologies and methods which directly address hermeneutical concerns (Denzin and Lincoln 1994).

3   Cf. analytic induction (Robinson 1951, Znaniecki 1934), grounded theory (Glaser and Strauss 1967), generative analysis (Huberman and Miles 1994), interactive synthesis (Fischer and Wertz 1975) and others.

4 Harris (1979) speculates about the difficulties of counting the number of people in a university oval without applying some form of theoretical construct to define what a human being is.

5 Naturalistic research is best defined in terms of what it is not; that is, research conducted by experimental or other researchers in artificial conditions. I explore the whole notion of artificiality of data collection in Chapter 9.

6 Guba and Lincoln (1989: 114) argue that: 'the former set [credibility, transferability, dependability and confirmability] represents an early effort to resolve the quality issue for constructivism; although these criteria have been well received, their parallelism to positivist criteria makes them suspect. The latter set [fairness, ontological authenticity, educative authenticity and catalytic authenticity] overlaps to some extent those of critical theory but goes beyond them, particularly the two of ontological authenticity and educative authenticity.' Nevertheless they go on to suggest that these criteria are not yet fully developed and need further critique.

7 Hammersley (1992) in fact develops twin notions of validity and relevance. I have concentrated on the first because I am more concerned here with the relations between text and reality.

8 Mortimore and Blatchford (1993) claim that smaller class sizes contribute to improved conditions for learning in schools. Much of the evidence is based on studies conducted in the United States of America.

9 Technical rationality or instrumental rationality is understood by critical theorists (Marcuse 1964, Adorno 1967, Horkheimer 1972) as the dominant feature of the modern world. They describe it as constraining and distorting, and propose solutions which are emancipatory. Gibson (1986: 7) describes it in the following way: 'Instrumental rationality represents the preoccupation with means in preference to ends. It is concerned with method and efficiency rather than with purposes. Instrumental rationality limits itself to "How to do it?" questions rather than "Why do it?" or "Where are we going?" questions. It is the divorce of fact from value, and the preference, in that divorce, for fact. It is the obsession with calculation and measurement: the drive to classify, to label, to assess and number, all that is human. As such, it is the desire to control and to dominate, to exercise surveillance and power over others and nature.'

REFERENCES

Adorno, T. (1967) *Prisms: Cultural Criticism and Society*, London: Neville Spearman.

Bartlett, D. and Payne, S. (1995) 'Grounded Theory: Its Basis, Rationale and Procedures', in R. Usher and G. McKenzie (eds) *Understanding Social Research: Perspectives on Methodology and Practice*, Southampton: University of Southampton.

Bhaskar, R. (1989) *Reclaiming Reality*, London: Verso.

Bracht, G. H. and Glass, G. V. (1968) 'The External Validity of Experiments', *American Educational Research Journal*, 4, 5: 437–74.

Bulmer, M. (1979) 'Concepts in the Analysis of Qualitative Data', *Sociological Review* 27, 4: 651–77.

Campbell, D. T. and Stanley, J. C. (1963) 'Experimental and Quasi-experimental Designs for Research on Teaching', in N. Gage (ed.) *Handbook of Research on Teaching*, Chicago: Rand McNally.

Charmaz, K. (1983) 'The Grounded Theory Method: an Exploration and Interpretation', in R. Emerson (ed.) *Contemporary Field Research*, Boston: Little, Brown.

Denzin, N. and Lincoln, Y. (1994) (eds) *Handbook of Qualitative Research*, London: Sage.

Fischer, C. and Wertz, F. (1975) 'Empirical Phenomenological Analysis of being Criminally Victimized', in A. Giorgi (ed.) *Phenomenology and Psychological Research*, Pittsburgh: Duquesne University Press.

Geertz, C. (1973) *The Interpretation of Cultures*, New York: Basic Books.

Gibson, R. (1986) *Critical Theory and Education,* London: Hodder and Stoughton.

Gillies, D. (1993) *Philosophy of Science in the Twentieth Century: Four Central Themes*, Oxford: Blackwell.

Glaser, B. G. (1978) *Advances in the Methodology of Grounded Theory: Theoretical Sensitivity*, California: Sociology Press.

—— and Strauss, A. L. (1967) *The Discovery of Grounded Theory: Strategies for Qualitative Research*, Chicago: Aldine.

Guba, E. and Lincoln, Y. (1985) *Naturalistic Inquiry*, London: Sage.

—— and ——(1989) *Fourth Generation Evaluation,* London: Sage.

—— and ——(1994) 'Competing Paradigms in Qualitative Research', in N. Denzin and Y. Lincoln (eds) *Handbook of Qualitative Research*, London: Sage.

Hammersley, M. (1992) *What's Wrong with Ethnography?*, London: Routledge.

—— and Atkinson, P. (1994) 'Ethnography and Participant Observation', in N. Denzin and Y. Lincoln (eds) *Handbook of Qualitative Research*, London: Sage.

Harris, K. (1979) *Education and Knowledge*, London: Routledge and Kegan Paul.

Horkheimer, M. (1972) *Critical Theory: Selected Essays*, New York: Herder and Herder.

Huberman, M. and Miles, M. (1994) 'Data Management and Analysis Methods', in N. Denzin and Y. Lincoln (eds) *Handbook of Qualitative Research*, London: Sage.

Malinowski, B. (1922) *Argonauts of the Western Pacific*, London: Routledge and Kegan Paul.

Marcuse, H. (1964) *One Dimensional Man: Studies in the Ideology of Advanced Industrial Society*, London: Routledge and Kegan Paul.

Mortimore, P. and Blatchford, P. (1993) *Briefings for the Paul Hamlyn Foundation, The National Commission on Education*, London: Heinemann.

Rahkonen, K. (1991) 'Der biographische Fehlschluss', *BIOS* 4: 243–7.

Robinson, W. (1951) 'The Logical Structure of Analytic Induction', *American Sociological Review* 16: 812–18.

Rudduck, J. (1991) *Innovation and Change*, Milton Keynes: Open University Press.

Schwab, J. (1978) *Science, Curriculum and Liberal Education*, Chicago: University of Chicago Press.

Strauss, A. (1987) *Qualitative Analysis for Social Scientists*, Cambridge: Cambridge University Press.

—— and Corbin, J. (1990) *Basics of Qualitative Research: Grounded Theory Procedures and Techniques*, London: Sage.

—— and ——(1994) 'Grounded Theory Methodology: An Overview', in N. Denzin and Y. Lincoln (eds) *Handbook of Qualitative Research*, London: Sage.

Usher, R. (1993) *Reflexivity, Occasional Papers in Education as Interdisciplinary Studies* 3, Southampton: University of Southampton, School of Education

Van Maanan, J. (1988) *Tales of the Field: On Writing Ethnography*, Chicago: University of Chicago Press.

Walsh, P. (1993) *Education and Meaning: Philosophy in Practice*, London: Cassell.

Wood, R. (1987) *Measurement and Assessment in Education and Psychology*, London: Falmer.
—— and Power, C. (1987) 'Aspects of the Competence-Performance Distinction: Educational, Psychological and Measurement Issues', *Journal of Curriculum Studies* 19, 5: 409–24.
Znaniecki, R. (1934) *The Method of Sociology*, New York: Farrar and Rinehart.

Part II
Practices

6 Evaluation as realpolitik

Janet Harland

One of the problems in developing an analysis of evaluation in contemporary education research is that the term itself has been stretched and stretched to encompass an ever-widening range of activities, undertaken for an ever-increasing range of purposes. In so doing the notion of evaluation has, for many people, become part of their daily vocabulary. As recently as the mid-1970s evaluation seemed an esoteric term for a specialised and specialist activity. Yet ten years later teachers and all in the educational sphere had absorbed evaluation into their routine discourse. Just as the term curriculum became common usage for those who had previously talked of courses, or syllabi, or even timetables, so evaluation established itself in the landscape of educational talk.

Nevertheless evaluation is still a concept around which there exists some lack of clarity, some uncertainty and, all too often, some apprehension, even fear. The lack of clarity is caused by the uncertainty and even the ambivalence which so often surrounds the practice of evaluation. Frequently this is expressed by strengthening the word itself by constructing a compound term such as research-and-evaluation, or monitoring-and-evaluation ('M and E' in the working language of many agencies). Such strengthening hides unanswered (and maybe unanswerable) questions, such as whether evaluation is an acceptable form of research, and at what point evaluation becomes little more than a checking up or monitoring process. The only solution seems to be to unpack the term evaluation, accept that it has become over-extended, and endeavour to distinguish between different usages and practices in such a way as to clarify differences and to try to legitimise alternatives as alternatives.

For a long time most attempts to do this have concentrated on methodologies as a key determinant of difference: the qualitative versus the quantitative; the scientific versus the naturalistic (Guba and Lincoln 1981); the democratic versus the non-democratic. But much confusion has been caused by this conventional focus on methodology because while battle lines have been drawn up largely in terms of differences in the practice of evaluators, many current exercises in evaluation – some of which have a very considerable impact on

educational practice – are totally eclectic in their use of alternative methodologies. More useful amid the present confusions is, I suggest, a distinction based
on function, and this is the framework I shall adopt in this chapter.

In doing this I shall begin with a distinction drawn by Janet Finch in her
important book *Research and Policy: the Uses of Qualitative Methods in Social
and Educational Research* (1986). Using the work of Bulmer and others, she
distinguishes between an 'engineering model' of social research and an
'enlightenment model'. The former reflects a linear relationship between
research and policy, with 'research feeding into specific "decisions" by
providing the missing facts' (Finch 1986: 153) The enlightenment model on
the other hand emphasises 'intellectual and conceptual contributions rather
than the provision of facts' (ibid.: 153). Later she argues that there is evidence
that the impact of most research is more likely to be 'diffuse and indirect' rather
than immediate – 'the conceptualisations of an issue offered as a result of
research are more important than concrete findings'; and that this means that
the products of research will be used 'from below' as well as 'from above', in
other words 'by those who are the targets of policy and who are pressing for
change in their own situation' (ibid.: 230).

Finch's argument provides a useful starting point for the discussion which
follows. Her functional distinction between research as engineering and
research as enlightenment readily transposes into a distinction between
evaluation geared to action (i.e. to decisions) and evaluation geared to understanding, with more diffuse implications for decision making. Second, she
argues for a concept of policy making and hence policy critique at 'a very small
scale indeed', including presumably the daily classroom practice of teachers.
And third, although Finch (1986: 158) seeks to distinguish between the
evaluation of existing policies as a proper focus for qualitative social research
and a narrower notion of evaluation in which there is a 'direct commissioning
of research into the effects of a particular policy' (often requiring quantitative
measures), her overall definition of evaluation covers both the action and the
enlightenment functions of evaluation:

> to describe and understand the real effects of policies, to compare the
> assumptions on which policies are based with social experience, and to
> assist in a considered assessment of their viability and appropriateness.
>
> (Finch 1986)

The argument in this chapter will, however, go beyond Finch's analysis of
function. I shall suggest that a third and equally, if not more, significant
function of evaluation is concerned with *control*. Evaluation is now incorporated into a strategy of policy implementation; policy itself is enacted through
a process of resource allocation; and the deployment of resources implies an
obligation to be accountable. Evaluation thus becomes both stick and carrot in
the business of policy enactment and therefore of control.

We have therefore a model of function which offers three alternatives:

action, understanding, control. Different actors in different spheres undertake evaluations, with different purposes in mind. But in doing so they use overlapping methodologies. Moreover, these many enterprises operate at many different levels and on many different scales: all the way from a well-staffed project operating within a six-figure budget under contract to a major sponsor, to a voluntary, ad hoc project in a particular school or sub-section of a school, or a piece of personal research pursued for its own sake or as part of a dissertation or a thesis. Much of the confusion created around the practice of evaluation has arisen from the unproblematic way in which it has been assumed that observations and principles can be applied readily across functions, across levels and across scale, perhaps based on the naive assumption that methodological issues are the same no matter in what context they crop up.

The history of evaluation and of the theoretical debates which mark that history is an oft-told tale (Simons 1987, Norris 1990, etc). The history is a matter of fact, the theoretical debate one of impassioned argument which often conceals fundamental epistemological differences as well as conflicting educational and political philosophies. Words like values, ethics, democracy and power often feature early on in the analysis and, in my experience, can easily frighten the novice who seeks to know what and how, why and when. So at this point I shall summarise the history in terms of function.

Formal educational evaluation began in the USA in the context of finding explicit answers to specific questions about a range of educational programmes. It seemed a natural component of the drive to efficiency (Callahan 1962) and the task readily fell into the hands of the psychometricians. They naturally favoured quantitative data and their natural predilection was itself a shaping and constraining factor on evaluation practice. Essentially, evaluation was about checking and comparing outcomes, with a bias towards aggregated data rather than towards a focus on specificity or difference at the level of the individual or the institution. The focus was on what had occurred and rarely on why. And there was no suggestion that the quality of the programme itself, and not merely its outcomes, was to be the object of scrutiny. Even Tyler (1971, first published in 1949), much of whose writing now seems refreshingly liberal and sympathetic to the professionalism of teachers, saw evaluation as a commentary on the effectiveness of the teaching methods chosen rather than on the adequacy or appropriateness of the overall aims and the objectives derived from them.

The function of such evaluation was clearly to contribute to action. It was assumed that decisions would be taken in the light of the evaluation data. However, over time it became clear that evaluation might and should be more sophisticated in the way in which it clarified the implications for action. Two significant contributions here were the work of Cronbach (1963) and Stufflebeam *et al.* (1971), both of which have a continuing relevance today. Cronbach emphasised the contribution of evaluation to course improvement. The evaluator's data should not just record the effectiveness of teacher or pupil performance; it should feed back into questions about the course itself and lead to revisions of the teaching programme. Such ideas were later conceptualised as formative evaluation (Scriven 1967). They also laid the foundation for arguments subsequently developed by writers such as Patton (1978) that evaluation should be useful – in other words, should inform action.

Stufflebeam (Stufflebeam *et al.*1971) was more concerned to analyse the stages in decision making. He posited a rather idealised model of rational decision making and urged the evaluator to produce relevant and timely data to feed into each stage of the process, so that informed decisions would be reached. It is a truism among experienced evaluators that evaluation is rarely responsible for more than 20 per cent of a decision, the remaining 80 per cent being the product of personal, political and contextual factors. Yet the impact of this kind of thinking is also still in evidence: for example, it is worth considering the role of 'audit' and the later interlocking of 'implementation' and 'evaluation' processes in the model of school development planning advocated by Hargreaves and Hopkins (1991) where appropriate data are fed into the decision-making process at timely points in the planning cycle.

One of the early advocates of an approach to evaluation which emphasised understanding as opposed to the demands of action or the need for decisions was the 'reformed' psychometrician, Robert Stake. His countenance model of evaluation (1967) recognised that in relation to a specific programme there were issues to do with both the passage of time (before, during and afterwards) and with human agency (intentions, actions, effects) which we needed to grasp in order to understand the totality of a programme. It was Stake who also raised the issue of whose judgement was to count, and urged evaluators to think about whether their own judgement or that of the programme participants was of most relevance to the evaluation. Such questions later prompted the idea that evaluations should seek to 'illuminate' (Parlett and Hamilton 1972), paying attention to the context of a programme in order that the reader might understand it within its setting rather than abstracted from reality like a specimen on a laboratory bench. Evaluations should 'mirror' the reality of their study. And case study was, par excellence, a strategy which allowed a focus on the uniqueness of each institutional setting. Thus in the cause of understanding, evaluations focused down and down. The tendency was to see everything as sui generis, and this raised increasingly urgent questions about generalisability as understanding was sometimes bought at the price of excluding the rest of the world. At best the case study worker worked on the principle of generating 'grounded' theory from the field which could be of use elsewhere: at worst, weak claims were made about the value of evaluation reports as 'vicarious experience'.

These developments in educational evaluation practice fed a notion of the school as the site of innovation and teachers as the agents of change. In other words, the success or failure of a particular project or programme was crucially determined by the actions of the practitioners who adopted it. No project could be 'teacher proof'; no programme would succeed wholly on its own merits. As faith in centrally devised projects declined (the Schools' Council closed in 1984 but the impact and take-up of its programmes was in serious doubt by the mid-1970s), it was increasingly claimed that evaluation studies very often appeared to explain disappointing outcomes in terms of inadequate management of the change process, or of tissue rejection at the level of the classroom. If projects were failing on the ground – or if teachers chose not even to adopt those that were offered to them by outside experts – then we needed to understand not so much the supposed inadequacies of the programmes as the lack of adaptive and innovative behaviour at the institutional level.

In the field of curriculum development, such thinking generated the notion that the school itself should be the source and site of innovation – Hargreaves (1989) suggests that 'hope, faith and optimism' did not so much permeate as consume both the discussion and the evaluation of such initiatives. Moreover, in the field of teacher development, the findings of understanding-oriented evaluation sustained and developed the initially somewhat provocative notion of 'teacher as researcher' advocated by Stenhouse (1975) and the related concept of 'action research' developed by Elliott and others as a problem-solving strategy (see Elliott 1991, for an interesting advocacy of this concept). And finally, in terms of educational evaluation itself, this sharper focus on the innovation in context encouraged the view that evaluation might usefully be conducted by practitioners themselves as part of the developmental process. School self-evaluation flourished from the early 1980s both with and without positive encouragement from the LEAs. Incidentally, it is in those instances where LEAs required and even intervened in this process (often using the GRIDS procedures developed by the Schools' Council) that we can see early evidence of evaluation geared to control.

There is always a tendency to see developments in education in isolation from the wider scene but it may help us to understand shifts in the function of evaluation if we paint in some background. Early evaluation practice is best understood against the efficiency movement of the 1920s and 1930s and against the positivism of post-war social planning. Similarly, the reaction towards an evaluation practice geared to understanding can be interpreted as a reflection both of the growing currency of ideas concerning the construction of personal meaning, and of an increasing emphasis on participative styles of decision making. It also seems helpful to relate some of these developments to shifts in thinking about institutional management. For example, in the early 1970s Schön's Reith lectures argued that only 'adaptive' organisations would survive in a world which had passed *Beyond the Stable State* (1971). Yet change was not easy and frequently was actively resisted by a process of 'dynamic conservatism'. A decade later Peters and Waterman (1982) were arguing the significance of the individual in the health of successful companies and promoting the idea of delegating decisions to the lowest possible level. Alongside this came arguments that the most effective workers were self-managers, able to initiate and to critique their own contribution to the general good. For the professions the concept of the reflective practitioner (Schön again, 1983) promoted the notion that professional knowledge is generated through systematic reflection on practice. This was developed without reference to the education profession and yet has been assimilated rapidly into the rhetoric of teacher education, even where there seems to have been little attempt to explore the implications for action. (What is to be reflected upon? How? And with what results? See Zeichner and Tabachnik 1991.)

Space does not allow for more than this brief reference to broader thinking about organisational change: what is clear, however, is that within such a frame it is not surprising that the move to make evaluation studies more developmental in character fitted readily into what has been called the 'human relationships' school of management. It would seem that evaluation geared to enhancing understanding can contribute to the tasks of supporting, developing and empowering organisational members to be more creative and effective. Such models of good management seem to have persisted into the mid-1990s and many of the evaluation practices which sustain them have been assimilated into the working practices of all manner of organisations: public and private, profit-seeking and service-oriented, commercial and educational.

But the picture is not as simple and straightforward as this analysis suggests. Alongside this evolving philosophy of institutional management, there has developed a more hard-nosed approach well expressed through the triad: efficiency, effectiveness, economy. In this context evaluation has acquired a third function – that of control – and this will be the focus of the major part of this chapter.

It is always tempting to look for causes behind causes. But in an attempt to curtail that process, I shall make here a number of possibly uncontentious assertions without going into the reasons for each in their turn. Between them, however, they provide some clues about the emergence of evaluation as a means of control.

The first of these assertions is that there has been a move to reduce public expenditure or, at the very least, to secure more 'bang for the buck'. Expenditure constraints, spurred first by Hayekian economics and second by world-wide recession coupled with rising demand, have led to a chronic sense of resource limitation across the whole public sector.

Second, the globalisation of the economy, and the increasing pressures of international competition, have created concern in every nation about the quality of their workforce. Taken together these two factors go a long way towards explaining government attempts to steer educational policy, and to see that public expenditure on education is geared to what are judged to be national priorities. Over and above this, in Britain there has clearly been a political and an ideological agenda driving the Conservative government's educational policy – but few of us expect that to go away as and when there is a change of government; at best there may be a change in emphasis or direction.

It seems unlikely that any government will abandon a commitment to the three-E principles and it is this commitment which has transformed the practice of evaluation.

A further assertion is that since the middle of the 1970s government has learned new strategies for turning policy intentions into actual practice by shortening the time-line between the two and by finding a series of strategies to minimise resistance or Luddite-type wrecking at the regional, local or institutional level. It has largely achieved this by refining its strategies of resource allocation and resource control. In crude terms this might be characterised as a shift from block grant to specific grant, but in practice the move has been far more sophisticated and far more pervasive than this implies. The new mode of operation is built upon a series of quasi-contracts whereby government specifies the services it wishes to purchase, and others, whose existence and/ or survival depends upon the allocation of public monies, strive to deliver those services. We then move into a world in which the implementation of policy is achieved through relationships defined by terms such as customer–contractor, purchaser–provider, or spending department–executive agency; and we reach the logical point of conceptualising government as 'entrepreneurial'. Because these points have such a material effect upon evaluation, I shall expand this theme a little further.

I have argued elsewhere (Harland 1987a, 1987b, 1993) that the pioneer work in developing such techniques in Britain was done by the Manpower Services Commission (MSC), a satellite unit within the Department of Employment. From the mid-1970s, the MSC was in charge of substantial funds and had a brief to make a quick impact on the skills of the workforce and the problems of unemployment, especially among the young. Lacking any organisational or institutional structure of its own, it achieved this by signing contracts with employers, colleges, voluntary organisations, and all manner of training agencies. With the advent of the TVEI programme in 1982, it moved this mode of operationalising its broadly defined policies into the schools and the FE colleges. To cut a potentially long story short, the DES saw and admired (despite initial concern at the invasion of its territory). Similar strategies were therefore adopted for the Lower Attaining Pupils Programme in 1982, and a limited range of in-service grant schemes in 1983, 1984 and 1986. In 1984 came the Education Support Grant Scheme (ESG). In 1985 the DES asked the MSC to pilot a TVEI related in-service training programme (TRIST) which rapidly became the Local Education Authority Training Grant Scheme (LEATGS) under the control of the DES itself, and was later transmuted into a programme combining LEATGS and ESG, the Grants for Education Support and Training (GEST) programme. In the meantime, the department also funded a range of pilot (research and development) programmes into a range of topics such as the local management of schools, teacher appraisal and records of achievement, all fundamentally as contracted arrangements with evaluation programmes attached. Other agencies involved with developments in schools (the National Council for Educational Technology and the Health Education Council, to name but two) have employed similar strategies. So extensive has been the spread of such contractual arrangements (with their normal sequence of criteria, bid, contract, monitoring, evaluation and replication/impact) that it is possible to argue that the whole system of education is tied up in relationships of this kind. One might for example say that schools now manage their own budgets having contracted to provide the services required (the National Curriculum and more) and are subject to the quality standards imposed by the contractor (national testing plus OFSTED inspections); or that universities contract to provide degree courses for first degree students in line with the funded places allocated to them and at the price fixed by the Higher Education Funding Council, acting on behalf of government. Moreover, contracting now informs working practices at all levels of the education service, as it does in the health service and most other areas of public policy.

This picture of contractual funding in education is parallelled throughout all areas of social policy. In some ways it is surprising that it was not until the late 1980s that policy initiatives began to use the language of contract quite unequivocally because it is a concept which grows naturally out of the Conservative preference for market economics. Keith Joseph frequently argued that market strategies promote the good of individuals; Skidelsky (1989: 34) suggested that the term social market 'means that we turn to the market as a first resort and the government as a last resort, not the other way round'. To move beyond this rhetoric into action almost *requires* the use of contract.

An early sign of this philosophy in action was the mounting pressure on local authorities during the 1980s to put ancillary services out to competitive tendering, but this was primarily intended as an assault on profligate spending by intransigent authorities. Within government itself, the major shift came with the publication of the Efficiency Unit's *Improving Management in Government: the Next Steps* (Jenkins, Caines and Jackson 1988) which proposed that the executive functions of government should be carried out by independent agencies working within a specification and within a budget determined by the parent department. The aim was to complete this process by the end of 1993, thereby reducing very substantially the number of 'regular' civil servants.

Graham Mather, at that time the General Director of the Institute of Economic Affairs, published a pamphlet entitled *Government by Contract* in March 1991, in which he set out to argue that 'treating government service provision as a series of contracts presents new opportunities to improve service standards, set explicit performance standards, and improve customer entitlements . . . '. Such objectives, he claimed

emphatically will not be secured by the traditional techniques of public service ... The government of Britain is moving towards a series of contracts, in which a core of fewer than 10,000 civil servants will specify and buy public services from outside agencies, private contractors and consortia of former public sector managers. Separating policymakers from providers of services offers major opportunities to define more precisely and more frequently the range of public services.

(Mather 1991: 8)

It is precisely this philosophy which was reflected in the *Citizen's Charter* (HMSO), published in July 1991, four months after the IEA paper. Drawing parallels with the way in which many private companies have, it is claimed, decided 'to concentrate on their core businesses, and to buy in services in which they have no particular expertise from specialist contractors', the charter argues, sector by sector, for a major shift in 'contracting out' via 'compulsory competitive tendering' (HMSO 1991: 36). This means that in the public as well as the private sector, those who manage can 'concentrate on planning the future direction of service delivery and on setting quality standards and monitoring the service to ensure that the standard required is achieved' (ibid.: 36).

More recently similar arguments have been gaining ground in the USA. In 1993, Osborne and Gaebler published *Re-inventing Government: How the Entrepreneurial Spirit is Transforming the Public Sector*. The authors based their analysis on what they discerned as developments in the conduct of public affairs at the level of 'cities, counties, states and school districts', and not until p. 328 do they recognise that the United States might be following a trend and not inventing it. However, their book so impressed Washington that President Clinton set up a commission chaired by Vice-President Al Gore to examine the practical application of the Osborne and Gaebler argument to ongoing policy initiatives. (The same book has been circulated around Whitehall departments by government ministers.)

The central argument of this book is that governments should 'steer' more and 'row' less: in other words, that they should concentrate on formulating policy and specifying standards rather than on providing the services themselves.

Governments that focus on steering actively shape their communities, states and nations. They make *more* policy decisions. They put *more* social and economic institutions into motion. Some even do *more* regulating. Rather than hiring more public employees, they make sure *other* institutions are delivering services and meeting the community's needs.

(Osborne and Gaebler 1993: 32)

Later, in a telling phrase, they say 'leaders have to enforce the general interest over the special (i.e. vested) interests of those who want to preserve the status quo'; and again:

Steering requires people who see the entire universe of issues and possibilities and can balance competing demands for resources. Rowing requires people who focus intently on one mission and perform it well. Steering organisations need to find the best methods to achieve their goals. Rowing organisations tend to defend 'their' method at all costs.

(ibid.: 35)

Evaluation, or 'performance measurement' is clearly the link between those who hold the big picture and those who concentrate on their 'one mission'. Osborne and Gaebler conclude with a useful section on 'The Art of Performance Measurement' in which they make clear distinctions between outputs (process) and outcomes (results), between programme outcomes and policy outcomes, and between efficiency (output costs) and effectiveness (output quality). They also argue for a balance between quantitative and qualitative analysis. But here, as in Mather's ideas quoted earlier, as well as in the routine practice of contracting agencies, it is clear that monitoring and evaluation is about rounding off the entrepreneurial cycle: have the services specified in the contract been properly delivered and adequately achieved?

This digression brings us back to the issue of evaluation as a form of control. Of course, it is not only within the bounds of contractual arrangements that evaluation is used as a form of control. But so much commissioned evaluation is now of this nature that it seems useful to locate the discussion which follows against this background. Furthermore, it does not seem to make much difference whether we are talking about evaluations required by the sponsor but undertaken within the 'rowing' organisation, or independent evaluations commissioned (and contracted) by the sponsor, or indeed the sponsor's own personnel. The issue here concerns the function of evaluation rather than the perspective of the evaluator.

But the single word 'control' implies a monolithic function; it needs further refinement if we are to understand that in this context control has a complex and a shaping function and is not simply to be understood as a constraint. I therefore propose to distinguish four different aspects of the control function, concerned variously with compliance, patterning, surveillance and management.

Of these, compliance is the most obvious and perhaps the most straightforward. Evaluation addresses the question of whether you are doing what you should; and if not, why not (and the reasons may spread from intransigence, via incompetence, to a range of situational and human constraints). In other words, are the terms of the contract being observed in terms of the programme's objectives, processes and outcomes? Evaluation compares the what and how of the programme with the intentions, wishes and quality requirements of the policy maker. It is surely the essence of contract to legitimise such an activity.

Patterning is a more subtle process. The values of any project are expressed through and reinforced by the language in which its objectives and all its associated activities are expressed and implemented. Accepting a contract implies that the contractee accepts those values and indeed the bidding process requires the adoption of the language through which those values are expressed. Evaluation serves to reinforce that process by focusing on the project's objectives through the medium of the project's own language. The national and local evaluations of TVEI exemplify this to perfection; the achievement of the MSC in this programme was less about the installation of a particular programme (indeed, local variations in programme design and implementation were a key characteristic of TVEI) but rather were to do with the installation of a set of values expressed through a shared language. As such, evaluation conveys messages both to the practitioner within the project and to any outside observers about what the central concerns of that project are, and in doing so, it imprints those values upon both the observed and the observing.

The third aspect of this control function I have called surveillance. Surveillance reaches across the boundary between monitoring and evaluation: indeed the funding agency itself is often not entirely clear about the difference between the two, a problem well exemplified by the repeated and often contradictory attempts made by the DES to clarify the distinction for the benefit of LEAs within the LEATGS programme (Harland 1993). At the monitoring end of the spectrum, a high level of demand for information and statistical returns serves as a reminder that the funding agency is watching. Evaluation itself naturally focuses on the major goals of the project. We have already noted that programme participants tend to internalise the language and expectations of the programme. The exercise of continuing surveillance through the processes of monitoring and evaluation means that those concerned also come to anticipate the response of the funders to their actions, past, present and future, and thereby come to discipline themselves. Foucault, writing about Bentham's Panopticon, talks about the capacity 'to arrange things so that the surveillance is permanent in its effects even if it is discontinuous in action' (Foucault 1979: 201). Later he says that 'mechanisms of observation' ensure that there are 'gains in efficiency and in the ability to penetrate into men's behaviour' (ibid.: 204).

Perhaps this is not so surprising because one should not underestimate the satisfactions of being an insider rather than a long term outsider. Successful patterning reinforced by effective surveillance encourages identification with the programme's aims:

> On the whole, people have a marked tendency to adapt themselves mentally to success, or to what at a particular time holds out the prospect of it, not only... in regards to the means with which or the extent to which they seek to realise their ultimate ideals at that time, but in their abandonment of

these ideals themselves. In Germany, it is thought proper to dignify this attitude with the name of Realpolitik.

(Weber 1978: 89)

Finally, we need to remark on the way in which evaluation controls by influencing management. Sometimes this is quite explicit (as in the LEATGS scheme) because the development of management systems for the sponsored activity is a central objective of the programme. But the effect is often far more pervasive. Evaluation focuses on implementation strategies. It celebrates the successful, and speculates on the reasons for disappointing performances elsewhere. It serves constantly to remind project managers of the agenda set by the contract. It legitimates experimentation and site-specific development by demonstrating the link to project aims. Furthermore the evaluator can find his or her role extended into confidante of programme managers and management consultant to projects (McCabe 1987, Pole 1993). Evaluation becomes part of the message system between those who steer and those who row. Hence it not only supports the management of the project in its task of fulfilling the contract, but can also act to shape it as well. It is hard work to fulfil a contract and simultaneously to maintain a critical distance. Also, for reasons which are situational just as much as financial, evaluators are under serious pressure to become part of the system.

Evaluation thus becomes a tool of management and finds difficulty in escaping the technocratic imperatives of the system. As Apple (1979: 147) says, 'evaluators are "experts for hire"' and these experts are 'quite strongly influenced by the dominant values of the collectivity to which they belong and the social situation within that society that they fill'. He goes on to say:

> One of the tasks of the expert is to provide the administrative leader of an institution with the special knowledge these persons require before decisions are made. The bureaucratic institution furnishes the problems to be investigated, not the expert. Since the expert bears no direct responsibility for the final outcome of a programme, his or her activities can be guided by the practical interests of the administrative leaders ... And what administrators are not looking for are new hypotheses or new interpretations that are not immediately or noticeably relevant to the practical problems at hand.

(ibid.:147–8)

This passage describes very accurately the practice of evaluation as a form of control.

I now need to return to the original distinction drawn between evaluation for action, evaluation for understanding, and evaluation for control, in order to consider where this analysis takes us. First of all I want to concede that many evaluations in practice overlap these categories. Those whose task is to control are often keen to understand – providing, of course, they can live with the data presented to them because they too are subject to accountability pressures (see Kushner and MacDonald 1987, for a useful exposition of the vulnerability of scheme managers and even government officials). Those whose understandings are fed by the processes of evaluation often proceed to making decisions. Moreover, evaluations undertaken for one purpose may effectively serve another.

Second, I want to repeat that much of the confused thinking about the function of evaluation is the product of a highly eclectic use of methodologies. It would be simple if we could equate evaluation for action with, for example, quantitative measures, or evaluation for understanding with softer, more qualitative approaches. And it would be even more reassuring if we could equate the three functions defined here with the three political stances defined as long ago as 1974 by Barry MacDonald – the autocratic, the bureaucratic and the democratic. But most evaluation exercises now display a catholicity in their choice of methods which must surprise some of the early polemicists of evaluation theory. Indeed, many of those commissioning evaluations now specify evaluation strategies which combine what previously might have seemed to be conflicting approaches: for example, quantitative data relating to pre-specified performance indicators combined with anonymised and progressively focused case studies. Evaluations increasingly display a capacity for both ... rather than either ... or.

Third, I want to return to my opening remarks and identify yet another reason why the whole concept of evaluation increasingly presents us with difficulties and confusions as a direct product of the over-expansion, and possibly the over-use, of the term. This concerns the fact that evaluation activities can be found at every level and upon every scale imaginable. Thus we have a concept which has to encompass everything from a very public and very well funded operation to something which is very intimate and may involve only a few people (even one alone) and certainly no resources beyond those available for the task which is to be evaluated. For this reason, many teachers and other practitioners are exposed to ideas about evaluation (its methods, its problems) which are scarcely related to their concerns but are better understood as belonging to the professional research and evaluation community which generated them (see for example Guba and Lincoln 1981, Burgess 1993). Yet most teachers encounter evaluation at a much simpler level in the context either of some part of an internal process within their own institution or locality, or in the course of preparing a piece of independent work, possibly for an advanced degree. In addition, they are increasingly subject to other forms of evaluation of their work (including all the processes of description, interpretation and judgement) which go under a range of other names such as inspection, appraisal and the publication of test and examination results.

Perhaps it is time we abandoned the word evaluation or at least reserved it for very well-defined situations. The previous paragraph suggested two or three other practices which are part of the broad field of evaluative activities:

others in use include audit, review, performance measurement, quality assurance and even plain research (because I would argue that all educational research is geared to some notion of improvement and is therefore inherently evaluative in intent). But while we retain the one word for the many and varied tasks, it seems helpful to retain some clarity about its varied functions. That way we can accept the legitimacy of many different forms of evaluation undertaken by many different people in many different ways, while avoiding the danger of mistaking or confusing the underlying purpose of their actions.

REFERENCES

Apple, M. (1979) *Ideology and the Curriculum*, London: Routledge and Kegan Paul.

Burgess, R. (ed.) (1993) *Education Research and Evaluation: for Policy and Practice?* London: Falmer.

Callahan, R. (1962) *Education and the Cult of Efficiency*, Chicago: University of Chicago Press.

Cronbach, L. J. (1963) 'Course Improvement through Evaluation', *Teachers College Record* 64: 672–83.

Elliott, J. (1991) *Action Research for Educational Change*, Milton Keynes: Open University Press.

Finch, J. (1986) *Research and Social Policy*, Lewes: Falmer.

Foucault, M. (1979) *Discipline and Punish: the Birth of the Prison*, London: Penguin Books.

Guba, E. G. and Lincoln, Y. S. (1981) *Effective Evaluation*, San Francisco: Jossey Bass.

Hargreaves, A. (1989) *Curriculum and Assessment Reform*, Milton Keynes: Open University Press.

Hargreaves, D. and Hopkins, D. (1991) *Development Planning: a Practical Guide*, London: DES.

Harland, J. (1987a) 'The TVEI Experience: Issues of Control, Response and the Professional Role of Teachers', in D. Gleeson (ed.) *TVEI and Secondary Education*, Milton Keynes: Open University Press.

—— (1987b) 'The New INSET: a Transformation Scene,' *Journal of Education Policy* 2, 3: 235–44.

—— (1993) *From Policy to Practice*, unpublished PhD thesis, University of London: Institute of Education.

Jenkins, K., Caines K., and Jackson, A. (1988) *Improving Management in Government: the Next Steps*, London: HMSO.

Kushner, S. and MacDonald B. (1987) 'The Limits of Programme Evaluation', in R. Murphy and H. Torrance (eds) *Evaluating Education: Issues and Methods*, Milton Keynes: Open University Press.

McCabe, C. (1987) 'The External Evaluator – Inspector or Management Consultant?' *Evaluation and Research in Education* 1, 1: 22.

MacDonald, B. (1974) 'Evaluation and the Control of Education', in B. MacDonald and R. Walker (eds) *Innovation, Evaluation, Research and the Problem of Control (SAFARI)*, Norwich: CARE, University of East Anglia (reprinted in R. Murphy and H. Torrance (eds) 1987 op. cit.).

Mather, G. (1991) *Government by Contract*, IEA Inquiry No. 25, London: Institute of Economic Affairs.

Murphy, R. and Torrance, H. (eds) (1987) *Evaluating Education: Issues and Methods*, Milton Keynes: Open University Press.

Norris, N. (1990) *Understanding Educational Evaluation*, London: Kogan Page.

Osborne, D. and Gaebler, T. (1993) *Re-inventing Government: How the Entrepreneurial Spirit is Transforming the Public Sector*, New York: Plume.

Parlett, M. and Hamilton, D. (1972) *Evaluation as Illumination*, Occasional Paper 9, Centre for Research into Educational Sciences: Edinburgh (reprinted in R. Murphy and H. Torrance (eds) 1987 op. cit.).

Patton, M. Q. (1978) *Utilization-focused Evaluation*, Beverly Hills: Sage.

Peters, T. and Waterman, R. (1982) *In Search of Excellence*, New York: Harper & Row.

Pole, C. (1993) 'Local and National Evaluation', in R. Burgess (ed.) *Education Research and Evaluation: for Policy and Practice?* Lewes: Falmer.

Prime Minister's Office (1991) *The Citizen's Charter*, London: HMSO.

Schön, D. (1971) *Beyond the Stable State: Public and Private Learning in a Changing Society*, London: Maurice Temple Smith Ltd.

——(1983) *The Reflective Practitioner: How Professionals Think in Action*, London: Temple Smith.

Scriven, M. (1967) 'The Methodology of Evaluation', in R. Stake (ed.) *Perspectives on Curriculum Evaluation: AERA Monograph No 1*, Chicago: Rand McNally.

Simons, H. (1987) *Getting to Know Schools in a Democracy*, Lewes: Falmer.

Skidelsky, R. (1989) *The Social Market Economy*, London: Social Market Foundation.

Stake, R. (1967) 'The Countenance of Educational Evaluation', *Teachers' College Record* 68: 523–40.

Stenhouse, L. (1975) *An Introduction to Curriculum Research and Development*, London: Heinemann Educational.

Stufflebeam, D., Foley, W., Gephart, W., Guba, E., Hammond, R., Merriman, H. and Provus, M. (1971) *Educational Evaluation and Decision Making*, Ithaca: Peacock.

Tyler, R. W. (1971) *Basic Principles of Curriculum and Instruction*, Chicago: University of Chicago Press.

Weber, M. (1978) 'The Methodology of the Social Sciences', in W.G. Runciman (ed.) *Weber: Selections in Translation*, Cambridge: Cambridge University Press.

Zeichner, K. M. and Tabachnik, B. R. (1991) 'Reflections on Reflective Teaching', in B. R. Tabachnik and K. M. Zeichner (eds) *Issues and Practices in Enquiry-oriented Teacher Education*, Lewes: Falmer.

7 Action research and reflective practice

Ian Bryant

The ideas embraced by the terms 'action research' and 'reflective practice' have developed an increasing momentum within educational circles, attracting the attentions of front-line teachers, advisors, researchers, professional developers – and to a much less degree administrators and policy-makers – in the past two decades. As someone who tries to teach educational research students about such things, I recognise the seductive quality of these ideas. But they have never seemed to be entirely satisfactory to me, for reasons that I hope will become apparent in the course of this chapter. What exactly are these ideas, and why are they apparently so attractive? What meanings can we give to the terms 'action research' and 'reflective practice', and how are they related? Here, I examine a number of different accounts of action research and its justifications, by way of commenting on selected extracts from some of the standard texts in the educational action research field. A brief history of action research as a preferred mode of enquiry is followed by a specific consideration of the work of Cohen and Manion (1985), Carr and Kemmis (1986), and Winter (1989). As we shall see, these writers offer rather different justifications for action research. They also emphasise different perspectives on particular aspects of the process of engaging in such enquiry. Collectively, however, they are a good source, together with that of Elliott (1991), for an overall understanding of what is involved in this form of practitioner investigation.

Reflective practice is now taken to be a key ingredient of professional development in a variety of practitioner domains, including education. The work of Donald Schön (1983, 1987) in exploring the process of 'reflection-in-action' is briefly considered in relation to action research as reflective enquiry. A number of issues are highlighted for the would-be action researcher/reflective practitioner which need to be addressed *in practice* for those who decide to make a commitment to researching their own activities as educators. These include: dealing with the risks involved; challenges to the validity of the enterprise; problems associated with the generalisability, documentation and reporting of findings. Readers of this chapter who want practical details of how to go about conducting an action research project are especially referred to Nixon (1981), and to Elliott (1991). I do, however, offer four simple suggestions on how to begin to think about doing action research before actually making the commitment – always bearing in mind that the key to any successful action research lies in the quality and strength of that very commitment.

A BRIEF HISTORY

Action research has only a fifty-year history. Commentators are generally agreed that its origins are to be found in wartime operational research and the post-war development of Kurt Lewin's (1948) theories of change agency in formal organisations. Lewin's model of action research was based on a cycle or spiral of conceptual discovery, planning and executive and evaluative activities. In his schema, the distinction was preserved between researcher and researched. The primary change agent was to be the former, with the latter consigned to implementing the research evaluations. For twenty years following Lewin, theories of action research were cast within a positivist applications paradigm, notwithstanding their claims to be sensitive to the contingencies of action. Until the late 1960s, the theories of structural functionalism and the methodologies of experimentalism and survey analysis dominated educational research. As we shall see, these have left a residue of problems concerning the relationship between action research and reflective practice which are not accidental; they are an historical product of the unresolved tensions between action research and more conventional education research methodologies. From positivist and foundationalist perspectives, the 'problems' of action research were seen to lie in its inadequate theorising, and its lack of methodological control, according to the conventional scientific canons.

In the USA, action research was regarded as a species of applied, client-oriented research, unquestioning of the foundationalist claims of psychological and sociological theory during this period. By 1970, Rapoport (1970) was criticising existing understandings of action research as focusing too exclusively on the existence of a client with a problem to be solved, at the expense of scientific interests. He advocated a 'mutually acceptable ethical framework' to reconcile the competing academic claims of social scientists and the needs of their client practitioners without, however, questioning the basis of the former. At the end of the decade, Sanford (1981) judged that practitioner dissatisfaction with the institutional separation of research from practice and the increasing inter- and intra-disciplinary fragmentation of research had put action research back on the agenda through questioning an applications model of research utilisation which was not demonstrably delivering better educational practices.

Meanwhile in the UK, action research was beginning to develop the characteristics of a movement in response to the issue of making academic research relevant to practitioners' problems. The advocacy of 'teachers as researchers' by Stenhouse (1979), and the work of the Humanities Curriculum

Project (documented by Elliott 1991), as well as that of the Tavistock Institute in adopting group approaches to changing practices, were each instrumental in developing action research procedures explicitly distinct from 'scientific' research. Emphasis was now placed on case studies of situational understanding aimed at changing practices through negotiation involving all parties in an investigation. It can be shown that the resurgence in qualitative research and the collapse of the positivist paradigm (at least, in terms of its epistemological justifications) has been accompanied by a renewal of interest in action research both as reflective practice (following the work of Schön 1983), and as theoretical and action critique (following the work of Carr and Kemmis 1986, and Winter 1989).

There are practical reasons also for the recent trend towards action research as a preferred style of research in education. The dependence of educational research on outside funding offers the opportunity to be identified with initiatives of an apparently dynamic kind, promising both value for money and practical results. The value of research has now to be demonstrated within a discourse of 'relevance' which action research supposedly embodies. For the educator it offers a mode of enquiry and understanding in which the conventional dualisms and distinctions between internal and external accounts, subjectivity and objectivity, theory and practice, means and ends, teacher and taught, researcher and researched, are dissolved. It claims to be inherently 'educational' in emphasising the learning aspects of reflective practice. Action research also has a strong educational warrant in the interpretive requirement to study the situated aspects of human action by getting involved, not simply as a participant observer, but as an active change agent. Despite the proliferation of action research projects in recent years, many tensions remain between different understandings of what action research actually involves, and what it can and ought to claim on behalf of understanding and action.

In the three accounts of 'action research' which follow, I highlight some of the differences of meaning associated with the term. These differences are centrally related to the problematic status of this form of enquiry within the more conventional educational research community.

ACCOMMODATIVE ACTION RESEARCH – COHEN AND MANION

In their influential student textbook *Research Methods in Education* (1985) Cohen and Manion characterise action research as a 'style of research' which is situational, collaborative, participatory and self-evaluative. They also see it as 'a method' which is dedicated to adding to 'the practitioner's *functional knowledge* of the phenomena he [sic] deals with' (Cohen and Manion 1985: 208–9, emphasis in original). Comparing action research and applied research, the authors state that whereas

both utilise the scientific method . . . action research, by contrast, interprets the scientific method much more loosely, chiefly because its focus is a specific problem in a specific setting. The emphasis is not so much on obtaining generalisable scientific knowledge as on precise knowledge for a particular situation and purpose.

(ibid.: 209)

Reviewing the Humanities Curriculum Project as an example of action research, Cohen and Manion (ibid.: 211) conclude that 'although lacking the rigour of true scientific research, it is a means of providing a preferable alternative to the more subjective, impressionistic approach to problem-solving in the classroom'. They reproduce, without comment, the aim and premises of the project among which is one that 'the teacher should accept the need to submit his [sic] teaching in controversial areas to the criterion of neutrality at this stage of education, i.e. that he should regard it as part of his responsibility not to promote his own view' (ibid.: 211, Box 9.1). It is important to notice here how 'neutrality' is promoted as an unquestioned and realistic ideal and how it is discursively constructed.

Referring to Nixon's (1981: 212) guidelines for teachers on how to develop an action research 'style of their own', the stricture is reproduced that 'action research must be designed in such a way as to be easily implemented within the pattern of constraints existing within the school' (ibid.: 214, Box 9.2) – a recommendation of accommodative action research which does not question the situatedness of practice. Nevertheless, the goal of action research is taken to be the improvement of practice. In the school context, 'this can be achieved only if teachers are able to change their attitudes and behaviour. One of the best means of bringing about these kinds of changes is pressure from the group with which one works' (ibid.: 214). The Tavistock Institute approach is evident here. Consequently, for Cohen and Manion (1985: 215), 'action research relies chiefly on observation and behavioural data. That it is therefore empirical is another distinguishing feature of the method'. There is no discussion of reflection and/or critique in the authors' account.

Noting that action research takes 'a much more relaxed view of the scientific method' (ibid.: 215) they regard critiques of action research by opponents to 'hold in most cases' (ibid.: 216). Action research is appropriate, however, 'when a new approach is to be grafted on to an existing system' (ibid.: 216). With regard to the generalisability and validity of action research data, it is judged that since the data are situationally specific they cannot be extended beyond the case to stand as generally representative. They conclude therefore that 'the problem of *validity* cannot be side-stepped by arguing that the contexts are unique' (ibid.: 220). Reporting the problems associated with mounting the Humanities Curriculum Research Project, Cohen and Manion see these as stemming from

mistaken or incongruent attitudes and expectations on the part of the teachers in the experimental schools ... they failed to appreciate that the venture had a social science basis and that they would need to adopt a suitably detached stance in keeping with its experimental nature.

(Cohen and Manion 1985: 223)

We are left with a neutralised and accommodative version of action research, without critique and without reflection, one which in effect challenges neither teaching practice nor conventional research wisdom.

EDUCATIONAL ACTION RESEARCH AS CRITICAL SOCIAL SCIENCE – CARR AND KEMMIS

Practitioners who wish to change their practices by means of an action critique are provided with an extensive justification through the work of Carr and Kemmis on action research as a critical social science. According to Kemmis (1993: 177), 'action research is a form of research carried out by practitioners into their own practices ... [it is] a participatory democratic form of educational research for educational improvement'. Action research is seen as a form of practical enquiry characterised by 'a self-reflecting spiral of cycles of planning, acting, observing, and reflecting' (ibid.: 178). Kemmis characterises action research as an 'approach' rather than a 'method', emphasising its emancipatory potential as

> an embodiment of democratic principles in research, allowing participants to influence, if not determine, the conditions of their own lives and work, and collaboratively to develop critiques of social conditions which sustain dependence, inequality, or exploitation in any research enterprise in particular, or in social life in general.

(Kemmis 1993: 179)

This is a far cry from Cohen and Manion's understanding. Here, Kemmis emphasises practices as committed action, or *praxis.* 'Since only the practitioner has access to the commitments and practical theories which inform praxis, only the practitioner can study praxis. Action research, as the study of praxis, must thus be research into one's own practice' (ibid.: 182). There are important implications here for reporting the self as a researcher, i.e. not as a detached observer but as an engaged participant. Action research is eclectic in its choice of investigative techniques, though the interpretive, case study approach is most often used. The key feature is that whatever techniques are employed, action research 'expresses a commitment to the improvement of practices [practitioners' understandings, and the settings of practice]' (ibid.: 185). Furthermore, 'educational action research is a form of educational research which places control over processes of educational reform in the hands of those involved in the action' (ibid.: 189). The extent to which this happens can vary, producing three variants of action research, viz:

1 'technical' action research – which is concerned with the relative efficiency and effectiveness of practice. It has an outsider agenda, with the purpose of sustaining the commitment and collaboration of participants.

2 'practical' action research – which aims at the improvement of practitioners' understandings and action but does not necessarily develop collective responsibility for participants' practices.

3 'emancipatory' action research – in which 'the group itself takes responsibility for its own emancipation from the dictates of irrational or unjust habits, customs, precedents, coercion or bureaucratic systematisation'.

(Kemmis 1993: 187; Carr and Kemmis, 1986: 202–4)

Carr and Kemmis affirm that the purpose of action research is neither to prove nor disprove theory, but to improve practice:

There are two essential aims of all action research: to *improve* and to *involve*. Action research aims at improvement in three areas: first the improvement of a *practice*; second, the improvement of the *understanding* of the practice by its practitioners; and third, the improvement of the *situation* in which the practice takes place. The aim of *involvement* stands shoulder to shoulder with the aims of *improvement*.

(ibid.: 165)

They argue for a theory of action research which is dialectical. The moments of action research comprise a self-reflective spiral. In the self-reflective spiral, the plan is prospective to action, retrospectively constructed on the basis of reflection. Action is essentially risky, but is retrospectively guided by past reflection on which basis the plan was made, and prospectively guided towards observation and the future reflection which will evaluate the problems and effects of the action. Observation is retrospective on the action being taken and prospective to reflection in which the action will be considered. Reflection is retrospective to the actions so far taken and prospective to new planning.

The self-reflective spiral links reconstruction of the past with construction of a concrete and immediate future through action. And it links the discourse of those involved in the action with their practice in the social context ... In this way, action researchers come to develop their own educational theories from its basis in personal knowledge, through its expression in *praxis*, to its systematic development in the discourse of self-reflective communities of action researchers.

(Carr and Kemmis 1986: 186–7, 191)

Carr and Kemmis continue: 'In the action research process, reflection and action are held in dialectical tension, each informing the other through a process of planned change, monitoring, reflection and modification' (ibid.: 206).

Here we have an account of action research in which Carr and Kemmis build on a substantial theory of change through critique and reflection. Critique is theorised by means of a Habermasian assessment of knowledge claims in terms of their truthfulness, authenticity and prudence. But reflection, though asserted as an essential component of the spiral of practitioner research activity, is not itself theorised. Significantly, there are no references to theories of reflective practice and no mention of Schön in their work.

PRINCIPLES FOR THE CONDUCT OF ACTION RESEARCH – WINTER

In developing principles for the conduct of action research, Winter (1989: 4) prefers the hyphenated term 'action-research' to designate 'the basic unity of theoretical and practical knowledge'. He shares the view of Carr and Kemmis that 'the assertion of the viability of practitioner action-research is the assertion of a democratic social and political ideal, the ideal of a creative and involved citizenry, in opposition to the image of a passive populace awaiting instruction from above' (ibid.: 14). The cyclical format as a characteristic of action research is confirmed.

Reviewing some of the early work of Kemmis and Elliott which provided guidelines for would-be action researchers, Winter highlights the problem of casting action research within a positivist perspective. In addition, the formulation of the action research process is seen to be problematic, for there is 'the very cursory treatment given to the process of reflection' (ibid.: 25). 'Reflection' is oriented towards better understanding; practitioner development involves taking action which, when reflected upon, results in changes in practice. Winter (ibid.: 25) defines reflection as: 'the crucial process by means of which we make sense of evidence – whether from specific data-gathering procedures or from our practical experience as it occurs'. The problem is that

> reflection is tacitly assumed to be a straightforward familiar process, or one where the comprehensiveness of the data automatically guarantees the validity of the interpretation, or one which action research can simply *borrow* from elsewhere, i.e. from 'common sense' or from conventional research methods.
>
> (ibid.: 25)

Considering reflection to be *review* or *re-view*, Winter notes that its aim must be a reinterpretation of evidence and practice and that to be valuable it must open up new possibilities for understanding and action; in serving this function it does not merely confirm or disconfirm what is already 'known'. Therefore, 'we need a model for the process of reflection which is clearly different from the logic of natural science . . . otherwise action-research projects will merely seem to be incompetent versions of "real science"' (ibid.: 33). Reflection 'must build upon the competences which practitioners already possess' (ibid.: 35).

Reflection is an aspect of the inherent *reflexivity* of all practices insofar as they are routinely concerned with the negotiation of meaning and the interpretation of knowledge claims. Reflexivity is inherent in the process of making practice judgements. In 'ordinary practice' these often go unnoticed; meanings and claims are discursively hidden. Indeed, we cannot constantly be surfacing them for the purposes of review and critique, since practice would simply stall. Reflective practice is literally, therefore, extra-ordinary practice. One might therefore say that it is itself practically problematic. Nevertheless, as Winter shows, 'reflexive critique' can open up new lines of action, and this is why it is an essential part of action research dedicated to changing practice. He says, 'by showing that a statement is grounded in reflexive interpretive judgements, rather than in external facts, I make it possible to review other possible interpretive judgements concerning that statement, and thus to envisage modifying it' (ibid.: 43). By questioning claims, new lines of argument and possible actions are opened up.

Of Winter's six principles, 'reflexive critique' is the first. The second, 'dialectical critique' emphasises the understanding of 'reality' as a process of becoming and change, and practice as 'praxis' – the actions of an engaged self in which contradictions between the unity and diversity of phenomena are never finally resolved. To paraphrase the Marxist approach to dialectics, in action research there can only ever be a temporary 'synthesis' between different reflective interpretations of practice. There are no eternal truths nor absolute standards of validity that in themselves would privilege either specific practices or their interpretations. The third principle is that of 'collaborative resource'. No particular view is privileged. 'Reality' is negotiated between members and intersubjectively validated. The fourth principle is 'risk'. Researchers are active agents who put themselves at risk, and therefore more than just the disembodied hypotheses of the conventional researcher are at issue. In challenging the routine coping of practitioners, 'the micropolitics of the research process creates a series of rigorous requirements, where considerations of ethics . . . mesh with considerations of prudence' (ibid.: 61). Winter suggests that 'risk' can best be managed through reciprocity between collaborators (e.g. agreements between practitioners to research aspects of each other's practice). Principle five is 'plural structure' which raises questions about the status of different accounts and reporting considerations. Reports will take the form of a collage rather than a linear tale, to represent different views. No single account will be authoritative, and reports of action research will be questioning rather than assertive. Principle six is that of 'theory, practice, transformation'. In action research, theory and practice are not mutually opposed; theory questions practice and practice questions theory. Theory is based in practice and is transformed by transformations of practice.

With Winter, we have an elaborately theorised account of action research which is built up explicitly to incorporate reflection. His six principles are proposed as criteria for assessing the validity of action research in its own terms. Yet the nature of the relationship between action research and reflective practice still remains problematic, begging a number of questions: are 'action research' and 'reflective practice' really the same thing? Is it possible to engage in one without the other? What version, if any, of 'action research' and/or 'reflective practice' should the intending practitioner-researcher follow? In his own characterisation of action research, Elliott (1991: 49) states that 'the fundamental aim of action research is to improve practice rather than to produce knowledge. The production and utilisation of knowledge is subordinate to and conditioned by, this fundamental aim'. He suggests that action research and reflective practice are in fact equivalent. Speaking about reflection in relation to the collaborative aspects of action research, he notes 'this kind of joint reflection about the relationship in particular circumstances between processes and products is a central characteristic of what Schön has called *reflective practice* and others, including myself, have termed *action research* (ibid.: 50). His own interests lie in locating 'action research in the kind of reflective practice which aims to improve the realisation of process values' (ibid.: 51).

ACTION RESEARCH AND THE REFLECTIVE PRACTITIONER

Given the problematic status of reflection in action research, it is curious that in Carr and Kemmis, and in Winter, there is no place for the work of Donald Schön, who does not even merit a bibliographical reference. In order to try and resolve some of the above questions, here is yet another definition of 'action research', one which I suggest is less elaborate and potentially more fruitful. It offers a more promising synthesis between action research and reflective practice. Ebbutt defines action research as involving 'the systematic study of attempts to change and improve educational practice by groups of participants by means of their own practical actions and by means of their own reflection upon the effects of those actions' (Ebbutt 1985: 156).

This definition is useful in a number of respects. First, it emphasises that action research is carried out by practitioners or at least that researchers are actually participating in the practices being researched, and working collaboratively with practitioners. The point here is that action research is concerned both to understand and to change particular situations, and that researchers who are not in and of the situation are not in a position to do either. They cannot share the informal theory of practitioners and cannot possess the situated knowledge essential for change. By being detached from the situation, the researcher does not have to see the research through in all its possible consequences. This is not only a matter of ethics, it also means that the researcher cannot act 'rightly' or in a committed way in the situation, thus endangering the success and validity of the research.

Second, the use of the terms 'change' and 'improve' in the definition points to the importance of improving practice in action research through transformation of the practice situation. In action research there is a particular kind of relationship between transformation and understanding. Schön (1983: 14) puts it this way: 'the practitioner has an interest in transforming the situation from what it is to something he [sic] likes better. He also has an interest in understanding the situation, but it is in the service of his interest in change'. There is thus an interplay between understanding and change, such that understanding is oriented by the interest in change and the change itself increases understanding. Schön characterises this process as 'reflection-in-action'. The vital ingredient in this process is action: we can, therefore, see action research as akin to reflection-in-action. This implies that action research does not have to be something carried out by a special group of people called researchers but is in fact what any practitioner could do as part of everyday practice, given certain conditions. Reflective practitioners are *ipso facto* researchers into their own practice. Interestingly, Schön himself nowhere employs the term 'action research' in his accounts of reflective practice. In promoting reflection-in-action as an epistemology of practice, Schön questions the conventional relationship between research and practice. Rejecting the traditional view of professional knowledge, he re-casts the relationship, thus:

> research is an activity of practitioners. It is triggered by features of the practice situation, undertaken on the spot, and immediately linked to action ... Here the exchange between research and practice is immediate, and reflection-in-action is its own implementation.
>
> (Schön 1983: 308–9)

Third, and related to the above, there is the emphasis in the definition on reflecting upon the effects of actions. Reflection is a key aspect of action research *qua* research. The action research process has been compared to a spiral where action is followed by reflection, and greater understanding followed by more action and reflection. When we reflect we do not do so aimlessly, but because the situation towards which reflection is directed demands action. Reflection has intentionality, which is grounded in the situation and thus involves 'thinking', not in a purely abstract sense but thinking about something – in other words it has both form and content.

Reflection is not something that is just mental and subjective. It always involves action and therefore has a social dimension. At the same time it is not confined to mental problem-solving or thought experiments. This is not to deny that reflection cannot be part of the process of problem-solving, although to see it purely as this is to have a technical-rationality view of reflection, to see it only as a technique for solving problems more efficiently. Schön (1983: 56) puts it in the following way: 'reflection tends to focus interactively on the outcomes of action, the action itself and the intuitive knowings implicit in the action'. In action research as reflective practice, given the concern with change there is always an interest in the outcomes of action but, at the same time, given the concern with understanding, there is an equal interest in the 'knowing' or informal theory which is implicit in the 'doing' or action. Here, thought and action are united both in the practice which is being researched and in the practice of the research itself.

Schön identifies a number of kinds of research which can be undertaken in the service of reflection-in-action, under the umbrella term 'reflective research'. Such research includes

(a) analysing the ways that practitioners frame their roles and practice problems;
(b) building practice repertoires and exemplars through case presentations of specific practice problems and asking the question 'what is this a case of?';
(c) questioning fundamental theories and methods in the light of one's own practice experiences;
(d) engaging in meta-reflection, i.e. examining the process of reflection-in-action itself, through linking affective and situational to cognitive factors.

Action research is concerned with understanding action and its outcomes and with acting through understanding. In this process, reflection plays a key part, but as we have seen it is not the reflection of abstract or *post hoc* contemplation nor yet the reflection of instrumental problem-solving, but a reflection which is practical. The concern is with acting appropriately in a particular situation, given the circumstances and constraints of that situation which could be envisaged differently (i.e. re-framed) and thereby potentially changed.

Finally, Ebbutt's definition uses the term 'systematic study' which poses the question of the extent to which action research actually is 'research'. Practical reflection, since it is situated, is inevitably value-laden. Actions and understandings are always concerned not only with what is possible but also with what is desirable, and thus the ends towards which action is directed and the means used to achieve those ends are co-implicated within value frameworks. Understandings are not simply technical, of how to achieve a given end most efficiently and effectively, but of how to act rightly and appropriately in a particular situation. Since the consequences of action are a key consideration, this provides a further rationale for the involvement of practitioners in action research.

SOME SUGGESTIONS FOR THINKING ABOUT ASPECTS OF PRACTICE

Those who refer to the academic literature on action research and/or reflective practice are likely to be confused by some of the over-elaborate theorising of these processes, possibly even to the point where they decide not to pursue such lines of enquiry. Insofar as action research and reflective practice is about questioning experience and habitual ways of doing things, then a number of related themes and aspects of practice are readily available for questioning without the prior possession of any elaborate theory. They are (a) settings, (b) play, (c) scripts, and (d) communication. These are good places to start any action research or reflective practice project.

Settings

In every day practice, we read settings as the usual contexts in which our activities take place. They carry expectations that events will be organised in certain ways, that some things will happen and not others, and so on. A condition of any practice is that we cannot be constantly attending to settings but must take them for granted, at least for most of the time. But there are also occasions when the practitioner calls into question routine assumptions and asks 'What is going on here?'.

How might such a question be dealt with? It suggests a natural follow-on question of the form, 'What is/are he/she/they doing?' At this point, one might be satisfied with an answer in terms of other people's behaviour. Prudently, one might wish to check one's own reading of the situation with colleagues or others. Reflectively, one might ask oneself, 'How am I reading this situation, and are there alternative readings available?'.

This leads to a general affirmation about reflective practice. There are many possible readings of settings, and the reflective practitioner is one who has a range of readings to hand, those which point to others but also those which point to oneself as an interpreter.

Play

The usual idea of 'play' is that, discounting professional games players, it is an un-serious activity, something set aside from work. One could argue strongly for its therapeutic value precisely because it engages the self in non-critical matters and at the same time distances the self from day-to-day practice concerns.

If we consider practice as play, then we can look at the related ideas of game and rule. Other ways in which we could ask questions about settings include, 'What game is being played here?' or 'What game is she/he playing?'. Such questions normally carry negative connotations, for example 'power plays' and so on. But it is not this sense of 'game' that I want to commend; rather it is the positive metaphorical sense of the term. But first, some thoughts about rules.

Games imply rules that are both enabling and constraining. One way of looking at practice is in terms of the rules which permit and proscribe different activities. They create the action spaces that characterise what we do. Actions are guided not just by formal requirements but also by personal standards – our own rules. These are in principle more flexible. Inventiveness within the formal rules is commended; outside the rules it may lead to the equivalent of a 'red card' or possibly even a new game.

Thinking of practice as a game allows us to open up new action spaces, to be inventive within the rules or to create new 'play' with alternatives. At a mental level, thought experiments can rehearse practice alternatives virtually in the absence of formal rules; good brainstorming sessions attest to this. At an action level, gaming needs to be more prudent and to consider its own standards in relation to others. At the very least, the reflective practitioner will call some rules into question and may wish to take the risk, at an action level, of trying to change the rules or to start another game.

Scripts

Another aspect of play is that of performance. Action research involves the monitoring of performance when practice 'gets stuck' or 'goes wrong'. Practice is also activity which is scripted. In the performative sense of 'play', actions follow the script or score but at the same time allow considerable latitude in interpretation. Like rules, scripts both define and enable our practices; they are the texts which mark out but which do not completely define performance. They do not come to life except by being enacted. For example, a meeting is more than its formal, written agenda. Professionals are often required to produce scripts in their public roles, but anyone can be a private author of his/ her own practices by keeping a journal or diary as a medium for, and record of, reflection. The reflective practitioner is someone who reads practice as script and who also builds a public and personal practice through the creation and interplay of scripts.

Communication

Practice problems are often put down to 'difficulties of communication', as if all that was needed to put things right was the clarification of meaning and intent. Can I ever be sure that you have understood and share my meanings? No, because you are free to make your own interpretation. This illustrates an inherent problem with all language and not just a local difficulty with reading a particular message. The meaning I intend may not be the one you receive, including any message in this script (and this goes for everything that is said, has ever been said, or ever can be said).

Because language is performative, communication works to persuade as well as to inform. It has a rhetorical quality whose power lies in the fact that it is often hidden. I am trying to persuade you of the value of certain ideas about action research and reflective practice right now, partly by using the inclusive register 'we'. I hope that my rhetoric is obvious, but certain aspects of it may not be, either to you or to me. If I present things as 'facts', then I am trying to persuade you to accept them as the truth because of the association of 'facts' with 'things that are true'.

There is a moral here: be wary of anyone who says, 'these are the facts', which often carries with it the implication that 'there is nothing more to be said'. In action research and reflective practice, perhaps the most important message is that there is always more to be said.

A NOTE ON FURTHER SOURCES

Jean McNiff has written three non-technical books on various aspects of conducting action research: *Action Research: Principles and Practice* (London: Macmillan, 1988); *Creating a Good Social Order Through Action Research* (Poole: Hyde Publications, 1989); and *Teaching as Learning: An Action Research Approach* (London: Routledge, 1993).

Users of the Internet can find a vast amount of information and contacts concerning action research on Bob Dick's pages. The location is: http://www.digimark.net/educ/WWW/faculty/indexb.html.

REFERENCES

Cohen, L. and Manion, L. (1985, second edn) *Research Methods in Education*, London: Routledge.

Carr, W. and Kemmis, S. (1986) *Becoming Critical: Education, Knowledge and Action Research,* Lewes: Falmer.

Ebbutt, D. (1985) 'Educational Action Research: Some General Concerns and Specific Quibbles', in R. G. Burgess (ed.) *Issues in Qualitative Research: Qualitative Methods*, Lewes: Falmer.

Elliott, J. (1991) *Action Research for Educational Change*, Milton Keynes: Open University Press.

Heron, J. (1988) 'Validity in Co-operative Inquiry', in P. Reason (ed.) *Human Inquiry in Action: Developments in New Paradigm Research*, London: Sage.

Kemmis, S. (1993) 'Action Research', in M. Hammersley (ed.) *Educational Research: Current Issues*, London: Open University.

Lewin, K. (1948) *Resolving Social Conflicts*, London: Harper & Row.

Nixon, J. (ed.) (1981) *A Teacher's Guide to Action Research*, London: Grant McIntyre.

Rapoport, R. N. (1970) 'Three Dilemmas of Action Research', *Human Relations* 23: 499–513.

Reason, P. and Rowan, J. (1981) 'Issues of Validity in New Paradigm Research', in P. Reason and J. Rowan (eds) *Human Inquiry: A Sourcebook of New Paradigm Research*, Chichester: John Wiley.

Sanford, N. (1981) 'A Model for Action Research', in P. Reason and J. Rowan (eds) *Human Inquiry: A Sourcebook of New Paradigm Research*, Chichester: John Wiley.

Schön, D. (1983) *The Reflective Practitioner*, London: Temple Smith.

—— (1987) *Educating the Reflective Practitioner*, London: Jossey-Bass.

Stenhouse, L. (1979) *What is Action Research?* Norwich: University of East Anglia, CARE.

Usher, R. and Bryant, I. (1989) *Adult Education as Theory, Practice and Research: The Captive Triangle*, London: Routledge.

Winter, R. (1989) *Learning from Experience: Principles and Practice in Action-Research*, Lewes: Falmer.

8 Feminist approaches to research

Pat Usher

This chapter draws on the experience of exploring with a group of MPhil/PhD students what it means in practice to incorporate feminist approaches in research designs. All the students were following research training programmes in the School of Education or the Faculty of Social Sciences at Southampton University and all had an interest in, but not necessarily a commitment to, feminism. The aim of the research training is to heighten awareness of the relationship between epistemology and methodology, and provide information and critical insights into the efficacy of different methods, so that in shaping the design of their personal research topics they are able to exercise critical reflexivity about their choices.

As the tutor of this ten-week course, I began by asking students to identify those issues which they wished to study, and how, so that from the outset *we* set the parameters of the course. Previous knowledge of feminist theory among the students was varied and not a prerequisite. I am under no illusions that I took more of a lead in designing the course than the students did, but they acknowledged in their evaluations of the experience that their hesitancy about the issues, and their time commitment to their own personal research, meant that they were comfortable with these arrangements. I remain uncomfortable about the imbalance of responsibility for the direction of the course and the dangers of authoritarian teaching. They knew this and the pedagogic implications of learning and research relationships were a recurrent theme in our conversations.

The course was attempting to address three strands of thinking in parallel. First, it was designed to help students to understand the meanings and relationships between epistemology, methodology and method; in this, Harding's (1987) categories were particularly helpful. Second, it sought to examine the formative influences on feminist thinking, distinguish the characteristics of different kinds of feminist response, since it is not a unified discourse, and ask how the different responses were implicated in different approaches to research. Third, it attempted to assess the contribution which feminist theory has made in questioning the construction of all theory and knowledge: the inclusion of this latter point owes a great deal to my own view that feminism's most important contribution has been to ask that we all recast the way we understand the nature and product of knowledge. What impresses me most about the stages in feminism's development are those many feminists who are trying to understand how women and their interests have been excluded or devalued in the process of creating theory and knowledge about the world.

In what follows, I provide an outline of the content of, and approaches to, the course. My final section addresses those issues which emerged from discussions as the most significant for students: these issues raised questions about identity, positionality and authenticity in research, power/knowledge relationships, the importance of reflexivity and the tension between generalisable and specific 'knowledges'.

BREAKING WITH TRADITIONS OF KNOWLEDGE-MAKING

In the early weeks of the course we examined how feminism has evolved in different stages over the last thirty years since it is not a unified and homogenised set of ideas. It also became clear early on that students had already positioned themselves somewhere within the spectrum of feminist ideas but still could not sort out why they disagreed so vehemently, and denied that they were identifying with a feminist perspective. It was important to draw attention to how the construction of theory had always been allied to a politics of change and how each phase had defined the theoretical and political focus differently. For me this illustrated a major theme in the course's approach: that ideas evolve within specific historical contexts. The key strands which we examined are summarised below.

Liberal feminism

Liberal feminism is widely represented in the Euro-American world of academic scholarship today: since the 1960s it has been the relationship between liberalism and feminism which has underpinned the equal opportunities paradigm so prevalent in areas of education and social policy. Its concerns are to remove barriers to women's participation in all aspects of public affairs and to argue for a greater share for women in the rights, duties, privileges and responsibilities of men. This kind of feminism is derived from the emancipatory impulse of liberalism which in turn is an offshoot of Enlightenment thought. The key elements of this thought are a belief in an essential human equality, a scepticism towards prejudice and tradition, and trust in external standards of rationality and justice against which reality can be evaluated. Mary Wollstonecraft was the first recognisable liberal feminist, and her ideal world was one in which individuals possessed inalienable rights and the freedom to behave as they wished so long as they did not infringe the rights of others.

Liberal feminism espouses an egalitarian politics and argues that the problem of female subordination can be summed up as the operation of sexism. *Sexism* is defined as the unwarranted differential treatment of women: it is identifiable in empirical terms and could, it is argued, be removed. If men and women are treated equally in the political, social and personal sense, there is the rational possibility that women's views and activities could be invested with the same degree of significance as men's: equal but different is the sound-bite of the egalitarian paradigm.

Critique of liberal feminism

On the face of it, it seems that women are one of the groups who can justify their right to an equal share of political power because that right is grounded in their equal share of rationality. However, there is a strand in early liberal theory, particularly emanating from John Locke, that excludes women from the sphere of rationality and politics. This exclusion relies on the dualism between the public and the private, placing men in the former category and relegating women to the latter (Elshtain 1981, O'Brien 1981).

A different and more sympathetic account of the liberal position on feminism, found in John Stuart Mill's *The Subjection of Women* (1970) suggests that women have a 'nature' different from that of men and that, either as a result of a lack of opportunity or from natural difference, they do not demonstrate the capacity for rational abstraction which men do. Although Mill asserts women's equality with men, he also denies the existence of a domestic division of labour which positions women in the private world and handicaps their participation in the public world. It is unclear as to whether he sees the masculine pattern of thought as innately superior, but it is clear that Mill identifies rationalism as a masculine trait and at least suggests that woman's lack of this trait may be part of her nature.

Liberalism is therefore regarded as being based on a contradiction that cannot be resolved. Despite its emancipatory directions and its call for equal access and opportunity, it is rooted in an epistemology that effectively bars women from the political realm by defining them as irrational. By being rooted in the rational/irrational, public/private dichotomies, liberal feminism cannot achieve the equality it establishes as its goal because the categories of thought which structure it are inherently sexist. As Hekman (1990) succinctly argues, women do not fit the liberal definition of rationality and morality because the liberal definition of self is based on masculine values of separation and autonomy.

Those critical of liberal feminism argue that an epistemology that does not define women as fully rational or moral is not capable of reform, since its implicit patriarchal nature cannot be disowned and therefore must be rejected outright.

Marxist/socialist feminism

Marxist/socialist feminists argue that in concentrating so much on legal rights, political equality and affirmative actions in social policy, liberal feminists neglect the distribution of power in civil society and the significance of the value structure which masks and legitimates political, social and cultural inequalities. By focusing too much on the individual's rights, liberal analysis ignores economic inequalities and prohibits an analysis of class differences between men and women and among women. Marxist/socialist feminists draw selectively from Marxist theory and argue that the categories of Marxism are either sex-blind or under-developed in the ways that the economy and the state allow for men's domination of women. They argue that Marxist categories have considerable analytical power and that, allied with feminist critiques of patriarchy, they can reveal insights about the social role of the family and domestic labour, the economic subordination of women both in unpaid domestic and paid work roles, and the relationship between patriarchy, capitalism and the state.

However, in epistemological terms, many radical feminists (Hekman 1990) argue that both Marxist/socialist and liberal feminists are rooted in the dualities of Enlightenment thought. Both accept the rational/irrational dichotomy and both accept the modernist search for truth, progress and liberation. Although Marxists strongly attack the liberal political programme and argue that its reformist approach cannot possibly address the inequalities produced by capitalism, they believe emphatically that their political aims can achieve the Enlightenment dream. Rather than reject the epistemology altogether, they believe they can correct its sexist characteristics.

Essentialist feminism

A number of feminists from conservative and radical positions (McMillan 1982, Daly 1984 and Griffin 1978) have united around a position that advocates the privileging of traditional 'feminine' values: they accept the view that women's 'nature' is different from men's and that women excel in nurturing values.

Conservatives like McMillan argue a different but equal claim for feminine difference, while radicals like Daly and Griffin argue that if rationality is associated with domination and control of the natural world, with all the destructive implications that have emerged, women are fortunate not to be associated with it. They go on to argue that the characteristics associated with the feminine, such as caring, relatedness and community, should therefore be privileged above those of the male. In other words, they all, irrespective of emphasis, accept the rational/irrational dichotomy and its association with masculine/feminine difference, and argue that it can be reversed, with some advocating a privileging of the feminine above the masculine.

Critical theory

A few feminists espouse critical theory because it too is critical of the dualisms of Enlightenment thought, especially rationality. Habermas makes a qualified rejection of foundational thought by arguing that while foundations are required, they are historically defined. Fraser (1985: 37) makes a detailed examination of Habermas' critical social theory from a feminist perspective, and argues that some of the crucial categories of his social theory (like the social identities of workers, citizens, consumers and clients) ignore their gendered identity; and that the family, which he posits as part of the 'private-intimate' sphere in contrast to the 'public space' of political-public sphere, is not always a 'haven in a heartless world' but the site of 'ego-centric, strategic and instrumental calculation . . . exploitative exchanges of service . . . coercion and violence' (Fraser 1987).

She concludes that, while Habermas wants to be critical of male dominance, his analysis lacks an awareness of gender differentiation. Hekman draws attention to Habermas' own discussion of the feminist movement as a social force within the progressive tradition of a modernist programme (Hekman 1990: 163). However, the problem with this critique, as well as essentialist, Marxist and liberal approaches, is that all of them fail to dislodge the dualistic structures of thought which underpin Enlightenment thought. As a modernist, committed to the fulfilment of progressive ideals, he cannot recognise its patriarchal nature. For approaches which both critique dualistic structures of thought and allow for a discussion of sexual differences that avoid them, we must turn to the alliance between feminism and postmodernism.

Radical feminism

By the 1980s many feminists had become disillusioned with the political project of women's inclusion as male equals, because they found mainstream discourses such as Marxism, liberalism or psychoanalysis particularly resistant to their challenge or incapable of being broadened to include women. These experiences of being rejected and alienated facilitated a growing awareness of the *patriarchal* nature of such discourses. Even if sexism was eliminated and both sexes participated fully, the patriarchal nature of structures and value systems would still ensure that men and women were placed in unequal positions of power, and that female activity was defined as marginal and of lesser significance than male experience. Even if women were incorporated into patriarchal discourse, it was on the basis of their sameness to men: their specificity as women could not be recognised. In other words, women began to assume the role of surrogate men.

The development of a more radical feminism was a response to the perceived limitations of liberal and essentialist approaches, which, it was argued, were based on irresolvable contradictions from which women could not escape inferior definition.

The focus of study became the *phallocentric* nature of all systems of representation; that, whenever the two sexes are represented in a single model, the specificity of the female or the feminine is always collapsed into a single, universal model that is represented in male or masculine terms. In theoretical terms, feminists have analysed how the general concepts, assumptions and categories of Western thought have been organised around hierarchies which, by association, privilege masculinity and devalue femininity. Regardless of which academic discipline radical feminists are working within, there is a widespread recognition that philosophy has exerted a powerful influence on concepts, ideals and values in everyday life. The way we make sense of the world is through broad categories and central questions to do with the nature of reality, subjectivity, how knowledge is constructed, morality/ethics and political rights and responsibilities.

As feminist theory has developed, it has engaged in a dialogue with postmodernity and psychoanalytic approaches. This has led to questions about how philosophy is responsible for defining masculinity and femininity, how it defines the 'nature' of people, the values attached to their skills and capacities and how 'gender difference' is a category of analysis around which every society is structured.

FEMINISM AND POSTMODERNISM

In this section of the course we looked briefly at some of the convergences between contemporary feminist thought and postmodernism to show the similarities between the two critiques and why a dialogue between them may be fruitful.

For as long as it was held that there was only one truth, that its discovery was guaranteed by objectivity and the rigorous pursuit of a scientific methodology, the *gendered* nature of this discourse and its privileging of masculinity were disguised. Postmodern approaches are asking us to be sceptical with regard to traditional beliefs about truth, knowledge, power and the self, all of which have served as legitimation for contemporary Western culture. They question the following beliefs, derived from the Enlightenment, which have shaped modernist thought:

1 A coherent, unified self exists that is capable of using reason to understand its own processes as well as the laws of nature.
2 Reason and its application through science can provide an objective, reliable and universal foundation for knowledge.
3 Knowledge acquired through the right use of reason will be true and unchanging irrespective of time or culture.
4 Reason has a universal and transcendental quality and is not contingent.

5 By grounding all claims to truth and authority in the application of reason, conflicts between truth, knowledge and power can be overcome. By privileging reason, truth can serve power without distortion. By utilising knowledge in the service of power, both freedom and progress can flourish. As a result, knowledge can be neutral because it is grounded in reason and its effects are beneficial.

6 The scientific paradigm is the framework to guarantee truth, its methods are neutral and its contents socially beneficial.

What radical feminists like Hekman (1990) and Flax (1990a) have added to the above analysis is the insight that in deconstructing notions of reason, knowledge and the self, their gendered nature is revealed and concepts which had been seemingly neutral and universal are by association masculine.

Their argument is that knowledge is structured through a number of fundamental dichotomies such as rational/irrational, subject/object, nature/culture which constitute a hierarchical view of knowledge. The way that knowledge is constructed privileges certain concepts over others and rather than being a peripheral issue, the study of epistemology is central to the way the social sciences examine the relationship between human thought and social existence.

Hekman and Flax argue that the rationalism which is the source of modernist epistemology is a specifically masculine mode of thought. They argue that the positivists' claim that only rational, objective, abstract, universalistic thought can lead to the truth is in fact a specifically masculine claim. Further, they argue that each of the dualisms on which modernist thought rests is the product of the fundamental dualism between male and female. In each of the dualisms mentioned above: rational/irrational, subject/object, culture/nature, the male is associated with the first element, the female with the second. In each case, the male element is privileged over the female and maintains its position by its capacity to define itself as a universal standard against which the subjective, the emotional, the aesthetic, the natural, the feminine must be judged. In the very dualities of modernist thought women's significance is defined as inferior to the rational, objective, abstract qualities of the scientific method, which not only guarantees 'truth' but positions masculinity and 'man' as capable of finding the 'truth'. Once this kind of analysis is accepted, all the other common sense stereotypes about gendered identities, which we constantly attempt to counter, fall into perspective. As Flax (1993) shows, ' "woman" is defined as a deficient man in discourses from Aristotle to Freud'.

There are some interesting parallels between feminist analyses of modernist dualities and the irresolvable disputes between positivist and interpretive approaches in the social sciences. Many people working in an interpretive paradigm do not challenge the subjective/objective dichotomy on which positivism rests because they believe that the strength of social science research is that it can be objective in a subjective kind of way. Despite all their efforts, however, the objectivity of the natural sciences remains the gold standard against which all other variants (qualitative/interpretive approaches) are judged. By not challenging the dichotomy, the privileged concept maintains its power of definition. As I indicated earlier, for feminists the same dilemma applies. Some essentialist feminists try to exalt the virtues of 'female nature' and the related concepts of community, care, relatedness, as opposed to the 'male' values of control, mastery, rationality and abstraction. But, as the dispute in the social sciences reveals, these arguments are not convincing because such feminists cannot succeed in privileging the female over the male, since they have not challenged the very dichotomy through which the female is defined as inferior in the first place. 'Equal but different' simply cannot succeed in a world where knowledge is constructed through hierarchical meanings. Not that the reverse argument of valorising femininity over masculinity works either. What does emerge is the postmodern insight that if particular dualisms cannot be reversed, the aim should be to dissolve the structure on which those dichotomies rest.

By the mid-point in the course, after a number of presentations led by me and consideration of specific texts derived from the work of authors referred to in this text, it was clear to students where the loyalties and preferences of this tutor lay, but they were also beginning to locate themselves and their current thinking within stages of feminist development.

My own epistemological stance and my preferred perspectives derived from radical feminism. It is not the task of the social sciences to discover absolutes in the way that the Enlightenment defined epistemology (i.e. the relationship between knowledge construction and truth), but rather the task is the interpretation of social meaning and not a search for scientific truth: the search is for understandings of the social world and not for scientific laws about human beings.

In other words, I am challenging the view, derived from Enlightenment thought, that the purpose of research in the social sciences is to separate universal truth from historical and cultural influences, which, by implication, warp human thought. I am advocating an approach to research which recognises that all knowledge is produced out of a relationship between human thought and human existence; that in producing knowledge one cannot make a distinction between objective and subjective knowledge, that all knowledge is shaped by a mixture of historical and cultural influences.

Drawing on the work of Foucault (1972, 1978) and Gadamer (1975), I am arguing that modern science, far from offering the one true model of knowledge, is rooted in certain historically specific assumptions about the way the world is; assumptions which are not universally valid but related to specific contexts. This approach to knowledge undermines the universalistic claims of scientific, objective knowledge that are so characteristic of Enlightenment thought; rather, this approach shows that these claims derive from a specific moment in history and do not apply universally across time and culture. This illustrates a further important assumption which I make in my work: that *values, politics* and *knowledge* are *intrinsically* connected. Some perspectives state this clearly, while others do not, and indeed disguise the links in a seeming neutrality. If understanding is always from a particular *perspective*, researchers must acknowledge too that their values and prejudices are implicated in what they create as knowledge. So, as well as acknowledging the influence of socio-historical conditions and the interpretive role of social research, I am also arguing for a reflexivity which seeks to understand that power is not exterior to knowledge or to social relations but is embedded within their very conditions of existence.

In the first half of the course, the emphasis was on the critique which feminism makes of traditional epistemology. However, feminism's project cannot remain solely a reactive and critical one: to remain an anti-sexist project only would position feminism in a politics of sameness or equality with men. My belief is that feminism must develop alternatives to patriarchal discourse which are not merely adaptations of existing orthodoxies. In attempting to develop alternative discourses, course members drew on the work of Michel Foucault, in particular his discussion of discourses and power/knowledge. Space within this chapter does not allow for inclusion of the detailed considerations we entered into; however, the concepts and categories of his work which we found fruitful were discourse, power/knowledge, technologies of power, dividing practices, regimes of truth, the politics of truth telling, and disciplinary practices, through which seemingly neutral scholars define people and the nature of their 'problems', and exercise power over them.

All of these upsetting and disturbing categories of thought are immensely helpful for radical feminists. First, they allow a challenge to be made to Western philosophy's orientation around the appearance of oneness, unity and stability in the world: one truth, one method, one logic. Attention can then be drawn to the way that order is imposed and maintained by privileging culture, maleness, rationality through binary categories. Arising from this, the way is opened up for perspectives which acknowledge contingency: that truths are varied and relational but not relativist. Relativism only assumes a meaning by comparison with its binary opposite: universalism. If it is no longer assumed that absolute standards are possible, then 'universalism' loses its force and instead attention must focus on the conditions within which conflicting claims are made and within which disputes can be resolved.

FEMINISM'S CHARACTERISTICS AS A PERSPECTIVE

At this point in the course students were asked to consider the characteristics of feminism as defined by a radical discourse: such a perspective is increasingly being used by educators such as Walkerdine (1990), Kenway (1990, 1992), Jones (1993).

First, instead of being committed to truth and objectivity as privileged by both positivist and interpretive perspectives, feminism can argue for the insight that all discourses create subjects, objects, regimes of power and truth. Instead of being for or against the regimes of any one research tradition, one asks what conditions facilitated the development of a particular discourse and what criteria and assumptions were used and made.

Second, 'knowledges' must be reflexive in coming to understand their own self-development as 'knowledges'. Feminism must therefore accept its own status as context-specific, the product of socio-economic and historical movements. It has no more claim to speak *the* truth than any other discourse but must own up to its own points of view, specific aims, desires and political position within power relations. Feminism acknowledges that it is historically, politically and sexually motivated: its interests are those of women. Patriarchal theory fails to address the gender specificity of its theory and its motivations because to do so would undermine its rationale. Positivism disguises its gendered nature by claiming that its approaches are applicable across culture and history.

Third, no discourse can disassociate itself openly from a political position. Thus the political is always personal. Feminist theory does not claim to be subjective, or objective, either absolutist or relativist: it strives to occupy the middle ground excluded by these dichotomies. It argues that all theory is relational and connected to other practices (Grosz 1987). It is not a question of being neutral or indifferent to diverse experience as are so many approaches which adopt historic and universal criteria; nor is it the case that 'anything goes'. Feminism argues that we must recognise the functioning of power relations and the necessity of occupying a position that is political in both the public and the personal spheres of an individual's life.

Fourth, gender divisions are fundamental categories around which all social structures are organised and meanings created. Radical feminism rejects the 'add women and stir' approach of many interpretive approaches to research. Men and women should understand that all human thought is based on the dominant conceptions we have all internalised about masculinity and femininity. The context for thinking about gender is that we see it as a social relation rather than a set of opposite and different characteristics. In so doing we can illuminate how our thinking becomes implicated in power/ knowledge relationships both between the sexes and within each category: how men treat other men, and how women treat one another.

Fifth, feminist research has the potential both to express and to uncover relations of dominance. All types of feminism are attempting to show how gender relations operate in favour of a male hegemony and aim to redistribute power towards women. This may often imply the writing of histories or giving expression to voices and views that have been suppressed, unarticulated or denied by traditional discourse. Models of investigation which assume homogeneity as their starting point fail to acknowledge the variety of human beings and are oppressive in their phallocentric assumptions: that women can be represented as having the same characteristics and interests as men. It also implies that women do not all have some universal experience from which standpoint theories can emerge. The category of 'woman' is not unified: female experience is differentiated through other categories such as class, race, ethnicity and religion and so our enquiries need to be sensitive to the diversity of female experience and the power relations among women.

Sixth, the subject cannot be separated from the object of knowledge. In accepting objectivity one must accept a knowing subject free of personal, social, political and moral interest; a positivist subject unimplicated in a social context or uninfluenced by prior ideas and knowledge. Feminism must reconceptualise the inter-relationship between subjects and objects so that reason and knowledge include a recognition of history, context and specificity.

Finally, there is a need to deconstruct dichotomies and reconstruct them as continuities. Instead of organising thought through dichotomies which separate and exclude subject/object, reason/emotion, culture/nature, masculinity/femininity, a feminist position would argue for these terms to be regarded as continuities and for discourses to be created that avoid dualities, essences and the temptation to privilege the feminine over the masculine. The dualisms of masculine thought need to be displaced by a pluralism and fluidity that transforms categories which have continually positioned and named women as inferior. The modernist move of trying to incorporate women into the masculine definition of rationality should be avoided in favour of deconstructing the dualism on which it rests. Radical feminists argue that we do not need new 'truth' but a plurality of perspectives.

Scott's (1988) discussion of equality-versus-divergence illustrates the point well. Instead of accepting categories in fixed opposition to one another such as unity/diversity, identity/difference, presence/absence, universality/specificity, we argue for their interdependence so that we reverse and then displace the binary opposition. In this context we can refuse to place equality and difference in opposition to one another, and argue for a respect for differences 'as the condition of individual and collective identities, differences as the constant challenge to the fixing of those identities, differences as the very meaning of equality itself' (Scott 1988: 38). Challenging the way knowledge/power is constructed from the ground of difference is a crucial insight not only for all women but for all social scientists as well, if they are to arrive at valid understandings about the relationship between human thought and the nature of existence. Only by following this approach can women or any other subordinated group avoid being defined as inferior against the universalising categories of rationality, objectivity and masculinity.

WHAT ARE THE IMPLICATIONS FOR FEMINIST METHOD?

During the course we had looked at the relationship between epistemology and methodology. I defined epistemology as the study of how knowledge is constructed about the world, who constructs it, and what criteria they use to create meaning and methodology, in the sense used by Harding (1987), as a theoretical and conceptual framework within which research proceeds. In the final meetings we considered whether the themes we had identified amounted to such a thing as a feminist method; by which I mean, distinctive techniques of evidence gathering or pursuing inquiries.

Feminism is a perspective and it argues that all methodologies should recognise that they too are perspectives. Feminist researchers (Reinharz 1992) do not consider feminism to be a method; rather they see it as a perspective that can be infiltrated into all disciplines as a means of developing innovative methods. Feminist social research uses the methods supplied by the discipline – both quantitative and qualitative – and adds its own perspective in order to create diverse and innovative approaches to analysing human activity. At an earlier stage in the development of feminist theory it was argued that qualitative approaches were the hallmark of feminism because of their respect for the inclusion of women's experience which interpretive research methodologies advocated. However, for reasons I suggested earlier, feminist scholarship has identified the contradictions of methodologies which do not challenge the dichotomies that label women's experience as of lesser significance. Theories and methodologies which attempt to valorise the 'essential' nature of women and their experience were seen to pose no challenge at all to the phallocentric nature of both positivist and interpretive methodologies. Feminist theory now uses the full range of methods and immerses itself in the greatest range of subject matters, challenging the false homogeneity of much that passes for understanding of the social world.

The following themes are those characteristic of feminist research which should guide the development of new approaches.

The acknowledgement of the pervasive influence of gender as a category of analysis and organisation

Each of us understands our own identity through the meanings we learn to attach to gender differences: society's institutions and structures are organised around divisions that have a gendered nature. Irrespective of the area of research in which we work, feminism would argue that as a strategy in designing research one should be asking how meanings about gender are implicated in the questions and criteria that guide one's thinking. These are not the peripheral questions which can be added on after a long list of more important questions have been asked; not to address questions of gender difference is to adhere to patriarchal theoretical norms which collapse all issues of difference into unitary, homogenised categories. Such approaches cannot lead to intelligible meaning about the diversity of experience in the social world; patriarchal discourses disguise their own specificity by portraying their frameworks and questions as universally significant.

The deconstruction of traditional commitments to truth, objectivity and neutrality

This involves the reversal and then dissolution of the binary oppositions which structure thought and subordinate all the categories – the subjective, the privately emotional, community, practice-based – that are associated with the feminine and females. The aim is to expand and multiply the criteria for what is considered to be rational and true, and to be critical of norms which are discriminatory in their assumptions.

The adoption of an approach to knowledge creation which recognises that all theories are perspectival

Each methodology is the product of a specific combination of historical, socio-political influences, whether positivist or postmodernist. All of them make claims about the truth but none should be regarded as telling the truth. Feminism itself must be treated in this light: it is not telling a better story about social relations, but, in making its own claims, it expects each claim to be equally self-reflexive. This does not mean that each perspective is equally valid, but each has a point of view and should be interrogated from a stance which accepts that no perspective is producing disinterested knowledge, and each represents particular positions within power relations.

The utilisation of a multiplicity of research methods

Feminist research reaches into all disciplines and uses all methods; it does not concern itself solely with the study of gender but is concerned that research about any area of social practice is sensitive to the differential experience of female and male. Reinharz (1992: 245) agrees with a number of writers who suggest that feminism is accumulating stages in scholarship. The current emphasis on multiplicity of methods is because, in her view, feminists value inclusiveness more than orthodoxy. The outpouring of scholarly feminist literature has contributed to what Bernard (1987) calls the 'Female Renaissance' or 'Feminist Enlightenment'. A multiplicity of methods allows women to study the broadest range of subject matters and reach a broad set of goals. Their approaches may include interview and oral history methods, case studies, cross-cultural research, ethnography, surveys or experiments. Giving voice to experience, understanding variations within populations, or measuring behaviours and attitudes, are only a few of the methods utilised by feminists.

The inter-disciplinary nature of feminist research

The organisation of knowledge into discrete disciplines is a thorny issue that feminist researchers cannot avoid. Each of us is shaped by disciplinary approaches but, given feminism's critique of the dualities of modernist thought which disprivilege the feminine, feminists must be alert to the ways that disciplines function as discursive networks to ignore or deny female experience. By presenting theory as universally applicable, those working within disciplines can successfully disguise the specificity of their theory. Disciplines function as phallocentric discursive systems and collapse the differential experience of the sexes into universal models with homogenised categories. Yeatman's discussion of sociology's resistance to the feminist challenge illustrates the extent to which the social sciences, including sociology, economics, psychology and political science, are all structured by modernist dualisms:

> Its own particular versions of these dualisms – for example, structure/ agency, social structure/culture, social/psychological, family/society – are logically derivative of the basic dualistic structure of the modernist consciousness: individual/society; subjective/objective; reason/emotion, and so forth. Sociology cannot change this modernist framework of reference which has governed it as a specific intellectual enterprise without abandoning its whole tradition and approach, without, that is, becoming something other than itself. Yet it is precisely the nature of the contemporary feminist challenge to require sociology, as all expressions of modern science, to move beyond this dualistic ordering of reality in the direction of integrating what have been regarded hitherto as opposing terms.
>
> (Yeatman 1990: 286)

Resistance to change is deepest in those disciplines quoted above, which have a role in preserving and gate-keeping modernist conventions of ordering reality through hierarchical dualities.

Involvement of the researcher and the people being researched

Feminism challenges the claim that valid knowledge is only produced through a commitment to truth and objectivity and that in order to achieve this objectivity, a gulf is necessary between the researcher and the object of research. This gulf presupposes that researchers are subjects in the Cartesian sense: capable of forming rational knowledge, free of personal, social, political and moral interests, and standing outside the social context of the 'objects' of research. Instead of accepting such dichotomous structures which separate subject and object, teacher and pupil, supervisor and student, feminism regards the terms as continuities and does not think of objectivity and subjectivity in confrontation with one another.

Such an approach acknowledges the importance of personal experience and expects researchers to analyse how their own experience is implicated in defining research questions, organising its data collection, interacting with others. Far from being a distorting influence, experience is seen as an asset. The important point is that the researcher should develop a *self-reflexive* stance towards their own research: they must be accountable for their own cultural prejudices and disciplinary allegiance, and be alert to how these implicate them in the choices made in research practice.

Unlike those who adopt patriarchal approaches to research, feminists need to develop an *intersubjectivity*, a shared or collective response to research with those they study. It demands that the researchers establish an empathic understanding with the people they study in a non-exploitative manner. Relations of respect, shared information, joint involvement in the commentary and evaluation of their own lives, and openness are all the goals of a feminist researcher. Clearly these themes are not without ambiguity and controversy, but, if the task is to represent the complexity of social reality, researchers need to form relationships which allow for those who are the researched to express what is significant in their everyday lives. It is this which provides for the validity of the research, not pseudo-objectivity; it is from the intersubjective process that new meanings are created which interpret human experience more accurately than reliance on patriarchal categories.

The deconstruction of the theory/practice relationship

Feminist researchers need to deconstruct the traditional ways educators separate theory from practice. Theory is a practice and practice incorporates theory. Too many feminists shy away from an involvement with theory because they are nervous about challenging the mystique that attaches itself to definitions and theories about knowledge. Much of the literature about theory has assumed that theory can be mapped onto experience in practice situations and that professional knowledge is based on theory derived from general principles which can be applied to practice situations. Theory is viewed as real knowledge whereas practice is technical and skills-based. My emphasis on the need for self-reflexivity and intersubjectivity is therefore a plea for a different kind of relationship where understanding emerges from 'dialogical engagement between representation and explanation which can assist judgement, interpretation and understanding' (Usher and Bryant 1989: 93). By dissolving and refusing to accept the gap between theory and practice feminists would stand a better chance of moving on from understanding their world, to changing it.

PEDAGOGIC IMPLICATIONS

In the remainder of this chapter I am going to raise some of the issues which seemed to the students on the course to be the most significant ones for them as researchers.

Identity and learning

The first set of issues raises questions about the nature of identity and the link with learning. Most of the students on this course were drawn from practitioner-based disciplines; their occupational roles were in the sectors of education, the health services, community-based and social work settings; most but not all were developing research projects within an interpretive paradigm. However, for all of them the exploration of feminist perspectives was a re-learning about themselves and a re-evaluation of the significance of key moments in their personal and professional lives. They discovered how inseparable issues from the public and private spheres are, and how much of what we conventionally think of as personal is in fact political, and vice-versa. They used their own testimony to illustrate how they manage in their own lives the tensions caused by trying to separate the demands of family care from the public life of paid work.

Given their disciplinary backgrounds, many students were familiar with, and committed to, perspectives on experiential learning and were open to views that emphasised the central role that experience plays in the learning process. However, now that these same women had adopted the role of researchers in an academic environment, they were finding it difficult to resist the taken-for-granted status and power of rational, empirical epistemology within the academy, which devalues the role of consciousness and subjective experience. The process of working through the development of feminist theory over three decades illustrated how integrated their own lives were in the development of ideas about gender relations. By asking questions about what causes gender relations to change over time, how gender relations are constituted and sustained in their own lives, how power hierarchies in gender relations are sustained, how meanings are created about masculinity and femininity, students realised that gender is no longer regarded as a simple, natural fact: sex and gender are not identical and gender both as an analytic category and social process is relational. This demonstrated to them the extent to which ideas are not fixed and immutable but formed and re-formed through experience and re-learning.

Many of the students were familiar with the ideas of Kolb (1984) and Freire (1985) since they, like this writer, had been vocationally socialised in the theories associated with adult learning; but not until they looked at experiential learning in the context of their lives as women did the full significance of the experiential perspective impact on them. They could now appreciate with

much greater clarity the strength of those arguments which challenge im-
plausible theories of subjectivity; theories which portray the self as coherent,
rational, unified and as a mind operating according to a set of principles
which are accessible through self-knowledge. They knew from their own
experience how their identities had changed through the interaction between
concrete events and their experience of them. They also had first-hand
knowledge of shifts in gender relations and could add a gendered analysis
to experiential perspectives not offered by male writers like Kolb and Freire.
Against the backdrop of developments in feminist theory they were able to
illustrate how their own identities were shifting and fragmented, multi-layered
and contradictory; how they positioned themselves through the various
choices they made; how they constructed their own meanings about their
identity; and how they lived in gender relations.

Women as theorists

From this clarity about how personal knowledge is created, came an important
epistemological stance. Is it the case that all understanding is understanding
that is contextual and historical, taking account of cultural and social factors?
Does not understanding and re-learning occur as a result of thinking,
interpretation and application? Does this dynamic perspective challenge
fundamentally the over-reliance of contemporary Western culture on a model
of knowledge that privileges reason and the application of rational thought as
the guarantors of objective, fixed and universal foundations for knowledge? If
self-understanding entails critique and reflexivity, does this apply equally to
the pursuit of all knowledge?

Being open to postmodern philosophers who are raising important meta-
theoretical questions about the nature of creating theory is a profoundly
discomforting business. Women who choose to position themselves as researchers in an academic environment are taking a number of risks. Acker
(1994) documents the marginality of women within academic disciplines and
the relative exclusion of gender from sociological and educational research.
Writers such as Collins (1990) capture the dual vision which feminist thinkers
have in academic life 'learning from the outsider within'. To design research
with gender relations firmly located as part of the central analysis is a difficult
enough challenge, but to put that simultaneously within a perspective which
openly challenges patriarchal discourses and their ways of omitting or
devaluing the female voice is felt by many to be incompatible with their
desire to achieve academic validation from the academy. However, the
tensions posed by being 'an outsider within' are also capable of being explored
by women who wish to change the practice of academic scholarship. Adopting
the identity of the 'outsider within' offers the possibility of seeing anomalies
that arise from taken-for-granted assumptions. Where white males may
assume it is normal to generalise findings from studies of white males to

other groups, women are much more likely to view this as problematic; similarly, black women in the academy are more likely to challenge generalisations about all 'women' and to challenge stereotypical distortions of behaviour analysis which do not draw on the testimony of black women.

In being aware of how they actively constructed their own identities, perhaps the most difficult part of learning was seeing themselves as theorists and seeing how their work had the potential to challenge the universal claims of patriarchal discourses. Many women gain approval and validation from being practitioners, activists and problem solvers, and this often reflects itself in their chosen value structure which holds in high esteem helping and improving the lives of others. The insight that radical feminism offers is doubly disconcerting. Not only does it show that in an epistemological sense women have been oppressed by being barred from the spheres of rationality and morality, but in a practical sense it shows that women's own chosen identities fit within the 'feminine nature' that renders them incapable of abstract and theoretical activity. Being a theorist is an alien role for many women, and, as Walkerdine (1989) points out, however successful women are as thinkers, they rarely connect the success to their own abilities or accept that the 'thinking' subject can be female.

Women and power/knowledge relationships

The second set of issues which generated a lot of debate and enquiry within the group were centred around the relationship between power and knowledge which underpins certain understandings of truth and rationality. The work of Foucault (1972, 1978) was helpful because it allowed us to work with ideas about identity that were dynamic and relational, but at the same time it located them in a hierarchical context of power relations that operate at both the micro and the macro levels of society. It allowed us to think about identity and diversity both within and between subjects as well as to view the social and the personal as politicised. Some of the most insightful readings we analysed were by feminists using postmodernism to analyse the complex ways in which institutions, meaning, power, human subjectivity and gender come together (Walkerdine 1990, Kenway 1992, Jones 1993, Plumwood 1993). Foucault's (1972) view that it is through discourse that meanings and human subjects are produced and through which power relations are maintained and changed, were closely read and debated. His argument that power and knowledge are always found together in 'regimes of truth', and that knowledge and what counts as truth are constructed through discourse, were of assistance in illuminating how different traditions of research made knowledge claims, but not all had the same status. By analysing the structure of knowledge hierarchies, the binary oppositions, and the exclusionary categories which control what can and cannot be said and which position subjects in hierarchies, students could appreciate for the first time the conditions which privilege positivist and patriarchal claims to knowledge. By association they could then appreciate the negative positioning of the interpretive paradigm and how feminism becomes so successfully tagged with the criticism that it speaks specifically about female experience.

While the students found these ideas about how meanings are structured and people positioned in hierarchies enormously enlightening, they were also confronted with the tensions the ideas pose for their own work. For years we have understood that women were marginal in academic scholarship but in the 1990s we now have the benefit of feminist theorists (Grosz 1987, Yeatman 1990) who argue that traditional approaches to knowledge and the structures of meaning taken for granted by the disciplines, collapse the two autonomous sexes into a single model which equates with masculine experience. There is no space left for the autonomous female voice and the masculine voice serves as a universal standard which renders invisible or devalues 'the other' by comparison with itself. For the first time in history, feminists have the intellectual resources to challenge not only the masculinity of patriarchal discourse, but also its universal and over-arching claims. Male scholars are simultaneously being challenged to acknowledge how their masculinity is implicated in the theories they produce, and to accept less universalising claims for their versions of reality. What is asked for is a fundamental re-evaluation of intellectual values, and, as Yeatman (1990) argues, it remains to be seen whether male scholars can acknowledge their self-interest in creating and maintaining the structures, criteria and hierarchies within disciplines which combine to privilege masculine versions and exclude feminine versions of reality. For them to do so, men will have to give up their institutionalised intellectual practices which gatekeep and police what is recognised 'as the substantive and methodological canons for the discipline' (Yeatman 1990: 285). For obvious reasons female researchers are nervous about challenging the power relations within their disciplinary base. However, the same tension acts in reverse when they consider their own positions as designers of a research enquiry with the power to select categories for investigation and criteria for evaluating and assessing the nature and definition of people over whom they exert some control.

Feminism and critical reflexivity

The students were already familiar with concerns about how power was exerted in the researcher/researched relationship; and about control of content, drawing on direct experience, listening and negotiating outcomes. What was disconcerting was the claim that what every scholar and researcher wants 'is power in the world, not an innocent truth' (Flax 1993: 144). Researchers in fields of social enquiry like to believe that truth is on their side and that what they produce as knowledge is for someone else's improvement or benefit. Educators in particular are part of the Enlightenment dream of unending progress and self-improvement. But if feminists are to challenge the legitimacy of discourses which disguise their desire to control others through normalising structures and categories, women cannot then claim that they alone adjudicate on the truth claims of other discourse or that their own discourse speaks a better truth.

Through a strict adherence to critical reflexivity, feminist researchers need to avoid the condition of dominance by adopting criteria that appreciate and respect difference, diversity and empathy, particularly when in doing so they reveal more conflict than consensus. While it was relatively easy to accept that certain discourses disprivileged women, it was very disconcerting to lay aside the search for feminist certainty and acknowledge the potential which feminists had to suppress discourses that threatened to undermine the authority of their own preferred feminist positions.

However, this insight gained in intensity when individual women tried to understand why they feared and resisted the label of feminism despite being committed to most of its principles. Feminism has been misrepresented so successfully in popular culture that very few women are confident enough to affirm its principles in the face of pejorative, negative stereotypes. We had to confront the argument that feminists must respect the differences among themselves and avoid standpoints which claim they have a better or true knowledge. In order to destroy the hierarchies and interpretations which dominate women, feminists must also avoid perspectives which allow them to feel they have superior understandings and that other women are guilty of false consciousness.

Lather (1988) draws our attention to the insight that research designs with good intentions are no guarantees about good outcomes, and all we can do is to reflect endlessly on how our value commitments insert themselves into our work and how our own understandings need to be critically examined so that we understand our own tensions and contradictions.

As part of this critical reflexivity, we thought long and hard about how to avoid using hierarchy as an ordering principle in research designs. Deconstructing what we take for granted and refusing to structure around binary opposites were part of the process of respecting differences and creating a continuum of meanings from which one account was not held to be more authoritative than others. Critics decry this approach as 'relativist', but my preferred stance was to stop hankering after universal standards which give the illusion of certainty and order, and to deny ourselves the desire for power over meaning, and control over people.

Privileging female experience

These comments were particularly discussed in relation to the last set of issues I want to raise here: what are feminist researchers striving to do in giving voice to female experience? Giving voice to the silenced has always been viewed as a politically positive and empowering move, but a number of troubling questions do suggest themselves: does the researcher presume to question the truthfulness of the account they are being given? Should we view silence by women as a politics of resistance? In asking women to reveal their experience, are we also opening their views up to possible colonisation? In situations where women are marked by multiple differences (cultural, racial, sexual and class), the possibility of revealing a collective women's experience may be subverted by a hierarchy of identity politics. Efforts to centre feminine experience and knowledge can lead to what Luke (1994) and others call a 'hierarchization of oppressions'. Individuals and groups can 'one down' one another on the oppression scale. In such a hierarchy, is there such a thing as 'women's' experience? Which knowledge is more authentic? Which experience embodies a more real oppression? In respecting such diversity, is one losing the opportunity to say anything meaningful and becoming politically inert in the process?

It was to the insights of Foucault that we turned for an approach to those issues that did not claim a resolution to the problems but was a preferred strategy for interpreting their significance. Experience can only ever be understood through interpretation. Instead of assuming that people speak the truth, we should ask about the discursive conditions in which they have constructed their meanings. This tied in with the epistemological stance which argues that all knowledge is context specific and related. Hollway (1989) draws explicitly on Foucault's work to argue that subjectivities are produced within the terms of a discourse and that in producing a narrative about their experience, individuals speak a discourse and produce their own subjectivity. This is not a deterministic analysis since people internalise the rules of many discourses and do not accept them passively; they invest in some, reject others, create their own meanings for the choices they make, and position themselves in hierarchies. The researcher's task is to analyse the processes by which definitions and interpretations gain cultural approval, how power hierarchies are implicated in them, and whose interests are being served.

QUESTIONS FOR THE FUTURE

Where does this leave us in looking for a politics of change and strategies to follow as educators if we renounce the comfortable certainties offered to us by liberal definitions of gendered relationships and traditional approaches to knowledge creation? For women who had been committed activists on a number of political fronts, it was particularly hard to resist the need to believe in resolutions, conclusions and political positions which they think hold a superior epistemology and moral ground.

Writers who locate their enquiries in a postmodern condition (Flax 1990b, Usher and Edwards 1994) encourage us to forego 'totalising conclusions', the privileging of some theories and the domination of one view or group over others. Usher and Edwards (1994: 207) summarise their task as 'how to cope with, operate within and challenge the openness, uncertainties and diversities of the postmodern moment'.

What I am hoping for in my enquiries is that we become much more aware of the character and links between gender, knowledge, self, power and justice; that as researchers we engage with critical discourses which challenge meanings associated with the power of reason and rationality within modernist discourse; that we remember our location in history and context in making claims about the nature of our social enquiries; that we understand the complex ways in which 'Man' retains his privileged place in creating texts and meanings about Himself, his world, and representing women as a reflection of his definitions; that we place ourselves firmly within discourses which resist oppressive disciplinary practices, and in a critically reflexive mode, search for ways of translating our critical ideas into political statements that are less distorting than those we have learned too well for our own good.

I leave Jane Flax with the last word in this particular text:

> Feminist theories ... should encourage us to tolerate and interpret ambivalence, ambiguity and multiplicity as well as to expose the roots of our needs for imposing order and structure no matter how arbitrary and oppressive these needs may be.

> (Flax 1990b: 56)

Woman was ever the subversive category!

REFERENCES

Acker, S. (1994) *Gendered Education*, Milton Keynes: Open University Press.

Bernard, J. (1987) *The Female World from a Global Perspective*, Bloomington, Ind.: Indiana University Press.

Collins, P. H. (1990) *Black Feminist Thought*, Boston: Unwin Hyman.

Daly, M. (1984) *Pure Lust: Elemental Feminist Philosophy*, Boston: Beacon Press.

Elshtain, J. (1981) *Public Man, Private Woman*, Princeton: Princeton University Press.

Flax, J. (1990a) *Thinking Fragments: Psychoanalysis, Feminism and Postmodernism in the Contemporary West*, Berkeley: University of California Press.

—— (1990b) 'Postmodernism and Gender Relations', in L. Nicholson (ed.) *Feminism/Postmodernism*, London: Routledge.

—— (1993) *Disputed Subjects: Essays on Psychoanalysis, Politics and Philosophy*, New York: Routledge.

Foucault, M. (1972) *The Archaeology of Knowledge*, New York: Harper & Row.

—— (1978) *The History of Sexuality, Vol.1*, New York: Random House.

Fraser, N. (1985) 'What's Critical about Critical Theory?: the Case of Habermas and Gender', *New German Critique* 35: 97–131.

Freire, P. (1985) *The Politics of Education*, London: Macmillan.

Gadamer, H-G. (1975) *Truth and Method*, New York: Continuum.

Griffin, S. (1978) *Women and Nature: the Roaring Inside Her*, New York: Harper & Row.

Grosz, E. (1987) 'Feminist Theory and the Challenge to Knowledges', *Women's Studies International Forum* 101, 5: 475–80.

—— (1990) 'Philosophy', in S. Gunew (ed.) *Feminist Knowledge: Critique and Construct*, London: Routledge.

Habermas, J. (1972) *Knowledge and Human Interests*, London: Heinemann.

Harding, S. (1987) 'Introduction: Is There a Feminist Method', in S. Harding (ed.) *Feminism and Methodology,* London: Routledge.

Hekman, S. (1990) *Gender and Knowledge: Elements of a Postmodern Feminism*, Oxford: Polity Press.

Hollway, W. (1989) *Subjectivity and Method in Psychology,* London: Sage.

Jones, A. (1993) 'Becoming a "Girl": Post-Structuralist Suggestions for Educational Research', *Gender and Education* 5, 2: 157–66.

Kenway, J. (1990) 'Making Hope Practical Rather Than Despair Convincing: Feminist Post-Structuralism, Gender Reform and Educational Change', *British Journal of Sociology of Education* 15, 2: 187–210.

—— (1992) 'Feminist Theories of the State: To Be or Not To Be', in M. Muetzelfeldt (ed.) *Society, State and Politics in Australia*, Annandale: Pluto Press.

Kolb, D. (1984) *Experiential Learning*, Englewood Cliffs, NJ, Prentice-Hall.

Kuhn, T. (1970) *The Structure of Scientific Revolutions*, Chicago: University of Chicago Press.

Lather, P. (1988) 'Feminist Perspectives on Empowering Research Methodologies', *Women's Studies International Forum* 11, 6: 569–81.

Lerner, G. (1986) *The Creation of Patriarchy*, Oxford: Oxford University Press.

Luke, C. (1994) 'Women in the Academy: the Politics of Speech and Silence', *British Journal of Sociology of Education*, 15, 2: 211–30.

McMillan, C. (1982) *Women, Reason and Nature*, Oxford: Basil Blackwell.

Mill, J. S. (1970) *The Subjection of Women*, Cambridge, Mass.: MIT Press.

O'Brien, M. (1981) *The Politics of Reproduction*, Boston: Routledge and Kegan Paul.

Plumwood, V. (1993) *Feminism and the Mastery of Reason*, London: Routledge.

Reinharz, S. (1992) *Feminist Methods in Social Research*, New York: Oxford University Press.

Scott, J. (1988) 'Deconstructuring Equality-versus-Difference: or the Uses of Post-structuralist Theory for Feminism', *Feminist Studies* 14, 1: 33–50.

Usher, R. and Bryant, I. (1989) *Adult Education as Theory, Practice and Research: The Captive Triangle*, London: Routledge.

—— and Edwards, R. (1994) *Postmodernism and Education*, London: Routledge.

Walkerdine, V. (1989) 'Femininity as Performance', *Oxford Review of Education* 15, 3: 267–79.

—— (1990a) 'Some Issues in the Historical Construction of the Scientific Truth about Girls', in L. Yates (ed.) *Theory/Practice Dilemmas*, Geelong: Deakin University.

—— (1990b) *Schoolgirl Fictions*, London: Verso.

Yeatman, A. (1990) 'A Feminist Theory of Social Differentiation', in L. Nicholson (ed.) *Feminism/Postmodernism*, London: Routledge.

9 Ethnography and education

David Scott

Ethnography has its roots in anthropology, the study of primitive societies. Early practitioners such as Bronislaw Malinowski[1] studied the Trobriand Islanders, and in particular focused on the local economy (*Argonauts of the Western Pacific*, 1922), social order (*Crime and Custom in Savage Society*, 1926) and inter-personal relations (*The Sexual Life of Savages*, 1929). In time, sociologists such as Lacey (*Hightown Grammar: The School as a Social System*, 1970), Ball (*Beachside Comprehensive: A Case Study of Secondary Schooling*, 1981) and Burgess (*Experiencing Comprehensive Education: A Study of Bishop McGregor School*, 1983)[2] adopted similar methods in their detailed studies of the culture of schools.

The introduction and subsequent development of ethnographic methods were a deliberate reaction to the dominance of 'positivism' in social science research.[3] Reference has already been made (see Chapter 4) to the differences between quantitative methodologies (experimental, single-case, ex post-facto, correlational and survey) and qualitative methodologies (ethnography and condensed case study).[4] This schism can be characterised on the one hand by an emphasis on nomography, replicability, the use of public and objective criteria and the adoption of a neutral observation language; and on the other, by a stress on the meaning–making capacity and interpretive activity of the human actor. Hammersley and Atkinson (1983: 8), for instance, characterise ethnography in the following way: 'the search for universal laws is rejected in favour of detailed descriptions of the concrete experience of life within a particular culture and of the social rules or patterns that constitute it'.

Ethnographers have taken up different and contrasting positions on a number of important methodological issues. The first area of dispute focuses on the adoption of deductive and/or inductive data analysis strategies, with proponents of the former (cf. Hammersley 1992) arguing that ethnography should be concerned primarily with the testing of hypotheses. On the other hand, most ethnographic approaches have been centrally concerned with induction (Glaser and Strauss 1967, Denzin 1978), that is the development of theory from the data. Second, there is a scission between those who use structured (Galton, Simon and Croll 1980, Galton and Willcocks 1983) and those who use semi-structured data collection instruments (Burgess 1983), with the latter usually considered more appropriate. Finally, participant observers who reject methods which involve the collection of data in artificial settings can be distinguished from non-participant observers who claim that valid data can be obtained in this way. These methods would include formal and semi-formal interviews, that do not occur 'naturally'.

Traditionally, ethnographers attempted to behave like participants in the research. Interviews with those participants were never formalised; data collection and recording were snatched and incomplete. The favoured means was the keeping of a fieldwork diary, which Burgess (1984a) argues had three purposes. First, fieldwork notes were substantive. This was a detailed record of the events observed, and included an account of experiences the researchers had had in the course of their fieldwork. Second, these notes included a discussion of the methods proposed and used. This was a continuous record of the researchers' reflections on the progress of the research project. Finally, fieldwork notes were used as an ongoing analytical device. They therefore included hunches, insights, hypotheses, and theories which had developed during the course of the investigation. In short, lengthy and detailed accounts by participants given in the course of a formal interview were rejected as ecologically invalid.[5]

However, both types of ethnographers argue that descriptions of social reality are incomplete if they do not take account of the views and perceptions of social actors. In this chapter, I will focus on traditional ethnography, where data are collected by researchers who behave as far as possible like the social actors they are investigating and eschew the use of artificial settings for gathering data. Four areas will be explored: the participatory nature of the researcher's role, the stress on studying interaction in natural settings, the need to be reflexive during the investigation, and the way ethnography relates to the practice of education.

PARTICIPANT OBSERVATION

The ethnographer may adopt the role of a participant observer during the investigation. Hockey (1991), for example, took on the duties of a 'squaddie' in the British Army as he went on night patrols in the streets of Belfast and training exercises in the Canadian wastelands. Burgess (1983) became a teacher as he spent long periods of time in a Roman Catholic Secondary School in the United Kingdom.

Gold's (1958) widely used typology refers to four participant observer field roles. The first is the complete participant, where the researchers conceal their identity. It is doubtful, however, that they are fully committed to their new role, since, at the end of the fieldwork, they will return to their universities and research institutes. Their data collection activity may involve them in secretive excursions to record those data, and they may have to restrict their participation, if, in order to maintain their credibility as a member of the group, they are required to perform dangerous or illegal acts. Inevitably, there are ethical problems with adopting covert roles since permission to collect, record and ultimately publish data will not have been sought from any of the members of the group being observed.

The second role identified by Gold is that of participant-as-observer. Educational ethnographers more frequently adopt this role. They are open about their purposes, and therefore have to negotiate access at every level of the research. The emphasis is still on participation, as they seek to experience for themselves the activities under investigation, be they teaching, being taught, being a parent at an open evening, a participant in a staff meeting, or a member of the staff room. The distinction between the first and second types lies in the degree of concealment. However, even if researchers adopt an open stance, they are rarely able to give a complete picture of their purposes and intentions at the beginning of the research, as these develop during the fieldwork and are responsive to the initial data collected.

The third role referred to by Gold is that of observer-as-participant. A more detached stance is adopted, where researchers will not attempt to experience the activities for themselves, but make close and detailed observations. Contact is maintained between observer and observed. However, if we take the case of classroom researchers, they are unlikely to do any teaching. They are more likely to sit at the back of the classroom and make notes, while at the same time accepting interruptions by students.

Gold's final role is that of the complete observer. Researchers adopt a passive role and concentrate on minimising their 'contamination' of the setting. A deliberate distance is maintained between the researcher and participants in the research. Ethnographers typically adopt either of the first two stances as they seek to investigate the setting through direct experience or through close involvement in the life of the individual or institution.

In the light of this, there are three possible epistemological positions that can be adopted by participant observers, of which, I will argue, only one is sustainable. They are: cultural incommensurability, tradition-bound rationality and universal rationality. In essence, Winch (1958), Archer (1988) and Macintyre (1988) represent these three positions. In addition, two versions of the 'ethnographic' argument will be discussed. Proponents of the strong version argue that full participation is possible and necessary for the collection of valid data. We have already suggested that this position is logically and empirically unsustainable. In the light of this, a weaker version is proposed, which is that the ethnographers participate as fully as they can, with the intention of acquiring empathetic understanding of the activities they are investigating.

The ethnographers divest themselves of their conceptual apparatus and take on new ways of understanding. They phenomenologically bracket out their values and 'go native', because to do otherwise would make it impossible to understand another way of life in terms of its underlying rules. Winch is one social philosopher who has argued that the observer cannot stand outside an alien culture and understand the way it works by utilising categories and values which do not belong to it: 'Logical relations between propositions themselves depend on social relations between men' (Winch 1958: 126). As a consequence, basic category systems, these 'logical relations', are socially and culturally specific. He is therefore arguing that it is simply not possible to do anything other than go native. Different worlds are paradigmatically incommensurable. Knowing another culture can only be achieved by direct immersion over a long period of time, and understanding only occurs as a result of imbibation of its beliefs and values. The most basic organising components of thought for Winch are social constructions. As a consequence, his epistemological stance is relativist.[6]

Macintyre (1988), in opposition to this, argues from a position of tradition-bound rationality. Within any historical moment there may be dominant traditions of thought, rival traditions that demand less allegiance and traditions which are going through epistemological crises. But these traditions cannot be subsumed under one overall conception of rationality. They are incommensurable, though translation is possible. But this simply means that observers can understand another tradition even if they continue to operate from within their own. As Macintyre himself argues when he writes about four different traditions of justice and rationality,[7] he does so through the lens of one of them: 'we either have to speak as protagonists of one contending party or fall silent' (Macintyre 1988: 356). These traditions are competing and do involve conflicting understandings of rationality. If they did not, they would not constitute different traditions. There would only be right and wrong ways of seeing the world: 'but genuinely to adopt the standpoint of a tradition thereby commits one to its view of what is true and false and, in so committing one, prohibits one from adopting any rival standpoints' (Macintyre 1988: 367). It is not that one party is more correct than another, or that members of one tradition understand rationality better than members from other traditions. Rival traditions are genuinely in competition with each other.

Macintyre is anti-Cartesian: Descartes (1949) argued that there are a number of axiomatic principles, that there is a logical way of proceeding, and that therefore systems of knowledge can be built on firm foundations. Macintyre is not prepared to accept that it is possible to discover foundational principles for any rational enquiry. Members of rival traditions may share beliefs, images and texts; but what they do not share is criteria by which participants decide the practical conclusions they come to about how to live, or 'practical rationality questions' as Macintyre calls them. They may share an agreement to give a certain authority to logic, but what they agree upon is insufficient to resolve their disagreements.

What Macintyre has done is to lay himself open to the charge that since the truth or falsity of statements is contingent upon particular historical and social traditions, those tradition-bound notions of what constitutes truth and falsity are themselves context-bound and therefore have no universal validity. This argument, of course, does not provide conclusive proof of the falsity of Macintyre's claims, only that, since the thesis asserts that we cannot know anything to be absolutely true, we cannot then know whether our thesis is true or not. But it still may be.

Macintyre defends himself against charges that he is a relativist or a perspectivist. He argues that he cannot be accused of either of these simply because he refuses to accept universal notions of rational discourse. The relativist challenge is that there are no rational standards. Every set of standards has as much or as little claim to our allegiance as any other. The perspectivist challenge is that rival traditions are mutually exclusive, but do provide different but complementary perspectives on reality.

He argues that these two positions and the rationalist position, that is the belief in universal rational standards, are mirror images of the same false epistemological stance. They all assume correspondence versions of our relations with reality.[8] Relativists argue that there can be no correspondence or no knowing of that relationship; no reality as such, therefore our thought cannot correspond with it. The perspectivist likewise disregards reality, but would want to argue that different perspectives may offer complementary perspectives about life, which do or do not conform more or less with reality. The rationalist position is also false because it posits a connection between reality and the judgements we make about it, and that in theory, though we might not always be right, we can know that reality. So Macintyre (1988) can argue that:

> what is and was ... highly misleading, was to conceive of a realm of facts independent of judgements or of any form of linguistic expression, so that judgements or statements could be paired off with facts, truth or falsity being the alleged relationship between such paired items.
>
> (Macintyre 1988: 358)

Macintyre wants to substitute a different type of relationship between our judgements and reality. In pursuit of this, he argues that one should not try to distinguish between the judgements we make and what they refer to and that it is inappropriate to say that the one corresponds to the other. He wants to replace this correspondence theory with one involving the relations between sets of meaning located within traditions. Traditions do develop and change, not because they correspond more or less with a static and never changing reality, but because contradictions and inconsistencies appear which demand resolution. They also change because they compete with rival traditions. There is always the possibility of epistemological crises, because rational enquiry is always contingent upon the relations of the particular tradition within which it exists. Knowing, therefore, always has to be located within particular ways of knowing, and is therefore always context-bound.

This middle position then is anti-relativist, anti-perspectival and anti-realist. Its most important implication is its acknowledgement that strangers, as Schutz (1964) argues, are never able to step outside themselves and live as natives. They are not able to 'bracket out' their beliefs and epistemological frameworks through which they understand the world. The stranger always retains vestiges of his or her original position, and therefore never quite behaves as a native. Translation, the key perhaps to understanding and then representing another way of life, is only possible from the standpoint of a set of values which are alien to the society which is being studied.

For Macintyre, these values are located within historically bound traditions. For Archer, who argues from our third perspective, they can be described as universal, which means that they refer to all types of knowing. In some essential respects, researchers investigating unfamiliar settings will always operate in similar ways; that is, they will utilise common and universal tools to investigate social reality. For Archer (1988) the ascription of these rules as universal is necessary to successful translation, and she argues that:

> Successful translation is a pre-condition of employing logical principles to attribute contradiction or consistency amongst alien beliefs or between those and our own. Unless we can feel confident in the beliefs we ascribe cross-culturally, nothing can be said about their relations. This confidence rests on the conviction that it is possible to produce adequate translations of the alien beliefs.
>
> (Archer 1988: 121)

Though Archer accepts here that criteria for making successful translations must be based on values which can be applied to a wide variety of settings, and not simply to the one which is being investigated, the argument she is proposing does not stand or fall in terms of the universality of those values. It is equally sustainable with regard to tradition-bound notions of rationality.

Furthermore, rationalist social philosophers such as Archer rarely distinguish between base logical rules and other values, assuming that if a case can be made for the one as being of universal applicability, then a case can be made for all the others. Successful translation makes use of a range of rules and resources which are located within specific traditions of thought and enquiry. The difficulty for the participant observer is that either they then have to find a solution to the problem of translation, or they have to accept that they will use concepts, categories and ways of seeing which may be alien to participants in the social setting being studied. Therefore they cannot in this sense participate fully, as they are involved in the act of translation and at the same time are making judgements (utilising their value system) about a society which must forever remain tantalisingly out of reach.

If this argument is accepted – that translation is not possible if the researcher acts as a full participant – then we need to examine the weaker case, which is that a measure of participation in the research setting allows the observer to experience events as they are experienced by participants. Here we refer to an act of sympathetic imagination or empathic identification which will allow the observer 'to grasp the psychological state (i.e. motivation, belief, intention or the like) of an individual actor' (Schwandt 1994: 120). It has been suggested (Schutz 1967) that this gives a false picture of the process by which the researcher comes to understand social reality. For Schutz (1967: 59) it is much more a question of grasping the intersubjective meanings given to their actions by social actors: 'the thought objects constructed by the social scientist, in order to grasp this social reality, have to be founded upon the thought objects constructed by the common-sense thinking of men, living their daily lives within their social world'. It therefore has little to do with experiencing the same types of activities, and developing understandings by generalising these empathised experiences, or intuitively getting inside that person's head. Consequently, there is bound to be a gap between the activities (intentions, beliefs, etc.) that precede actions and the observer's ability to grasp them. This has implications for the oft repeated claim by ethnographers that their method is superior to other methods because it allows actors and actions to be studied in their natural settings.

NATURAL SETTINGS

Ethnography can be contrasted with those methods which allow the study of human beings in 'experimental' conditions or by the use of retrospective data collected from interviews. What these experimental subjects or interviewees do and say therefore, can be generalised to other, real-life settings. Ethnographers argue that there are serious problems with this approach; that human beings do not always behave in laboratory or interview settings as they do in real life. Thus to generalise from the one to the other is suspect. Bracht and Glass (1968), adopting a realist ontology, have described this as 'ecological invalidity', and suggested that invalid conclusions are sometimes drawn by researchers when observations made in experimental situations are applied to human actors in natural settings.

As Hammersley (1992) points out, there are degrees of artificiality about the adoption of all types of research methods and techniques. Indeed, experimental researchers have developed validity criteria which take account of this (Bracht and Glass 1968). The first of these is internal, where in order for researchers to be sure that their research is valid, they need to eliminate seven types of threats – history, maturation, statistical regression, testing, instrumentation, selection and experimental mortality (Cohen and Manion 1989). The second is external, and in a similar way, in order for researchers to be certain of their ability to generalise, six threats need to be neutralised – failure to describe independent variables explicitly, lack of representativeness of available and target populations, the Hawthorne effect, inadequate operationalising of dependent variables, sensitisation to experimental conditions and interactive effects of extraneous factors and experimental treatments (Cohen and Manion 1989).[9] In the first instance, they are concerned with those factors which affect their ability to be certain that experimental effects observed in the data actually refer to the phenomena under investigation and have not been generated by other variables. In the second, they are concerned with whether their conclusions can be generalised across space and time and to larger populations than they are dealing with in the experimental setting; whether in fact, they can infer from one case to another.

The philosopher, David Hume (1963), distinguished between logical and empirical inference. If we take the well-known syllogism: all ravens are black, Peter is a raven, therefore Peter must be black; we can see that the conclusion follows logically from the premisses and could not be otherwise. On the other hand, it was believed a hundred years ago that all swans were white, until early explorers to Australia observed black ones (cf. Sayer 1992). The original premiss was therefore refuted by further observation. This and other examples led to a reformulation of the problem of generality: empirical inferences and predictions can only be made within probable limits. Experimental researchers generalise from their study of one case to others (this is what they mean by ecological validity), but its success or failure is subject to degrees of error. If there are clear differences between the experimental setting and the setting to which these empirical generalisations refer, then the transfer is suspect. It is suspect because of the poor match between the two settings, and not because one is more real than the other. We are therefore referring here to the problem of generalisation or transposition from one setting to another, across time and space, and not to its artificiality or genuineness.

How does this differ from the ethnographic or participant observation method? Participant observers establish close relationships with participants in the setting being studied. They have an influence on what happens. Furthermore, they have already made a series of decisions about which methods to use, where to be, and what to record. Their values are central to the direction the fieldwork takes, and their account therefore represents a positioned view of a particular culture or cultural setting. However, the ethnographer makes no attempt to control the relevant variables so that causal relationships can be established. Their self-imposed task is to develop understandings of human interaction within prescribed spatial and temporal boundaries.

Ethnographers have developed various methods to reassure themselves that their theory-building relates to their subject matter. Denzin (1978) itemises these as: data, researcher, theory and methodological triangulation. All have the same function, which is to reassure the researchers about the reliability, validity and generality of their findings. By using a variety of methods (questionnaires, as well as observations and interviews), or more than one researcher or data analyst, the researcher can be more certain of his or her conclusions. Two problems present themselves. The use of triangulated methods demands that like is compared with like. But researchers do not and cannot triangulate at the same moment, so the comparison that is made is between perceptions, conceptions and descriptions of evolving structures at different times. Furthermore, if researchers decide to triangulate, they are assuming that their methods (and these would include how close the researchers are to their sources of data) do not determine the type of data that is collected: that method is in some sense independent and thus can be discussed, modified and manipulated in isolation from, and without reference to, those data. This argument can only be sustained within the framework of a realist ontology.

Another measure of reliability is respondent validation,[10] and here the researcher cross checks that the data, the analysis of those data and the development of theory from those data fit the ideas and preconceptions of participants in the research. There is a similar problem, which is that the judgements made by participants are always partial and positioned. This, of course, does not mean that they should be construed as false or artificial; but what it does mean is that, however secure the researchers feel about their conclusions, they still may not be applicable to other settings.

Despite this, case study researchers operating from an ethnographic perspective may conceptualise the idea of generalisation in similar ways to experimental or survey researchers. Hammersley (1985) describes three styles of case study research. The first style is where the researcher studies typical cases, which represent a larger whole or aggregate. Honigmann (1973), for instance, argues that ethnographers must identify their selection criteria to enable the reader to determine the relationship between the sample and its intended population. In a similar way, Woods (1986) cites the need to make 'the case' as representative as possible to improve external validity. The second style of case-study research cited by Hammersley is where researchers want to use cases to test theories. They study more and more cases until they are satisfied that the theory holds.

On the other hand, ethnographers may seek to preserve the uniqueness of the case. They are not concerned, and this is Hammersley's third style, with its representativeness. But they are interested in how the workings of particular processes are illuminated by single cases. Mitchell (1983) brings out the tension which underlies each of these three research styles:

> The basic problem in the use of case material in theoretical analysis, however, is that of the extent to which the analyst is justified in generalising from a single instance of an event which may be – and probably is – unique.
> (Mitchell 1983: 189)

For Hammersley, the fieldwork is completed to test a theory or theories (Hammersley and Scarth 1986). Theory for him is explanatory in a retrospective sense, but it is not predictive. Testing theory allows generalisability, though as he admits in his discussion of the differentiation/polarisation thesis, the theory may become so circumscribed by context that it loses its power to generalise (Hammersley 1985).

Mitchell (1983), in contrast, writes about theoretical sampling: formal theory is developed which has explanatory power, but it is based on the uniqueness of each case. Though qualitative researchers frequently concern themselves with the typicality of their cases in relation to a larger population, analysts such as Mitchell argue that the selection and study of cases can be justified by using a different modus operandi. Here, the case being studied is an exemplar of the workings of a process, which has its own internal logic. The ethnographer seeks to uncover and make explicit this interior geography. However, prior to fieldwork, researchers have already identified the case to be studied (even if it later undergoes transformation). Therefore they have already set limits to the way they will understand, and subsequently describe, the internal workings of their case.

Indeed, we have already noted that ethnography is derived from anthropology and thus one way of distinguishing it from other approaches is the emphasis it places on a bounded cultural system. Later ethnographers have sought to apply this principle to smaller units of people, such as schools and classrooms. A number of assumptions are made. First, that both societies and institutions of various sorts are peopled by social actors who share common values and operate within systems of rules by which they can be identified. Second, that the categorising systems we use do in fact refer to identifiable areas of social life which can then be studied as holistic units.

Societies, whether primitive or modern, have been categorised in this way by social scientists and others. Archer (1988: 2) refers to this as 'the myth of cultural integration', and she argues that it has created 'an archetype of culture(s) as the perfectly woven and all-enmeshing web ... the perfectly integrated system, in which every element was interdependent with every other – the ultimate exemplar of compact and coherent organisation'. Two examples of this are Marxism and structural-functionalism, both of which have exerted an important influence on sociological thought over the last hundred years. Marxist and neo-Marxist approaches[11] have prioritised the infrastructure over the superstructure; and though more recent adherents have modified the dominating influence of the former over the latter, the dominant ideology thesis expressed by them still treats social actors as operating as and within a totality. Likewise, structural functionalists[12] designate the norms of society as so integrative that social actors struggle to assert themselves and in the end are reduced to a plasticity that denies their ability to behave intentionally.

At a micro, rather than macro, level, the same problem arises. Educational institutions are investigated as distinct cases, whereas it is possible to understand them as competing and cooperating groups and individuals who interact in various ways, and form and reform in different configurations and confirmations at different moments and places. However, the ethnographer frequently identifies the 'case' as an holistic entity before fieldwork begins, and this colours the way it is eventually inscribed in the research text.

REFLEXIVITY

In the light of this, we need to examine the notion of reflexivity, central to the ethnographic enterprise. The spoken texts of both the researched and the written texts of the researcher are constructed – in the latter case by a set of rules which constitute 'the academic text'. The latter is therefore embedded within a set of social and political arrangements, which are transitory. Usher (1993) argues that the form an academic text generally takes is realist and representative, thus conveying the impression that the researched account stands in some way for a set of phenomena that exists outside it and can be understood without referring to the way it was constructed. He further argues that if this fiction is to be exposed, all types of research should include reflexive processes.

The postmodern or linguistic turn (Giddens 1987) has influenced ethnography, with the emphasis placed on the way ethnographers express themselves. This has concentrated attention on the text and the way the textual form mediates the ethnographer's view of reality. It is possible to identify a number of different types. The text may be continuous or broken. A continuous text gives the impression that the series of events which are being described is logically and causally sequenced, and comprehensively accounted for. A broken text (by which I mean a text which deliberately eschews a narrative form) is designed to represent the unsystematic and serendipitous way data are frequently collected, and suggests that research is both a value-embedded and social activity.

Van Maanan (1988) identifies another type of text, the confessional, and distinguishes it from the realist. The traditional academic text deliberately excludes the author. The authorial 'I' is muffled, and the text now seems to represent unproblematically that segment of reality to which it refers. Furthermore, the traditional academic text excludes the confessional, and treats the biography of the researcher as ectopic. Recently, ethnographers (Burgess 1984b, Walford 1987, 1991) have sought to provide separate confessional accounts which deconstruct and lay bare the processes the researcher went through to collect the data and create the research account. This has by necessity included biographical data, though it is of course a textual account of biography. This works in two ways: first, the biographical account is presently constituted, and has thus been mediated by processes of time. Second, the biographical account has been textually constructed in terms of the conventions of the written text, which exclude other ways of portraying it. For Usher (1993) however, this does not mean that the researcher simply has to supply a series of biographical facts to enable readers to contextualise the account they are reading. The reflexive posture is more fundamental:

But the reflexive understanding which is always potentially present in doing research is not primarily the gaining of an awareness of one's subjectivity, one's personality, temperament, values and standpoints. The desire that structures research is not the produce of a psychology which has been made 'public' through honest introspection. Rather it is the effect of sociality and the inscription of self in social practices, language and discourses which constitute the research process.

(Usher 1993: 9)

The expression of that reflexive understanding is therefore always socially and textually inscribed.

Research texts employ devices which are transparent or opaque. The transparent text focuses readers on the text and allows them to understand the way it has been constructed. The opaque text seeks to cloud the issue of how it was constructed and to focus on the events to which it refers. It thus conveys the impression that textual representation is always a neutral medium: we do not read the text, we are in the presence of the events to which it refers. However, even here we cannot escape from the text, since both types of devices are textual constructions.

Texts are differently constituted. In Barthes' (1975) words, aspects of these texts are 'readerly'. The textual meaning is unequivocal, not subject to interpretation, non-writerly and therefore prescriptive. The text compels certain forms of action and proscribes others. On the other hand, texts such as these are not uni-dimensional; any text is likely to contain 'readerly' as well as 'writerly' aspects. In the latter case the text is so constructed that the reader is allowed interpretative space. Their options are not foreclosed by the text. Indeed, one form the 'writerly' text might take is dialogic.

The monologic/dialogic divide (Hammersley and Atkinson 1994) is an important way of understanding how texts are constructed. The monologic form refers to the dominant voice of the ethnographer which overwhelms the voice/voices of participants in the research. The dialogic form refers to the attempt to disprivilege the authorial voice and give equal standing to a multitude of voices. Though on the surface this would seem to be more democratic, the authority of the author is still sustained through his or her selection of voices, central role in the data collection process, and choice of focus. However, the author may deliberately disprivilege his or her voice by using a number of linguistic and organisational devices. This is most evident in ethnographies in which the author minimises the comment and analysis which connects those voices (though of course, the latter are always mediated expressions and have been chosen by the researcher). As a consequence, the account is more open and 'writerly'.

Broken, confessional, opaque, 'writerly' and dialogic forms of textual representation are all attempts at embodying reflexivity in the text, and they point to the way that ethnography demands a level of introspection both about how the data were collected and the positioning of the researched account in those social and political arrangements which constitute society. These types of approach are different from those which seek to suggest that research involves the collection of data uncontaminated by the presence and activities of the researcher, and as a result, are a-theoretical. All data involve theoretical assumptions, the uncovering of which constitute the reflexive process.

THE PRACTICE OF EDUCATION

Reflexivity is not just expressed in texts, but in practices, and in particular, the practice of education. This last can be distinguished from other practices, discourses or traditions in a number of ways. Education is a contested concept: different individuals and groups conceptualise it in different ways. Walsh (1988) seeks to circumscribe this position by suggesting that it is open-loaded dialectical rather than essentially contestable. This, he argues, rescues the 'objectivist' account of education from absurdity. He does, though, suggest that objectivist accounts of such concepts are not incompatible with ideas which are 'uncertain, adaptable, permissive, vision-dependent to the extent of being incommensurable in its variants, and interminably debated' (Walsh 1988: 32). If we accept this view (whether we call it 'objectivist' or not), the open-loaded dialectical nature of the discourse compels us to locate it within competing systems of values and evolving discursive traditions. As a discourse therefore, it expresses relations of power. It is not a neutral medium of expression and ideas. Educational discourses operate as closure devices: they restrict and prohibit what can be said about their subject matter. It is in this sense that Foucault (1980) wants to tie power and knowledge closely together.

However, educational discourses can be distinguished in a number of other ways. The practice of education always refers to something other than it is. It always looks outside itself at some future ideal: the child will become an educated citizen; the student will become a trained employee. This has certain implications. Formal education is seen as a means rather than as an end (though there have been many accounts of education as an end in itself: cf. Whitehead 1932), and thus methods seemingly iniquitous to the practice of education have been deemed acceptable to produce the 'educated' man or woman. Second, understandings of it are always utopian. Educational discourses are value-laden, but always with reference to an ideal future state.

More importantly, however, the practice of doing education and finding out about education are inextricably bound together. Ethnographers research themselves as they research their subject matter. They are therefore educating themselves, as well as developing understandings of education. This self-referential element to the study of education sets it apart. It refers to the notion of 'narrativity' developed by Ricoeur (1991) in which he suggests that human beings locate themselves in the present by a continual process of revision and re-working of the past. They thus develop narrative versions of their past through their present activity. The account of the past is always a lived account. Narrative discourse is therefore 'performative' (White 1991). This dialectical relationship between the practice of education and research (in particular ethnography) is its most important distinguishing feature. The ethnographic text is therefore always located in the practice of education and is reflexively made.

NOTES

1   Malinowski (1922: 25) argued that data should always be collected in real-life settings, and that the ethnographer should attempt to: 'grasp the native's point of view, his relation to life, to realise his [sic] vision of his [sic] world'; a position which I argue against in this chapter.

2   Though these three authors adopted methods which were similar in some respects, in other ways they were prepared to use more eclectic data collection methods. For instance, Ball (1981) makes use of a number of enumerative devices, in addition to collecting data of a more traditional ethnographic type.

3   Denzin (1989) lists five characteristics of positivist research: objective reality can be grasped, researchers can remain neutral, with their values separate from the descriptions of reality they provide; observations and generalisations are a-situational and a-temporal; causality is linear; and enquiry is an objective activity.

4   In Chapter 4, I argue that the division between qualitative and quantitative methodologies is real, despite recent attempts to sublate it.

5   The notion of ecological validity has been developed by Bracht and Glass (1968) to refer to the validity of conclusions drawn from experimental and other 'artificial conditions' when they are applied to other settings.

6   Since the publication of his celebrated book in 1958, Winch (1979) has sought to defend himself from a charge of relativism. However, Archer (1988) has suggested that, unless he wants to abandon his whole thesis, he cannot escape from it. Critics such as Rorty (1980) have argued that debates such as these are irrelevant, since postmodernists do not locate their ideas within traditional epistemological frameworks.

7   These four traditions are: the Aristotelian account of justice and practical reasoning, the Augustinian version of Christianity, Humean empiricism which synthesised Calvinist versions of Christianity and Aristotelianism, and modern liberalism.

8   Though few now advocate a position of naive realism, various forms of mediated realism have been adopted by social philosophers, such as Hammersley's (1992) subtle realism, Bhaskar's (1989) transcendental realism and Sayer's (1992) realist approach.

9   In Chapter 5, I provide a fuller explanation of those factors which define notions of internal and external validity.

10   In Chapter 4, I set out the arguments for the use of respondent validation processes at different stages of the research project.

11   Cf. Miliband (1969), Gramsci (1971), Marx (1978), Abercrombie *et al.* (1980).

12   Cf. Parsons (1951).

REFERENCES

Abercrombie, N., Hill, S. and Turner, B. (1980) *The Dominant Ideology Thesis*, London: Allen & Unwin.

Archer, M. (1988) *Culture and Agency*, Cambridge: Cambridge University Press.

Ball, S. (1981) *Beachside Comprehensive: A Case Study of Secondary Schooling*, Cambridge: Cambridge University Press.

Barthes, R. (1975) *S/Z*, London: Jonathan Cape.

Bhaskar, R. (1989) *Reclaiming Reality*, London: Verso.

Bracht, G. H. and Glass, G. V. (1968) 'The External Validity of Experiments', *American Educational Research Journal* 4, 5: 437–74.

Burgess, R.G. (1983) *Experiencing Comprehensive Education: A Study of Bishop McGregor School*, London: Methuen.

—— (1984a) *In the Field: An Introduction to Field Research*, London: Allen & Unwin.

—— (1984b) *The Research Process in Educational Settings: Ten Case Studies*, Lewes: Falmer.

Cohen, L. and Manion, L. (1989, third edn) *Research Methods in Education*, London: Routledge.

Denzin, N. K. (1978) *The Research Act*, New York: McGraw Hill.

—— (1989) *Interpretive Interactionism, Vol. 16, Applied Social Research Methods Series*, London: Sage.

Descartes, R. (1949) (translated by John Veitch) *A Discourse on Method*, London: J. M. Dent.

Foucault, M. (1980) *Power/Knowledge: Selected Interviews and other Writings 1972–1977* (C. Gordon, ed.), Brighton: Harvester.

Galton, M., Simon, B. and Croll, P. (1980) *Inside the Primary Classroom*, London: Routledge and Kegan Paul.

—— and Willcocks, J. (1983) *Moving from the Primary Classroom*, London: Routledge and Kegan Paul.

Giddens, A. (1987) *Social Theory and Modern Society*, Cambridge: Polity Press.

Glaser, B. G. and Strauss, A. L. (1967) *The Discovery of Grounded Theory*, Chicago: Aldine.

Gold, R. L. (1958) 'Roles in Sociological Fieldwork', *Social Forces* 36: 217–23.

Gramsci, A. (1971) *Selections from Prison Notebooks*, London: Lawrence and Wishart.

Hammersley, M. (1985) 'From Ethnography to Theory: A Programme and Paradigm for Case Study Research', *Sociology* 19, 2: 187–211.

—— (1992) *What's Wrong with Ethnography?*, London: Routledge.

—— and Atkinson, P. (1983) *Ethnography, Principles in Practice*, London and New York: Tavistock Publications.

—— and —— (1994) 'Ethnography and Participant Observation', in N. Denzin and Y. Lincoln (eds) *Handbook of Qualitative Research*, London: Sage.

—— and Scarth, J. (1986) *The Impact of Examinations on Secondary School Teaching*, Milton Keynes: Open University.

Hockey, J. (1991) *Squaddies*, Exeter: University of Exeter Press.

Honigmann, J. (1973) 'Sampling in Ethnographic Fieldwork', in R. Burgess (ed.) *Field Research: A Sourcebook and Field Manual*, London: Allen & Unwin.

Hume, D. (1963) *Enquiry Concerning the Human Understanding: 1748*, Oxford: Selby-Bigge.

Lacey, C. (1970) *Hightown Grammar: the School as a Social System*, Manchester: Manchester University Press.

Macintyre, A. (1988) *Whose Justice? Which Rationality?* London: Duckworth.

Malinowski, B. (1922) *Argonauts of the Western Pacific*, London: Routledge and Kegan Paul.
—— (1926) *Crime and Custom in Savage Society*, London: Routledge and Kegan Paul.
—— (1929) *The Sexual Life of Savages*, London: Routledge and Kegan Paul.
Marx, K. (1978) 'The German Ideology', in D. McLellan (ed.) *Karl Marx: Selected Writings*, Oxford: Oxford University Press.
Miliband, R. (1969) *The State in Capitalist Society*, London: Allen & Unwin.
Mitchell, J. (1983) 'Case and Situation Analysis', *The Sociological Review* 1: 187–211.
Parsons, T. (1951) *The Social System*, London: Routledge and Kegan Paul.
Ricoeur, P. (1991) 'Life in Quest of a Narrative', in D. Wood (ed.) *On Paul Ricoeur: Narrative and Interpretation*, London: Routledge.
Rorty, R. (1980) *Philosophy and the Mirror of Nature*, Oxford: Blackwell.
Sayer, A. (1992) *Method in Social Science*, London: Routledge.
Schutz, A. (1964) 'The Stranger: An Essay in Social Psychology', in A. Schutz (ed.) *Collected Papers, Vol. II*, The Hague: Martinus Nijhoff.
—— (1967) (M. Natanson, ed.) *Collected Papers, Vol. I*, The Hague: Martinus Nijhoff.
Schwandt, T. (1994) 'Constructivist, Interpretivist Approaches to Human Inquiry', in N. Denzin and Y. Lincoln (eds) *Handbook of Qualitative Research*, London: Sage.
Usher, R. (1993) *Reflexivity, Occasional Papers in Education as Interdisciplinary Studies*, 3, Southampton: University of Southampton, School of Education.
Van Maanan, J. (1988) *Tales of the Field: On Writing Ethnography*, Chicago: University of Chicago Press.
Walford, G. (1987) *Doing Sociology of Education*, Lewes: Falmer.
—— (1991) *Doing Educational Research*, London: Routledge.
Walsh, P. (1988) 'Open and Loaded Uses of Education and Objectivism', *Journal of Philosophy of Education* 22, 1: 23–24.
White, H. (1991) 'The Metaphysics of Narrativity: Time and Symbol in Ricoeur's Philosophy of History', in D. Wood (ed.) *On Paul Ricoeur: Narrative and Interpretation*, London: Routledge.
Whitehead, A. (1932) *The Aims of Education*, London: Benn.
Winch, P. (1958) *The Idea of a Social Science and its Relation to Philosophy*, London: Routledge and Kegan Paul.
—— (1979) 'Understanding a Primitive Society', in B. Wilson (ed.) *Rationality*, Oxford: Blackwell.
Woods, P. (1986) *Inside Schools: Ethnography in Educational Research*, London: Routledge and Kegan Paul.

10 The purposes and processes of biographical method

Michael Erben

Biographical method is an educative exercise, its axiomatic purpose being not only the accumulation of information and the interpretation of data but also a development in the moral reasoning of the researcher.

INTRODUCTION

The purpose of using biographical method as a research tool is to explore, through the analysis of individual lives, the relationship between social forces and personal character. The individual in this procedure is regarded as a highly singular and highly complex articulation of the cultural and, as such, research proceeds in a deductive rather than inductive manner. Denzin (1989: 7) has summarised the biographical method as 'the studied use and collection of life documents ... These documents will include autobiographies, diaries, letters, obituaries, life histories, life stories, personal experience stories, oral histories, and personal histories'.

We may therefore say that a studied life is the study of a temporal journey. This journey, the journey of life, is an enacted drama of selfhood that is empirically unpredictable. Although there may be some societally derived routes for the journey, the experience upon them – the happenings and persons encountered – are in large part unforeseeable. As Gadamer (1992) states:

> It cannot be known in advance whether the experiences to be had *en route* may outweigh the journey's end in their eventual importance and impressiveness. Nor can one know in advance whether the journey may change one utterly, in body or in mind. In this particular sense, it is clear that life itself is an adventure.
>
> (Gadamer 1992: ix)

The experience that selves undergo is reflective as well as naturalistic – that is, as people experience their lives they are aware that they are doing so, they are self-conscious. Self-consciousness as it proceeds through lived experiences becomes constitutive of self-formation. To investigate the way the self-consciousness of others is utilised to produce self-formation lies at the heart of the biographical method. The human subject can only interpret itself by interpreting the signs found in the surrounding world. There is no such thing as a notion of self-hood or self-identity that is genetically transferred. We are joined to the past and to the future because it is a constituent feature of mind to have memory and to have projection. The past then is always categorically linked to the future and when that future becomes the past it will, similarly, be linked to another future. However, selves are not free agents within this temporal schema. They arrive in a world already made, in a language already in existence. When individuals interpret or decipher their condition they are already partly socialised and are always in a state of prior signification. As Ricoeur (1988: 168) has said, 'all understanding is of necessity mediated by meanings which are not constituted by the self alone'. Subjectivity is therefore the product of a variety of social discourses and a unique, personal, life history. It will then be clear that the biographical method has an intra-reflexive aspect and that researchers should be aware of the normative facet of their own cultural position.

Biographical method, the study of life history and life courses, as we may call it, is concerned with the hermeneutical investigation of the narrative accounts of lives and selves. Hermeneutics is, quite simply, the theory or science of interpretation, and hermeneutical investigation is a method of analysis applicable to all forms of cultural life. For hermeneutical research, cultural life is regarded as a composition of cultural texts. Texts are areas of signification having cohering and recognisable cultural identities, e.g. a hockey match, *Hamlet*, a hospital ward, the class system, Mrs Thatcher, an unemployed school leaver. In the case of a biography, a life or self is regarded as a text. Further, part of the hermeneutical approach is the establishment of what has been termed the 'hermeneutical circle'. This represents an acknowledgement that cumulative interpretations of a text may supply increasingly refined explanations, but not complete knowledge of the text. Additionally, that the consciousness of the interpreter is always necessarily implicated in the analysis of the text. It is for this reason that biographical method is increasingly referred to as auto/biographical method (*Sociology* 1993). The hermeneutical procedure is employed in biographical research to understand the narratives of lives. By narratives is meant the types, varieties and patterns of the accounts or stories that compose life-course experience. Hermeneutical analysis of narrative takes Time and its passage as a universal feature of individual and social lives. Lives, as such, are composed of the narratives by which time is experienced. These narratives place upon existence – past, present and future – a cohering feature constituting the reasons for thoughts and actions.

The points raised in this introduction will now be further analysed in the following two sections: Background and Development, and Applications. Finally, there will be a third section comprising a summary.

BACKGROUND AND DEVELOPMENT

One of the best ways to understand the purposes of the biographical or life-history approach to research is to examine its development. This is of particular relevance to the biographical method because its conclusions are arrived at through the cumulative layerings of past hermeneutical considerations as well as the requirements of current research projects. The first modern treatise on biographical method is a short article by Samuel Johnson (1709–84) which appeared on 13 October 1750 in *The Rambler* (Johnson 1968). In Johnson we find a mind of rare hermeneutical insight that has been seriously neglected by sociologists of biography. The opening sentence to his *Rambler* article has the acuity of the most sophisticated contemporary hermeneutical narratologist:

> All joy or sorrow for the happiness or calamities of others is produced by an act of imagination, that realises the event however fictitious, or approximates it however remote, by placing us, for a time, in the condition of him whose fortune we contemplate; so that we feel while the deception lasts, whatever motions would be excited by the same good or evil happening to ourselves.
>
> (Johnson 1968: 168)

The reasons for the emergence of a marked degree of biographical sensitivity in the mid-eighteenth century need not detain us other than to say that the rise of modern biographical method and the rise of the novel were simultaneous events, linked by a desire to narrate the *complexity* of lives in terms of a relationship between phenomenological interpretation and structural cause. Johnson, in speculating upon the biographical method, immediately recognises the point where self identifies with other selves – not through the observation of an exact empirical replica, but through the engagement of mimesis. He observes, 'I have often thought that there has rarely past a life of which a judicious and faithful narrative would not be useful' (Johnson 1968: 169). Johnson's use of the word 'judicious' is of interest here because it comments directly upon the importance the researcher must give to the balance between description and interpretation. In fact he goes on, 'the biography must keep an eye out, not for trivia, but for the significance of the trivial' (Johnson 1968: 169). In other words, private preoccupations, modes of dress, speech patterns, mannerisms, etc. *may* be useful in biographical method but are not ends in themselves, must never become moments for the researcher to fetishise. Johnson (1968) was the first to articulate the normative and sociological reasons central to biographical method when he wrote that they may,

> be found in narratives of the lives of particular persons [and that, therefore,] no species of writing seems more worthy of cultivation than biography, since none can be more delightful or more useful, none can more certainly

enchain the heart by irresistible interest, or more widely diffuse instruction to every diversity of condition.

(Johnson 1968: 168–69)

For Johnson, then, biography is the realised form of an engagement with narrative, the benefits of which are both empirical and ethical. Its efficacious results are an increased knowledge of human variety and a deepened appreciation of the lives of others.

These themes were later taken up by the two formally acknowledged founders of modern biographical hermeneutics – the theologian Friedrich Schleiermacher (1768–1834) and his student, the sociologist Wilhelm Dilthey (1833–1911). This is not the place to discuss their work in detail but to note that both laid stress upon the importance of utilising narrative understanding as a method for deriving the most meaning from the ultimately hidden. For Schleiermacher (1977), access to the divine was axiomatically hidden, but was capable of being apprehended through the narratives of Christ's life, and for Dilthey (1976) (in a secularised version of the argument) access to the human was by the biographical re-creation of individual lives. Dilthey did not claim that a life could be perfectly replicated, its social context perfectly represented, its psychic acts vicariously experienced, but rather that the attempt at verisimilitude produced an approximation of that life sufficiently complex to do justice to the meaning it held.

It was Schleiermacher who introduced, and Dilthey who further elaborated, the term 'hermeneutical circle' which regards (in one of its variants) understanding of human expression to be possible only by other selves. That is, human cultural expressions are located in the same orbit of understanding as those wishing to interpret them. As such the interpreter or researcher is at once close to that which is to be interpreted but simultaneously distanced from absolute objectivity. The exploration of the advantages and disadvantages of this position, in terms of the analysis of human lives, is the role of the hermeneutical approach within biographical method.

In recent years the most sustained discussion of biographical narrative has been offered by Paul Ricoeur in the three volumes of his *Time and Narrative* (1984, 1985, 1988). This work, which White (1991: 141) has described as, 'the most important synthesis of literary and historical theory produced in our century' concerns the indissolubility of the relationship between historicity and human agency. For Ricoeur the understanding of social forces and personal outlooks is not *primarily* between true and false consciousness, between ideology and correct ideas, but is located in the irreversibility of time as expressed in narrative. The claim here is not that there is not mystification and domination in society, that there are not power relations, but that they are best understood as the expression and upholding of corrupted and corrupting narratives; that is, narratives that do not lay themselves open to the interrogation of, or benign appropriation by, other narratives. In biographical terms,

therefore, the understanding and meaning of lives can in Ricoeurian hermeneutics only be approached through narrative analysis.

In this narrative analysis we are concerned not only with the accurate
documentary of a life but also with the development of a plot, or an act of
emplotment (*mise en scène*). An emplotment is the charting of a narrative by
way of an engagement with the temporal. The act of adding a narrative
dimension to the seriality of events is the way in which individual identity is
established and made comprehensible, the way it is emplotted. However, as
another life cannot be replicated it is approximated and allegorised through an
ensemble of themes and facts that are the empirical links joining the researched
life to the process of interpretation. As such, to emplot is to perform narrative
biography and 'effect a mediation' (White 1991: 144) between events and the
human experience of time.

Ricoeur argues that emplotment is a poetic activity. By this he does not
mean that it is ungrounded in the world of facts but that the contour lines
joining facts are a geometry belonging to the imaginative realm. Ricoeur is in
effect arguing, then, that the imaginative integrity of the biographer is always
grounded in the emplotment of the biographical subject's narratives and not
the emplotments of the purely researching self. As we have seen the distinction
between biography and autobiography is not a clear one at either the
theoretical or empirical level. However, the starting place for biographical
research must always be the subject's life. The illumination of social reality
must be sought initially in the other, that is, in a conflation of subjectivities and
the social structure. Narratological research does not attempt to separate
structure surgically from subjectivity but to represent them as the first step of a
dialectic. It is as such that the researched life comes about as a network of
meanings (emerging from a montage of beliefs, behavioural practices and
records), the interpretation of which the researcher is advantageously and
ethically implicated within.

However, there will be accounts of selves that remain ambiguous, myster-
ious, discordant and confused – that, in short, cannot be resolved. For Ricoeur
it is in a recognition of this situation in our subjects and in ourselves that we
admit a deepened appreciation of the unknowable, that we recognise that we
can never articulate a would-be expressive or communicative ideal in the
understanding of a researched life or the nature of existence. The researcher, in
an attempt to approximate the lives of others, makes the incomprehensible part
of a comprehensible mode of enquiry. In this task, in recognising the speeding
impermanence of life in time and a sadness in the human condition, we may see
the importance of pathos for the conduct of our own lives and so climb another
interpretive spiral of the hermeneutical staircase. As such we may legitimately
employ the skills of literary and aesthetic criticism as well as the usual ones of
social science.

Like Ricoeur the contemporary moral philosopher Alasdair MacIntyre in
his *After Virtue* (1985) has joined the complexity of selves to narrative. He

recommends, as does Ricoeur, a concept of selfhood whose 'unity resides in the unity of narrative which links birth to life and to death' (MacIntyre 1985: 220). In consequence interpretations of a self's intentions may be understood both synchronically and diachronically. That is, the intentions of individuals (given the various contexts and settings in which they find themselves) are the perpetual guiding and layering goals that constitute life history. Coming from a different philosophical tradition to Ricoeur, MacIntyre (1985: 208) arrives at similar conclusions, namely that 'Narrative history of a certain kind turns out to be the basic and essential genre for the characterisation of human actions'. It is, for MacIntyre, the complexity of this position that allows the individual life to emerge in the dual nature, first, of its distinctiveness (person 'X' can never be person 'Y'), and second, its connectedness (person 'X' can 'recognise' the narrative of person 'Y').

If life ceases to be temporally or causally related to some recognisable narrative, it is, literally, not possible for it to be understood. The interpreter is, 'both intellectually and practically baffled ... [the] distinction between the humanly accountable and the merely natural has broken down' (MacIntyre 1985: 209). We may observe this state of dislocation when dealing with the mentally distressed and, possibly, also in encounters with 'alien cultures or even alien social structures within our own culture' (MacIntyre 1985: 210). As such, MacIntyre is arguing that mutual intelligibility is built on the notion of shared narrative, from the most banal to the most exceptional, from the most formally brief and instrumental to the most lengthy and expressive. It is to underscore this point that MacIntyre (1985: 211) cites Barbara Hardy thus, 'we dream in narrative, day-dream in narrative, remember, anticipate, hope, despair, believe, doubt, plan, revise, criticise, construct, gossip, learn and love by narrative' (Hardy 1968).

However, while the narrative road can be a long, varied and discursive one it is also undoubtedly one of limitations and forced marches. As individuals we are constrained by social circumstances: 'We enter upon a stage we did not design and we find ourselves part of an action that was not of our making' (MacIntyre 1965: 213). In addition, while selves are the centres of their own narratives, they are only part players within other narratives. The complex of activity these mutually intelligible, partly intelligible, and mutually unintelligible narratives represent (alongside the pressures of abstract social forces) is the background for the comprehension of actions. MacIntyre suggests that the *concept* of an action is dependent upon the temporality of an action because an action is always, inescapably, a moment in a narrative. In other words, an action is *conceptually derived* from an occurrence within a narrative. If, as MacIntyre argues, this is the case, then it must follow, as he also argues, that the lived narrative must have a certain teleological character. However, while the enacted drama of selfhood may be theoretically teleological it may also be empirically unpredictable.

When MacIntyre (1985: 216) says that 'unpredictability and teleology coexist as part of our lives' what he means is that unpredictability is a *technical* feature of existence but that selves have a notion of a past, present *and* future in which they situate themselves and from which they feel and intellectualise the experience of their lives. We can therefore argue that not only do human beings recount stories but that they are constituted as story telling creatures. It is through the hearing of stories, from the tiniest narrative scraps to a society's most prominent historical representations, that our own narrative selves are slotted into an engagement with culture. MacIntyre (1985: 216) clearly feels, and here he is close to the work of Basil Bernstein (cf. Dickinson and Erben 1995), that a reduction or a neglect of narrative accounts will restrict the ability of a self to produce a sense for itself of the temporal and causal: 'deprive children of stories and you leave them unscripted, anxious stutterers . . . '.

The centrality of the meaning of narrating to the practice of biographical methods and the pertinence of hermeneutics for an interpretation of those narratives should now be reasonably clear. It may now be useful to examine some empirical examples of how different scholars have used a broadly hermeneutical approach in the study of selves and life courses.

APPLICATIONS

There now follow three examples of biographical narrative analysis demonstrating some of the approaches outlined above. The three examples are all different pieces of investigation, demonstrating that biographical research attempts to suit its method to its subject. Advances in biographical method are predicated upon the articulation of its *purpose*. The first example is a short study by Hilary Dickinson (1994) in which she employs biographical methods to examine the experience of learning difficulties. The second example is an article by Christine Mann (1994) on adolescent girls studying for A-levels, in which she fuses her own autobiographical experience with those of her respondents. The third example is an examination by Anna Jackson (1994) of the meaning of that conceptually slippery document of selfhood, the diary.

Hilary Dickinson and learning difficulties

The *purpose* of Dickinson's article (1994) is the utilisation of a number of autobiographical accounts of learning difficulties to provide us with a better understanding of how such problems are experienced and understood. Dickinson argues that what at one time appeared as an unmitigated disaster can at a later point be viewed as a stage within a series of events culminating in a fuller appreciation of selves in society. Dickinson examines, among other things, four autobiographies by parents about a daughter or son with learning difficulties (Hardie 1991, Philips 1991, Fletcher 1992, Creasy 1993).

A critical dimension to Dickinson's analysis is the fact that the four autobiographies are autobiographies by proxy. That is, although they are the stories of the authors they have, nonetheless, been produced as consequences of the importance of other lives – those of the affected children. As such the theoretical issues surrounding the nature of autobiography and biography are highlighted and issues of selfhood become dramatically adumbrated. Through an encounter with a mentally 'handicapped' child a world is often turned upside down and selfhood shifts its previous boundaries. As Dickinson (1994: 95) says, 'to have a child with learning difficulties is for most families a traumatic event – an extreme example of Denzin's notion of epiphany . . . which permanently alters their way of life and perception of the world'.

This conclusion allows Dickinson to note the remarkable consistency in the autobiographies under discussion whereby *constative* narrative features (the record of events) later become translated into *performative* narrative features (that is, past events having an unforeseeable dimension that eventually gives meaning to the present). The author further notes that this process in the case of her subjects is not unlike sociological analyses of religious conversion. The accounts all describe painful, traumatic and important happenings as constative events of a performative narrative in which the original events are relived and realigned within a purposive whole. However, there is an important difference between the route to religious conversion and coming to terms with a child with learning difficulties. Religious conversion narratives are stories in which the stages on a journey are explicit and which finally achieve resolution in terms of a better present reflecting upon a worse past. In other words the self-world achieves congruity with a religious world.

However, this achievement of congruity does not occur in the narratives of learning difficulties. While the completed journey has parallel features to that of religious conversion it also has too many singular qualities for it to offer more than idiosyncratic resolutions. The reasons for this may be, in part, found in epistemological complexity but they lie also in the fact that learning difficulties are still too little understood to be accurately defined. Further, as Dickinson shows, the ways in which the public narrative of 'mental handicap' has translated into the public narrative of 'learning difficulties' has intensified the already noted idiosyncrasy of the corresponding life histories, which consequently now have more resemblance to the 'normal' population than hitherto. That is, 'the image of the simple, but affectionate and docile recipient of paternalistic care' is being replaced by a view 'which sees people with learning difficulties as having a right to responsibility and autonomy' (Dickinson 1994: 97–8).

Dickinson's article reveals in action the point made in the introductory section concerning the biographical method as an investigation of the ways the self-consciousness of others is utilised to produce self-formation. One of the problems in self-formation which the parental/family authors of the narratives experience is an interruption in the ordinary course of self-formation. It is interrupted in three respects, first by the apparently reduced self-consciousness of the family member with learning difficulties, which means that a greater burden of interpreting what the person is 'like' is taken on by the parent. This is connected with the second interruption, which is that the parent is constrained by existing 'cultural texts' (Denzin 1989) of what learning difficulties are 'like'. The reduced self-consciousness (or reduced ability to articulate consciousness) of the person with learning difficulties is in part a cultural construction, and is thus connected with texts of what such a person is like. This Dickinson shows by including an oral account by a man with learning difficulties. The third interruption for the families is a cultural text which may be designated as, 'family with normal healthy children'.

These interruptions of a 'normal' family life mean that the parents work harder and more self-consciously at constructing the narrative of the trans-formation of their lives. The life transformation is initially negative but ultimately, through particularly strongly marked performative aspects of the narrative, is translated into a positive conclusion of fulfilment and tranquillity. It should be noted that this summary of Dickinson's work of necessity emphasises ideal typical features of the parents' accounts. There is in fact a great deal of variation in the ways in which the parents' accounts, mediated by different individuals and different social universes, reach a resolution, and, further, in the degree to which such resolutions are positive. Dickinson's work exemplifies particularly clearly those interconnections between social dis-courses and a unique personal life history that are at the heart of the biographical method.

Dickinson's detailed analysis of the autobiographies is much less concerned with being judgemental concerning the various ideologies of learning diffi-culties than accounting for the manner in which those with learning difficulties and those most closely associated with them produce narrative accounts that make their experiences comprehensible and manageable. In this process the interplay of the constative and performative features of the narratives are highlighted in such a way that the method of biographical analysis is enhanced.

Christine Mann and adolescent girls

The *purpose* of Mann's paper is to provide insight into the adolescent lives of girls studying A-levels. In this process she examines a particular autobiogra-phical account in detail as a positive intervention into the discovery of the subjectivities of young women. Mann (1994: 61) argues that women's auto-biographies within patriarchal systems are likely to reveal, 'a fragmented self that is sometimes seen, sometimes not seen, sometimes labelled or categorised, sometimes approved of, sometimes controlled and *always* defined in relation-ship to others'. In an attempt to tap the empirical character of such a way of being in the world, Mann adopted a methodology (much influenced by the work of Carol Gilligan (Brown and Gilligan 1992)) in which she would 'stay in relationship' with her respondents. She emphasised to them that the research was a cooperative venture and collected data using a variety of methods including the recording of dialogue and the interpretation of such dialogue by the subjects themselves.

In the section of her research data that Mann provides us with we are given parts of an autobiography produced by Sally and are then offered various levels of analysis of this text. In the autobiography itself we are told of the story of a child of a single parent family moving to the Fens and being picked on in primary school. Great emphasis is placed by Sally on the encompassing importance of her mother's practical help and loving support during difficult times. We are informed of a developing confidence in Sally and a desire to go on to university after A-levels. Sally is vehement in her opinion that an absent father is no hindrance to her. As with many a 'traditional' narrative we are given here as Mann (1994: 64) says, 'a programme from dark to light': in spite of the odds, the put-upon child succeeds in becoming a reasonably integrated and confident young woman whose problems have become manageable.

Using a combination of textual analysis and her own experiences of a marginalised childhood, Mann investigates the life of her respondent in a manner that gives an autobiography its due while leaving it open to additional interpretive practices. It is clear that Mann's own reflections upon her girlhood sensitise her to the codes, rules and strategies that all marginalised children need to develop as they progress to young adulthood. For Mann these strategies are not devices to mask selfhood as much as part of the relationship that *is* selfhood. We may say that Sally over-compensates for being the child of a single parent by declaiming the virtues of her mother and by negating her father, but at the same time we recognise that Sally incorporates this stance in the development of her purposive attitudes to education which in turn becomes a constitutive element of her selfhood. Nonetheless, this selfhood in turn plays itself back to the social arena where it allies with a progressive, developmental public narrative that hinges on the advantages of social mobility and self-assurance.

This last point emphasises for Mann the way in which subjectivities operate within social contexts and which are particularly likely to manifest themselves at a time of adolescence. At this period we see a marked interrelationship between social expectations and personal feelings. As such, an adolescent girl studying for A-levels (the educational summit of adolescent life) is unavoidably at a threshold of self-definition. The question of the authenticity of such self-defining voices is best seen in terms of the authenticity of the text and its relationship with other texts. Sally's voice is authentic to the degree that it is both individual *and* relates to elements within the social structure. However, the nature of the relationship, for Mann, is better begun and understood through a sociology of selfhood rather than a sociology of contexts.

The high degree of control that Mann gave to her subjects was not so much a novel research method as a way of inaugurating a series of narrative accounts that offered some congruence between the intentions of the researcher and her respondents' data. The product of such a research protocol will be information that may give accounts of progressive, regressive, coherent or disintegrated selves, or, more likely, combinations of these. In Mann's (1994: 68) case she sees her research as 'consciously interventionist', as a way of asking each subject 'to see herself as a Heroine of her Own Life' and, further, to 'experiment with the idea of assigning new roles to herself'.

Anna Jackson and the diary

It is the *purpose* of Anna Jackson's paper (1994) to acknowledge the rewarding use that a psychoanalytic perspective can have for biographical research, particularly in relation to the examination of diaries. As Jackson points out, the diary is an especially intriguing document of selfhood. While an auto-biography might be revealing and interesting it is nonetheless a production within a given genre, and while letters are less easily located within a genre they do still have an addressee. The diary on the other hand is an altogether more equivocal cultural product. Frequently it is never entirely certain for whom a diary is written – whether self, a circle of intimates, an imagined audience, or a mixture of all three. However, this very uncertainty, while it can sometimes prove an impenetrable textual riddle, can also provide a stimulating example of the twists and turns of a self attempting to identify its own biographical existence.

Jackson uses the letters of Charlotte Brontë (Fraser 1988) and Emily Dickinson (1958) as a comparative measure to examine the diaries of Anaïs Nin (1973, 1974, 1976) and Sylvia Plath (1983). She argues that the most subjectively expressive moments contained in the letters have a rhetorical strength that is found in a routine way in the diaries. It is clear that while time and context will always partly determine the content of both diaries and letters, nevertheless diaries have more liberty to be both stylistically wilful and openly demonstrative than do letters. Jackson (1994: 159) is not arguing that diaries are therefore of equal aesthetic value to more conventional forms of literary production, but she is suggesting that the diary's 'volcanic writing of expression without strategic address' is a markedly pertinent document of self-writing.

The hinge on which Jackson's argument depends, and upon which she examines the relationship between the writer and reader of a diary, is Freud's concept of Transference and Lacan's later revision of it. By Transference Freud meant the process of the actualisation of unconscious wishes. 'In the Transference, infantile prototypes re-emerge and are experienced with a strong sensation of immediacy' (Laplanche and Pontalis 1973: 455). These feelings are transferred unconsciously from the subject to the analyst. While Transference seemed to be a hindrance to the psychoanalytic process, Freud came to see that the analysis of it was the central task of the analyst (Kuper 1988). According to Jackson (1994: 160), Lacan's definition of Transference –

'Transference is love addressed to, directed to, knowledge' – heightens the original definition and allows us to see the intensity of the subject/analyst relation at both the affectual and epistemological level. For Jackson's analysis the diary (having a definite but confidential existence) becomes a version of the object of Transference. She argues that the epistemology of affect makes the text (the diary) take the position of the analyst, thereby becoming the object of the Transference. The readers (ourselves) are then eavesdroppers upon a corpus of selfhood. From our observation of this intensity we as readers cannot but reflect upon the workings and character of our own identities.

The advantages for Jackson of the Freudian/Lacanian formulation of Transference is that it contains both the straightforwardly affectual (love) *and* the need to know and comprehend – each forming the component parts of an unresolved selfhood characteristic of all persons. If, as Freud argues, the Transference relationship includes not only love in its rehearsal of infant/parent feelings but also jealousy, anger, frustration, etc., it would seem an apt model for analysing the nature of the diary. In this situation the diary is turned to by the diarist with an 'investment of emotion similar to the investment of emotion a patient makes in analysis' (Jackson 1994: 161). The diary becomes a place for the emotion to be expressed but it is also the textual evidence (knowledge base) of that emotion – the case notes of the Transference event. The researching reader then conducts an 'interview' with the text. Jackson, in her analysis of the two well known diaries of Anaïs Nin and Sylvia Plath, argues (with many other points) that they reveal a constant unfulfilled adumbration of an irreconcilable duality in identity. As such the Transference metaphor seems methodologically particularly appropriate.

In the case of Nin, her long diary becomes in large part a vehicle for the expression of her feelings concerning a missing father. Nin's father deserted her when she was eleven, only to meet her again in her thirties and to initiate a (mutually sanctioned) incestuous affair. The astonishingly candid nature of Nin's diary is an example of the way she attempts to lay bare and articulate her detailed search for a resolved identity: 'she is looking for a father figure to be the site of knowledge, but no man is satisfactory for the place' (Jackson 1994: 164). What adds strength to Jackson's suggestions concerning the double nature of the text as both the expressive medium and the document of analysis is that Nin's incestuous consummation does not provide a resolution to her problem of identity. In short the text remains *conceptually* 'superior' to the action of the life but it provides only an occasion for Transference and not its resolution. Whether or not the 'fact' as reported by Nin that she was unable to experience orgasm with her father is a symbol for resigning herself to a search for an unfindable object or is merely a mundane event in a shocking story does not methodologically matter. Were the whole episode shown not to have taken place, its presence in the diary is beyond dispute and therefore its capacity for textual analysis relating to the complexity of the *meaning* of personal identity is evident (Erben 1994).

Plath, like Nin, 'lost' her father at early age. In the case of Plath this was literally the case, her father dying unexpectedly when she was eight years old. However, unlike Nin, Plath is the very opposite of a sentimentalist. The emotion caused by her father's death if anything polishes her predisposition to be a remorseless and technical analyst of self. The controlled but vituperative anger she displays in her journals is above all directed at herself. As Jackson (1994: 167) puts it: 'Perhaps the anger she directs at herself in the journals is transferred from her as yet unrecognised feelings towards her father. The writer who would make her name with the shockingly powerful poem *Daddy* assaults her powerful self in her journal'.

The sense of devastation that Plath feels and the cool, angered eye with which she sees it, makes her knowledge of her irresolution too transparent for the consolations of counselling. The resentment she felt at her father's 'desertion' and the way she used his scientist's sight (her father had been professor of biology at Boston) are evident in the accomplishments of her journal:

Here I am, a bundle of past recollections and future dreams, knotted up in a reasonably attractive bundle of flesh . . . And I think I am but one drop in the great sea of matter, defined with ability to realise my own existence. Of the millions, I, too was potentially everything at birth, I, too, was stunted, warped, by my environment, my outcroppings of humanity . . . I think of myself as worthwhile just because I have optic nerves and can try to put down what they perceive. What a fool.

(Plath 1983: 18, 20)

If Plath is as cerebral and sceptical as Nin can be sentimental and gushing, both diaries give evidence of an enduring act of Transference. The important point is not that the textual evidence in Nin and Plath is the same – clearly it is not. However, it may be analysed using the suggestive model of Transference advanced by Lacan. In this approach to the diary we may observe that the research methods of social science (in this case psychoanalysis) and those of literary and aesthetic criticism can provide a joined interpretive method for biographical investigation.

SUMMARY

1 Denzin's (1989: 7) definition of *biographical method* is accepted as a very useful one: 'I define the Biographical Method as the studied use and collection of life documents . . . These documents will include autobiographies, biographies, diaries, letters, obituaries, life histories, life stories, personal experience stories, oral histories, and personal histories'.

2 Closely related to biography is the term *narratives*. By narratives we mean the types, varieties, and patterns of the accounts or stories that compose life-course experiences.

3 To understand or come to terms with narratives we have to interpret them. The theory and practice of interpretation is referred to as *hermeneutics*. (Hermes was the messenger of the Greek gods, whose task it was to communicate messages to the mortals.) The hermeneutical method, in its attempts to interpret and understand, involves an appreciation of *both* that which is interpreted and the interpreting self.

4 The biographical method attempts to reconcile the positivistic and the interpretive, and the structural and the phenomenological; further, biographical method regards the individual as a *complex social identity* – a highly singular and highly complex articulation of the cultural.

5 Whether documentary, acted, spoken (or pictorial), *cultural texts* are social products and individual creations. Texts are areas of signification having cohering and recognisable cultural identities. From the point of view of biographical research, texts (e.g. a transcription of an interview, a research report, a novel, a wedding video, an autobiography) need to be examined using the tools of sociological and literary and aesthetic analysis.

6 *Single lives and social structure.* Biographical method attempts to resolve the tensions between structural and individualist interpretations by employing *narrative analysis*. In other words, biographical method attempts to utilise both positivistic (quantitative) and phenomenological (qualitative) analyses in so far as they contribute to the building up of a biographical picture. Not only does biographical method not reject information gathered in a wide variety of ways using differing investigative approaches, it also accepts relevant information derived from sources not usually exploited by social scientists – e.g. literature, history, art, etc.

7 *Narrative analysis.* Narrative analysis takes Time and its passage as a universal feature of social life. Life is composed of the narratives by which time is experienced. These narratives place upon existence – past, present and future – a cohering character that forms the reasons for thoughts and actions.

8 *Versions of lives.* It is never possible to replicate a life exactly. In one sense there is no such thing as the successful completion of the biographical method – just as there can never be a full-size map. The object of the biographical method is to provide more insight than hitherto available into the nature and meaning of individual lives; and given that individual lives are articulations of the cultural, it will provide insight also into the nature and meaning of society itself. The biographical method may be employed as small-scale research or large-scale research. In fact, the objects of the research in both cases could be the same – e.g. the biographical routes by which individuals decide to become teachers, nurses, mothers, fathers, etc. What is at stake is not the scale of the research but the *purposes* for which it is required. The small-scale piece of research can provide efficacious insight into a practical issue or question. The large-scale piece of research can provide information of a more detailed kind and is likely to contain material

scrutinising and advancing the principles of biographical method itself. However, these distinctions between small- and large-scale research are only indicative and are certainly not watertight.

ACKNOWLEDGEMENTS

I would like to thank the BSA study group on Auto/Biography, my research students, and Jackie Belenger.

NOTE

The British Sociological Association has a study group concerned with biography and autobiography. Details of the group may be obtained from Michael Erben, School of Education, University of Southampton, Southampton SO17 1BJ, UK.

REFERENCES

Bertaux, D. (1981) (ed.) *Biography and Society*, Beverly Hills: Sage.
Brown, L. and Gilligan, C. (1992) *Meeting at the Crossroad*, Cambridge, MA: Harvard University Press.
Burnside, M. (1991) *My Life Story*, Halifax: Pecket Well College.
Chanfrault-Duchet, M-F. (1991) 'Narrative Structures, Social Models and Symbolic Representation in the Life Story', in S. B. Gluck and D. Patai (eds) *Women's Words*, London: Routledge.
Creasy, C. (1993) *My Life is Worth Living!* Cornwall: United Writers.
Denzin, N.K. (1989) *Interpretive Biography*, Newbury Park, Cal.: Sage.
Dickinson, E. (1958) *Letters of Emily Dickinson*, Cambridge, MA: Harvard University Press.
Dickinson, H. (1994) 'Narratives in the Experience of Learning Difficulties', *Auto/Biography* 3, 1/3, 2 (double issue): 93–104.
Dickinson, H. and Erben, M. (1995) 'Bernstein and Ricoeur: Contours for the Social Understanding of Narratives and Selves', in P. Atkinson *et al.* (eds) *Discourse and Reproduction: Essays in Honour of Basil Bernstein*, Cresskill, NJ: Hampton Press.
Dilthey, W. (1961) *Meaning in History*, London: Allen & Unwin.
—— (1976) *Selected Writings*, Cambridge: Cambridge University Press.
Erben, M. (1994) 'Incest in Auto/Biographical Accounts', *Auto/Biography* 3, 1/3, 2 (double issue): 173–86.
Fletcher, G. L. (c.1992) *Peter, My Son*, London: Private publication.
Fraser, R. (1988) *Charlotte Brontë*, London: Methuen.
Gadamer, H-G. (1992) *Gadamer and Hermeneutics*, London: Routledge.
Hardie, S., Hardie, H. and Hardie, A. (1991) *Why Me? Autobiography of Sheenagh Hardie, a Down's Syndrome Girl*, London: Excalibur Press.
Hardy, B. (1968) 'Towards a Poetics of Fiction: an Approach through Narrative', *Novel* l2, 1: 5–14.
Jackson, A. (1994) 'Transference, Personal Letters and the Diary', *Auto/Biography* 3, 1/3, 2 (double issue): 157–71.
Johnson, S. (1968) 'The Rambler No. 60', in *Selected Writings*, Harmondsworth: Penguin.

Kuper, J. (1988) (ed.) *A Lexicon of Psychology, Psychiatry and Psychoanalysis*, London: Routledge.

Lacan, J. (1988) *The Seminar of Jacques Lacan – Book 1*, Cambridge: Cambridge University Press.

Laplanche, J. and Pontalis, J.-B. (1973) *The Language of Psycho-analysis*, London: Hogarth Press.

MacIntyre, A. (1985, 2nd edn) *After Virtue*, London: Duckworth.

Mann, C. (1994) 'How Did I Get to Here? Educational Life Histories of Adolescent Girls Doing A-Levels', *Auto/Biography* 3, 1/3, 2 (double issue): 59–70.

Nin, A. (1973, 1974, 1976) *The Journal of Anaïs Nin, 3 Vols*, London: Quartet Books.

Philips, C. (1991) *Mummy, Why Have I Got Down's Syndrome?*, Oxford: Lion.

Plath, S. (1983) *The Journals of Sylvia Plath*, New York: Ballantine Books.

Ricoeur, P. (1984, 1985, 1988) *Time and Narrative, 3 Vols*, Chicago: University of Chicago Press.

Schleiermacher, F. (1966) *Brief Outline on the study of Theology*, Atlanta: John Knox.

—— (1977) *Hermeneutik und Kritik*, Frankfurt: Suhrkamp.

Sociology (1993) *Auto/Biography in Sociology*, Special issue 27,1.

White, H. (1991) 'The Metaphysics of Narrativity: Time and Symbol in Ricoeur's Philosophy of History', in D. Wood (ed.) *On Paul Ricoeur*, London: Routledge.

11 Afterword

The politics of educational research

Robin Usher and David Scott

In educational research, problematising the practice of research is now a reasonably familiar process. To some extent, this is due to the influence of practices such as action research and practitioner-based enquiry where a completely unreflexive positivism is inappropriate. These ways of doing research have helped to produce an awareness of the need for care in the selection and use of methods in relation not only to their appropriateness but to their consequences as well.

Yet the natural attitude of researchers is still to want to get on with research and not bother too much with epistemological meta-questions. Educational researchers tend to think that it is much more important to concentrate on how best to go about research rather than with what effects it might have. Even those who want research to be beneficial or emancipatory adopt this 'natural' attitude as a matter of second nature. In other words, research is seen as primarily a technical process rather than a constructed practice.

In education there is a particular need to be aware of epistemological questions because the credibility of educational practice depends on knowledge of people and their relationships as these are expressed by educational researchers. Within this world the effects of research are therefore critically important. Researchers may think of their research purely as a neutral contribution to knowledge, or as useful for the development of policy and practice, or even as emancipatory. Whatever the aim, however, research remains an 'objectifying' practice, still a matter of 'speaking for others', unless the epistemological questions are properly foregrounded and the practice of research interrogated. Without this, what remains hidden is the implication of research in dominant and oppressive discourses through an unconsidered acceptance of its neutrality, pragmatic usefulness, or emancipatory potential.

In the natural sciences, researchers practice within a disciplinary matrix and a research tradition. These are also important influences in the practice of research within the social sciences, although here the boundaries and demarcations are much more fluid. Education is not itself a discipline in any traditional sense, although, insofar as it is located in any kind of disciplinary matrix, it is that of the social sciences. Equally, in terms of the practice of research, education is located in the research traditions and paradigms of the social sciences. The latter, however, do not themselves have a unified disciplinary matrix, nor do they operate from within a singular research paradigm. There is undoubtedly a strong tendency in the social sciences to base research on the 'scientific' model and to strive for knowledge which has the apparent certainty and universality of the natural sciences. However, as we have seen, there is a strong countervailing tendency which refuses to go down this positivist road.

The practice of research can be seen as a search for order: an attempt to systematise the flux of lived experience with its uncertainty, ambiguity and indeterminacy. Disciplinary matrices and research paradigms provide a means of doing this through imposing closure. Different disciplines and different research paradigms and traditions impose different closures and thus order the world differently. But whatever the differences there is one common consequence: that it is no longer possible to argue that the relationship between knowledge and the world is simply one of reflection or correspondence. The knowledge generated by research 'represents' the world but representation is not simply a problem of adequacy. A representational practice such as research is always embedded within epistemological conceptions and commitments which are themselves necessarily immersed in ethical and political discourses and concepts. To this extent research is always political, although it is important to emphasise that what we mean by this is not that research is always political in a partisan sense nor indeed that it is deliberately biased and distorted so that it serves the interests of dominant groups. What we are emphasising rather is that since research imposes a closure of the world through representation, it is always and inevitably involved with and implicated in the operation of power.

The political immersion of research as a representational practice has a number of aspects and meanings and is discernible at a number of different levels. First, epistemology has traditionally been concerned with providing strategies by which beliefs can be justified. This has involved formulating conditions for who can be a knower, what kind of things can be known, and how beliefs can be legitimately counted as knowledge. However, conditions of this kind work by excluding; thus, for example, although the scientific model of knowledge posits the universal knower, in practice this knower has always been far from universal. The universal knower is in effect the white, male, middle-class researcher, normatively if not always empirically. The representational practice of research therefore involves the construction of a particular kind of 'scientific' self whose particularity is concealed, and correspondingly, the systematic exclusion of 'others' whose particularities exclude them from being counted as legitimate knowers. The epistemological injunction to eliminate subjectivity and particularity therefore instantiates power under the guise of objectivity.

As well as the exclusion of 'others' as legitimate knowers, research also constructs 'others' as objects of knowledge and control. As authors in this book have noted, research, whether in the positivist or interpretive paradigm, is a process of objectification. One could extend this further and even include research influenced by critical theory which aims to give oppressed groups a voice – making them as it were into subjects. But here the point made by Game (1991: 30) is apposite: it is researchers themselves who give them a voice. Researchers do not place themselves 'in the same critical plane' (Harding 1987: 9) as those they research. Since questions of social power are involved in the research, the unequal self–other, subject–object relationship inherent within it is not so easily abolished. Harding (1987: 8–9) tellingly exemplifies this in the comment: 'psychiatrists have endlessly studied what they regard as women's peculiar mental and behavioural characteristics, but women have only recently begun to study the bizarre mental and behavioural characteristics of psychiatrists'. In any event, it is extremely doubtful whether the aim of giving voice to oppressed groups is ever best realised through the conventional research text. As Usher points out in Chapter 3, the very textuality of research, the very way in which research texts are constructed and presented as orderly, coherent and logical, ensures that the researched are always objectified (and hence deprived of a voice) whatever the emancipatory intentions of the researcher.

We have commented earlier on how research is commonly seen as a technical process. This technicised depiction of research is influenced by an idealised model of the algorithmic procedures of research in the scientific mode. Even when this model is refined to take some account of the interaction between methods and data, there is still an implicit assumption that the process of moving from data collection to interpretation is not simply a matter of 'reading out' a meaning which is already there. Rather, meaning is read *into* the data and this is not simply a matter of elucidating it by applying neutral techniques. Interpretation is a social act and the meaning that is read into the data is dependent on the paradigms and research traditions within which the researcher is located. It is this which makes the researcher the 'great interpreter' with privileged access to meaning. The seemingly neutral procedures and rules of validation which legitimate research conclusions and make interpretation simply a matter of drawing out a pre-existent meaning can be seen as a way of imposing an abstract order on the complexity, confusion and struggles of life as they are researched. Even in ethnographic and critical theory research, both of which consciously attempt to move away from the technicised model of the research process, the researcher's imposition of an abstract order is still an act of power.

Second, research always takes place within settings whose structuring depends on certain micro-political processes. The rules which govern these processes result from the arrangements of allocative (material features of the environment and the means of material production and reproduction) and authoritative (the organisation of time–space, the body and life-chances in society) resources (Giddens 1984). Actors draw on such resources and operate within these rules as they seek to produce and reproduce society through their interactions. These micro-political processes include the commissioning of research, the type of field relations that are possible, the available financial resources, the way time is understood and controlled, and the means of dissemination.

These processes, which contribute to the type of research report that is written and the way research is conducted, have been understood in three distinct ways. In the first, the central authority disguises its intentions, but always operates to maximise capital accumulation (cf. Sarup 1978). This view implies a coherence of intention among key players and involves the ascription of a hidden psychological mechanism which compels social actors to behave in certain ways. As a result, it unjustly conflates the socio-cultural and cultural systems (Archer 1987), and reduces social actors to automatons by denying their ability to exercise agency.

The second view is pluralist, where different interests compete on equal terms and on a level playing field. However, as we have suggested, all the relevant interests are not equally represented and social actors do not have equal chances of influencing decisions made about research at whatever level or site (government, university, research institute, etc.). The third view therefore understands the infrastructure of research as being a constructed affair, moreover one constituted by social actors interacting within constraining contexts. Power operates, as Foucault (1972) reminds us, not as an externality, not as an overwhelming coercive force, but through networks, integral to every human deliberation, including deliberation about research cultures.

There is a more profound sense though in which 'the political' is always present in educational research discourses. Epistemological cultures are social constructs and therefore in history. In Chapter 10, Scott makes reference to MacIntyre's (1987) 'traditions of knowledge', which are self-maintaining, incommensurable and the locus of the rules by which our understandings of the world are constructed. Educational research is embedded within disparate discourses and traditions; hence there is no single correct practice and no superordinate methodology. Some would see this as a weakness, arguing that this is why educational research never seems to succeed in progressively building knowledge of the world of education. Others, on the other hand, see this as a strength since it allows educational research to be both eclectic in its methods and approaches, and potentially more reflexive about its outcomes.

However, though this is undoubtedly true in comparison with other research discourses (e.g. those of the natural sciences), it is possible to identify discrete moments when particular research methodologies have been in the ascendant. It is important to understand that this genealogy of discourse is marked neither by progression nor by teleology (cf. Hegel 1942). Before and immediately after the second world war educational researchers adopted methods inspired by a strong positivist culture. The 1970s and the 1980s were dominated (in terms of the bulk of influential studies completed) by alternative methodologies which were self-consciously oppositional, having more in common with interpretive anthropological models (cf. Hammersley 1989).

The 1990s, influenced by the increasing control of funds from the central authority and the quality control mechanisms set up to force the universities and research institutes to be accountable to outside bodies, have tended to be marked by discourses which stress natural scientific procedures, disinterested researcher roles, the generalisability of research knowledge and the need for replication. This is translated into prescriptive activity which demands the use of both quantitative and qualitative approaches and the marginalisation of evidence which cannot be expressed enumeratively. Furthermore, contemporary discourses, although apparently privileging the procedures of natural science models of research, actually emphasise performativity and the managerial usefulness of research knowledge.

The genealogy of the educational research practice shows that, far from being a-political or outside relations of power, epistemological cultures are located firmly within political discourses. It does, though, extend the definition of the political *from* those activities engaged in by important and influential social actors in the polity *to* the context in which all social actors interact.

Fourth, educational research, alongside other types of social research, cannot be free of the value commitments of those who conduct it: social research is always valued research. Authors in this book have written from a number of different perspectives, but always conscious of this value-impregnated stance. As we have noted, this is a controversial position, seemingly implying that objective knowledge of education is impossible if this is defined as knowledge which transcends the value perspectives of the social actors who are responsible for its construction.

Hammersley (1995), for instance, argues that research can provide views of the world which correspond and thus reflect the world as it is and are thus separate from researchers' individual perspectives of the world. But it is hard to see how the researcher in the field can ever sustain, either at the time or retrospectively, a bracketing of their value positions, so that the decisions they make about the parameters of the case they are studying, the methods they use to collect data, and the means they appropriate to analyse and write up those data, do not reflect in a fundamental sense the way they understand the world. As we have seen, this understanding is not primarily individualistic but flows from the class, gender and ethnic particularities of the researcher – particularities which are more apparent to the researched than the researcher. At the same time, and related to this, researchers speak through particular discourses, paradigms and traditions which understand and 'close' the world in particular ways.

Educational research then is always political, not least in terms of its effects. Whether deliberately (as in critical theory) or implicitly, research always has effects since it changes the amount and type of intellectual and cultural resources with which social actors operate. There is always a potential for control and regulation as well as a potential for enhancing these resources and democratising the distribution of knowledge. Were this not the case, there would be little point in doing research. However, which potentiality is most fully realised depends on the micro- and macro-political arrangements and activities which constitute social life and education systems in particular. Educational research seeks to provide not better knowledge of the system (though researchers always strive to produce good research – see Chapter 5), but more coherent textual re-presentations which feed into and are responsive to the practice of education. The argument that these re-presentations are not designed, indeed should not be designed, to provide new ways of seeing does a disservice to the efforts of those who produce them. Yet those who carry out educational research need to realise that they are not engaging in a neutral activity but rather in a politics of knowing and being known where power is never absent.

REFERENCES

Archer, M. (1987) *Culture and Agency: The Place of Culture in Social Theory*, Cambridge: Cambridge University Press.
Foucault, M. (1972) *The Archaeology of Knowledge*, London: Routledge.
Game, A. (1991) *Undoing the Social*, Milton Keynes: Open University Press.
Giddens, A. (1984) *The Constitution of Society*, Cambridge: Polity Press.
Hammersley, M. (1989) *The Dilemma of Qualitative Method: Herbert Blumer and the Chicago Tradition*, London: Routledge.
——(1995) *The Politics of Social Research*, London: Routledge.
Harding, S. (1987) 'Introduction: Is there a Feminist Method?', in S. Harding (ed.) *Feminism and Methodology*, Milton Keynes: Open University Press.
Hegel, G. F. W. (1942) *The Philosophy of Right* (trans. T. M. Knox), Oxford: Oxford University Press.
MacIntyre, A. (1987) *Whose Justice? Which Rationality?*, London: Duckworth.
Sarup, M. (1978) *Marxism and Education*, London: Routledge and Kegan Paul.

Name index

Subject index